Praise for

The Head Game

"The title refers to the battle of wits between pitcher and batter, which is the essence of baseball. Kahn sides with pitching, and in a narrative that is both analytical and anecdotal, he rewards the reader with what amounts to a scholarly treatise on the craft.... This book is Kahn at his best, which is pretty damn good."

—*Sports Illustrated*

"An agreeable ramble through the history of baseball as seen from the point of view of its brainiest players, the pitchers.... [A] loving tale of baseball that is as lively and familiar and old-shoe as the game itself, even today."

—*Los Angeles Times*

"Roger Kahn reveals something new about the most important part of the game. In *The Head Game* he puts a fresh and original twist on the battle between the pitcher and the hitter, and I thoroughly enjoyed it."

—Tim McCarver

"Kahn elegantly traces the art of throwing across the years and through its many evolving grips.... Highly recommended for lovers of literate sports history and for bruised pitchers needing inspiration."

—*Library Journal*

"*The Head Game* skillfully blends the mechanical and the biographical to make a clear and lively picture of the baseball pitcher's art."

—Heywood Hale Broun

"*The Head Game* is part history lesson, part chatter over cocktails."

—*USA Today*

"A hot-stove league ramble, well lubricated with fine wines, on the subject of pitching, by a baseball writer who has seen it all. . . . [Kahn's] prose gleams like the grass at Ebbets Field in October. Opinionated, rambling, occasionally arbitrary, and always biased by the author's roots—in other words, everything a baseball book should be."

—*Kirkus Reviews* (starred review)

"Meticulous research about baseball's early days combined with interviews of prominent modern-day hurlers form this lively look at the evolution of pitching. . . . Kahn's love and knowledge of baseball is evident throughout this latest work in his baseball oeuvre, and his many fans will be especially pleased by his examination of the head game."

—*Publishers Weekly*

"Roger Kahn's new book, *The Head Game*, is a worthwhile and well-timed effort, especially in this, the era of the hitter. It's worth the sale price just for the concluding chapter on today's Atlanta Braves pitching staff."

—*Sun-Sentinel* (South Florida)

"Roger Kahn writes about baseball with a perfect ease. . . . [His] latest volume is part notebook-emptying, part fresh reportage, part history lesson and part physics primer with splashes throughout of personal memoir reminiscent of his 1973 bestseller, *The Boys of Summer.*"

—*Palm Beach Post*

"A terrific part of the baseball reading season . . . filled with musings, trivia, insights, interviews and asides, making for an entertaining and illuminating read. . . . A classy book full of information and opinions. Roger Kahn has complete control of his stuff and little wasted effort. Put this fine baseball book on your shopping list."

—*Harvey Frommer's Sports Book Review*

the head game

THE head game

BASEBALL SEEN FROM

THE PITCHER'S MOUND

Roger Kahn

Illustrations by Murray Tinkelman

A Harvest Book
Harcourt, Inc.
San Diego   New York   London

Requests for permission to make copies of any part of the work should be mailed to the following address: Permissions Department, Harcourt, Inc., 6277 Sea Harbor Drive, Orlando, Florida 32887-6777.

www.harcourt.com

Description of Warren Spahn by Paul O'Neil reprinted courtesy of *Sports Illustrated,* copyright © Time Inc. All rights reserved.

Library of Congress Cataloging-in-Publication Data
Kahn, Roger.
The head game: baseball seen from the pitcher's mound/Roger Kahn.—1st ed.
p.   cm.
Includes bibliographical references and index.
ISBN 0-15-100441-2
ISBN 0-15-601304-5 (pbk.)
1. Pitching (Baseball) 2. Pitchers (Baseball)   I. Title.
GV871.K35 2000
796.357′22—dc21   00-032014

Text set in Fairfield LH Light
Designed by Susan Shankin
Printed in the United States of America
First Harvest edition 2001

K J I H G F E D C

To Katy, for suffering a writer gladly

and

To Clem, for fifty years of friendship and one title

Nothing flatters me more than to have it

assumed that I could write prose—unless it be

to have it assumed that I once pitched

a baseball with distinction.

ROBERT FROST

CONTENTS

the head game

CASTING THE

FIRST BASEBALL

In the waning days of Harry Truman's presidency, I rode a noisy, bumpy, propeller-driven aircraft out of an uncertain New York March and into the torporous warmth of Miami, Florida. There the Brooklyn Dodgers, of sainted memory, were working their way through spring training and, it would develop, toward winning four pennants across the next five seasons. I had been dispatched by the *New York Herald Tribune,* another sainted memory, to cover this remarkable baseball club, an assignment that offered boundless promise and also the corollary possibility of falling prone and flapping like a flounder each morning, in full view of half a million readers.

This particular Dodger team had so firmly established itself that the eight-man starting lineup was set in stone—sod, actually—before spring training began. Indeed, the lineup had been set by the night before Christmas. The names are such stuff as dreams (and nostalgia shows) are made on: Reese and Robinson, Snider and Campanella, just to mention those players who have won places in the Hall of Fame. I was a student in a Brooklyn grade school when Pee Wee Reese broke in as shortstop; the prospect of reporting professionally on one whom I had idolized was daunting. I was a college boy when Jackie Robinson broke the color line, and I rooted passionately for this arrow of dark fire. Even the somewhat lesser names, Carl Erskine, Gil Hodges, Billy Cox, Carl Furillo, Preacher Roe, filled me with veneration, even awe. In a sense I was being asked to ascend into heaven and report accurately but not luridly on the doings of the gods.

I wrote my first story, neither very good nor very bad, for the editions of March 17, 1952, and that night I found myself standing in the lobby of the Hotel McAllister wondering how the editors in New York had liked the piece. The topic was pitching. I wondered also what I was going to do with all the time on my hands in a strange, hot, languid and intimidating city. I felt too overstimulated to read. I didn't want to drink. Women cruised in and out of the bar, but they seemed elderly. Some may have been as old as twenty-eight. *This is a great opportunity,* I told myself as I stood alongside a de rigueur potted palm, watching portly necktied tourists amble about. So why on earth, I wondered, did I feel so tense and lonely, so bloody lonely.

"Want to see a movie?" Clem Labine asked. He was a handsome, strong-jawed, crew-cut, right-handed pitcher of twenty-five. We had met and talked for a few minutes as I gathered data earlier in the day.

"Sure. What's playing?"

Labine had a poised, assured manner. He was a young major league star. He had served as a paratrooper. He had a lot to be poised and assured about. *"Moulin Rouge,"* he said. "It's the story of the French painter Toulouse-Lautrec." Labine made a little grimace. "I, uh, only know about that because my family is French." I didn't want to appear as tense and lonely as I felt. Labine, in our macho baseball setting, did not want to appear as artistic as he was. We proceeded down Biscayne Boulevard toward some forgotten movie house, where Labine insisted on paying for my ticket. Within, we enjoyed the movie hugely, the gorgeous Lautrec colors and the squealing cancan girls, the prime of Miss Zsa Zsa Gabor, and the acting artistry of José Ferrer. Afterward we had a drink and talked about the world that lay ahead. Clem and I have been friends ever since, through separate lives and loves and wars and deaths.

Back then, baseball apprenticeships ran long, and Labine had spent seven seasons in minor leagues, ranging from Colorado to the Carolinas, before establishing himself on the Dodgers late in the summer of 1951. That was the season of the New York Giants' storied pennant drive which reached apotheosis with Bobby Thomson's famous home run, called and recalled and recalled, "the shot heard round the world." While the Giants rushed onward toward the Dodgers, Labine pitched and won four consecutive games in August and September, finishing every start. Just up from St. Paul, of the American Association, Labine suddenly became Brooklyn's most effective pitcher. He appeared to thrive on the pressure of a pennant race. With certain other Dodger pitchers swooning, Labine became the team's sturdy Lancelot. Celebrity came to him in a seductive rush.

Red Barber told his listeners of Labine's poise. "Really extraordinary, folks. Way beyond his years. Way, *way* beyond." Dick Young, the reigning tough-guy baseball writer, nicknamed Labine "Chop-top," after the close paratrooper hairstyle. The newly famous pitcher made his fifth major league start on the night of September 21, against a strong Philadelphia team in Ebbets Field. These were the so-called Whiz Kids, a ball club strong enough to have clinched the National League pennant the year before by beating the Dodgers' power righthander, Don Newcombe, on the last day of the season. It was chilly. Labine had trouble getting loose. He loaded the bases in the first inning. Then, pitching to Willie (Puddin' Head) Jones, a Carolina strongboy, he saw the count go to 3 and 2. Charlie Dressen, the Dodgers' manager, called time, and stomped to the mound, his manner charged with the urgency of one about to deliver a philippic. The rookie pitcher waited, impatient to get on with his work. When Dressen reached the mound he said, "Don't walk him."

"You come all the way out here to tell me that?" Labine said. Dressen growled and walked back to the dugout, a small, irritated grizzly bear of a manager.

Jones hit the next pitch into the left-field stands, a grand-slam home run. The Phillies won the game, by 8 to 2. Dressen did not start Labine again or even send him to the bullpen until the second game of the play-off against the Giants, and Labine responded with a shutout, striking out Bobby Thomson with the bases loaded in a key situation.

A day later, with Thomson batting in another key situation, Dressen bypassed Labine for Ralph Branca. I believe it was Charlie Dressen's pique, as much as Thomson's bat, that tipped the 1951 pennant from Brooklyn to New York.

The following spring, the springtime of *Moulin Rouge* and Jane Avril, Zsa Zsa and Ferrer, Labine developed a walnut-sized muscle knot above the elbow of his pitching arm. He said the pain was minimal, but Manager Dressen told the legions of the press, "He ain't throwin' that good sinker no more, the sinker he trun last season." (Dressen's "trun" was the past tense of *throw*.) Neither the muscle knot nor the carping manager served the young pitcher's confidence, and Labine was hit hard in 1952. Dressen even sent him back to St. Paul for two weeks in August. That October, when the Dodgers lost a seven-game World Series to the Yankees, Dressen used him not at all.

Young stopped referring to Labine as "Chop-top." He had learned of Labine's artistic inclinations when the pitcher showed some nicely sketched designs for men's sportswear that he had drafted. "The guy turns out to be weak," Young told me. "Clothing designers can't make it in the big leagues. Baseball is a guts game and clothing designers don't have any guts."

If Young had moments of Neanderthal thinking, and he did, Charlie Dressen was an original American primitive. "I hear," he said, "that after Labine was born they had to put him in a incubator. That's his problem. Incubator babies can't go nine." Within a few seasons,

Dressen was gone and Labine had shown enough strength of character and arm to become the best relief pitcher in the National League. Pressed into service as an emergency starter in the 1956 World Series, he shut out the Yankees, 1 to 0. Couldn't go nine? That was a ten-inning shutout over the Yankees of Mickey Mantle and Yogi Berra.

When Labine retired in 1962, he had been a professional pitcher for nineteen seasons—thirteen in the major leagues—and he had collected six World Series rings. Teams for which Labine pitched, the Dodgers and later the Pittsburgh Pirates, won the pennant just about half the time. Dick Young's suggestion that Labine lacked courage was no more sensible than Dressen's comment on incubator babies; but Labine had to live with such wretched allegations, which he did in a dignified way. At length, after pitching in 526 big-league games, Labine returned to his native Rhode Island, where he designed clothing and managed the Deerfoot Sportswear Factory in Woonsocket. I thought he was a woefully underappreciated talent, and I believe I would have thought so even if he hadn't rescued me that long-ago night in Miami.

I visited Clem one day in 1990, thirty-eight seasons after we first met—my daughter was studying at the Rhode Island School of Design and we talked painting and ceramics and parenting and world affairs; but as soon as Clem and I broke away from the ladies, he said, "Do you still go to a lot of ball games?"

"Not that many. They're televising baseball pretty well."

"Do you get bored watching baseball after all these years?"

"As a matter of fact I don't get bored. Not at all. I study the pitcher. What's he going to throw? I study the hitter. What pitch is he looking for? I make myself become the pitcher and the hitter. Clem, they're playing chess at ninety miles an hour and that's not boring at all." Labine grinned. He was now a sandy-haired, trim executive of sixty-three, who looked like a well-conditioned fifty-year-old. "Me too," he said. "You know what I call that—the pitcher thinking, the catcher thinking, the batter, the anticipating, and all the rest? I call it the Head Game. I think that's the most interesting part of baseball."

In a single phrase, Labine had summed up the essential core of baseball magic. One man stands in the center of the diamond, surrounded by four umpires, eight teammates, and thousands of spectators. He is alone. The other, also alone but armed with a club, stares hard. The pitcher moves. The battle joins, and it is waged with wit and strength, with muscle, guile, and guts. Statistics? The numbers that fill fat record books are secondary stuff, commentary after the fact. The battle itself, the head game, is a duel.

I am grateful to Clem Labine for the title and to another good friend, John Herman, for his suggestion that I include in my considerations the metaphysics of pitching. *Metaphysics* is nicely defined as an inquiry into the relationship between mind and matter, substance and attribute, and for present purposes, a pitcher's head and a pitcher's arm. Art, science, and metaphysics is quite a bundle, and I had better add, as James Boswell did in his *Account of Corsica,* that the suggestions of friends are received with deference. "An author," Boswell writes, "should be glad to hear every candid remark. But I look upon a man as unworthy to write, who has not the force of mind to determine for himself. I mention this that the judgement of the friends I have named may not be considered with every passage in this book." Put differently, heed advice but call your own game. *Amen,* would say the good word worker Samuel Johnson, and perhaps the good righthander Walter Johnson as well.

R. K.

BOOK ONE

PITCHING IN

A PINCH

My eyes grow very misty

As I pen these lines to Christy;

Oh, my heart is full of heaviness today.

May the flowers ne'er wither, Matty,

O'er the grave in Cincinnati

Which you've chosen for your final fadeaway.

RING LARDNER, 1916

1.

"THE HELL IT

DON'T CURVE"

Ask them hitters about the curve. They'll tell you.
It's Public Enemy Number One.

CHARLIE DRESSEN

efore considering pitching as history, and pitching as combat, and indeed, pitching as life, it makes some sense to review a controversy that has spilled into baseball's modern times. On September 15, 1941, *Life* magazine, then the most popular weekly in the United States, published a dramatic photo essay which suggested that a baseball could not be made to curve. That year Lefty Gomez, a droll Californian who pitched for the New York Yankees, was fighting back from arm trouble and hooking his way across a season in which he would lead all American League pitchers with a winning percentage of .750. "Damn," Gomez said, as he stuffed a copy of *Life* into his locker in the catacombs under the grandstands at Yankee Stadium. "Here I am, trying to make a comeback, and what do they tell me? My best pitch is an optical illusion."

The old *Life,* a contentious, sexy, influential, self-important publication, was not above firecracker journalism, printing stories charged with more shock value than substance.* But the curve-ball piece, a copiously illustrated photo essay, appeared to be serious business. *Life* engaged a renowned photographer named Gjon Mili and hired two pitchers, including the Hall of Fame lefthander Carl Hubbell, who had been a twenty-game winner five times for the New York Giants. Both pitchers threw what were supposed to be breaking balls "under the scrutiny of three high-speed cameras." The magazine published eleven pictures and reported: "Mili's evidence fails to show the existence of a curve, raises once more the possibility that this stand-by of baseball is after all only an illusion." Details of Mili's methodology were left vague, but *Life*'s collective mind brooked no argument with its conclusion: Thrown baseballs always follow a straight path. The hop of Bobby Feller's fast ball did not exist, either, *Life* added. Feller had won twenty-seven games the year before, mostly with hopping

---

*In 1952, *Life* published an article under the byline of Ty Cobb titled "They Don't Play Baseball Anymore." Cobb argued that only two "modern" major leaguers, Stan Musial and Phil Rizzuto, could have played big-league ball in his era, 1905 to 1928. The premise—that Willie Mays, Ted Williams, Pee Wee Reese, Joe DiMaggio, Jackie Robinson, and Mickey Mantle lacked the discipline and/or the professional skills to have succeeded in an earlier time—is beneath rational discussion. But baseball fans talked about little else for weeks after the Cobb article appeared and that issue of *Life* sold out at newsstands.

fast balls. Like the curve, *Life* maintained, Feller's hopping hard stuff was "a batter's optical illusion." Honed to an edge, *Life*'s charge came down to this: Big-league pitching in America was a fraud.

Three months later the Japanese attacked Pearl Harbor.

Gjon Mili went on to other things. He induced Pablo Picasso to stand in a pitch-black room, holding a baton tipped with a light bulb. Mili set the time exposure on his Leica and said, "Draw." The subsequent photographs of Picasso's sketches in light were a wonder.

"But wait a minute, Mr. Mili," I said some years afterward, during an all-night Christmas party at his studio loft. "How do you think it's possible for people with just about the best vision in the world, major-league hitters, to be so consistently fooled by optical illusions? And why do some pitchers have better optical illusions than others?"

Mili shrugged. He was famous. His Christmas parties were famous. He held a wineglass in one hand. A dazzling Eurasian model clutched his arm. Salvador Dali, in cape and mustache, was entering. A Broadway actress, standing on a platform, announced that she was going to strip naked. Baseball must have seemed far away. "Please," Mili said. "Go get yourself a drink. We'll talk about curve balls some other time." We never did. Dali embraced Mili. I failed to catch the Eurasian model's name or eye. The Broadway actress stopped her striptease early when Walter Winchell arrived, talking loudly. She would undress for a wine-dark Soho party, but not for the hundred and fifty newspapers and all the ships and clippers at sea that were Winchell's glaring and prodigious syndicate.

People and publications are sure of one thing when they advance the hypothesis that a curve ball doesn't curve—or that a fast ball doesn't hop, or that a slider doesn't slide, or that an inshoot doesn't shoot in, or that a knuckleball doesn't "knuck." Putting this in Newtonian terms, they know that their action will produce a reaction. (When certain publications need attention, they move toward fireworks journalism. The old *Saturday Evening Post,* wanting to show special verve, once published an article entitled: "I Hate Dogs." *Grrrr.* Outrage arrived in a rush of mail sacks burdened with missives defending poodles, Chihuahuas, and wolfhounds and threatening to loose hungry Dobermans on the author.)

After about five decades of intermittent research, I have to conclude that articles in *Life* and elsewhere that deny the existence of a curve belong to the hoary I-Hate-Dogs genus, which does not mean that they will go away. *Look* magazine hired a photographer named Frank Bauman in 1953. This time, according to an anonymous *Look* writer, the pictures indicated that "Yes, a ball does curve, but in a gentle arc. No, a curve ball does not break." Different cameras. Different conclusion.

Within the past decade a scholarly batting coach, Ben Hines, who has worked for the Los Angeles Dodgers and the Houston Astros, undertook baseball studies from a different angle. Working with various ophthalmologists, Hines tried to find out precisely how a batter perceives a pitch. For example, which eye dominates the batter's vision at various points in the flight of the ball. One conclusion Hines reached was that sometimes a pitched ball moves faster than the ability of human eyes to focus. Calling a pitch a blur can be literally correct. This blur, Hines and his attending physicians decided, has the ophthalmological effect of slightly exaggerating the baseball's motion.

A hop seems higher. A curve ball, in the baseball phrase, "falls off the table." The vanquished batter then shakes his head and swears, "That last damn pitch musta broke three feet."

Hines' work suggested, no, that last curve didn't really break that much, any more than Babe Ruth could clout home runs "a country mile." But for either exaggeration to have a starting point, movement of the baseball—the hop, the curve, the long home run— first has to be there. As we shall see, scholarly physical studies of the 1990s prove that a hop, a curve, a slider, and a "knuck" are as real as the old *Life's* phenomenal newsstand sales. Put simply, a spinning baseball does veer in flight and sometimes sharply. That is physical fact. In addition, human vision, wondrous and imperfect, exaggerates the movement of the baseball. Voilà! Reality and illusion at the same instant, the stuff of magic, love affairs, and curve balls.*

Fun, games, and gainful employment have taken me from the very lowest levels of baseball to the very highest, and the curve ball, the curve ball that breaks, is a wholly consistent element in that experience. When I was no more than six years old, my father, once a strong-armed college third baseman, threw gentle wrinkles at me down the

*These recent physical studies also suggest that excluding meteorologically freaky conditions—a hundred-mile-an-hour tail wind—nobody, not Ruth or Mickey Mantle or Ken Griffey, Jr., or Juan Gonzalez or Sammy Sosa or Mark McGwire—nobody using a wooden bat could or can hit a baseball farther than 545 feet in the air, even when the pitcher messes up and hangs his curve ball high so that it looks as big as a pizza with anchovy stitches. Five hundred forty-five feet, though a considerable distance, is a country mile only in Andorra.

long upstairs hallway of the large whitestone house where we lived in Brooklyn. I remember the house on St. Mark's Avenue. I remember my father. I remember the curves. We played catch with a gray rubber ball that cost five cents at Horowitz Candy & Stationery around the corner on Kingston Avenue. Mr. Horowitz's Baby Ruth candy bars sold three for a dime. Our family always lived in corner houses. That way my grandfather could install small black-and-white signs, A. ROCKOW, DDS, on two streets, possibly increasing his dental practice during the Depression, when more people suffered from toothaches than could afford the drillings and fillings required to eliminate them.

THE BREAKING BALL
All pitching grips modeled by Stephan Rapaglia

In the long white upstairs hallway, I reached toward the spinning gray rubber ball. It drifted past my right hand. I said, "Dad, what was that?"

"Let's try again."

He threw three more three-quarter overhand wrinkles. Then he said, "Curve ball."

"How do you throw that?" I said.

He showed me a quick wrist snap; he was rolling his right wrist sharply clockwise at the moment he released the rubber ball over his index finger.

"Let me try." I had seen the glorious windup of Van Lingle Mungo, who kicked phenomenally high and struck out just about one major league batter an inning when he pitched for the Dodgers at Ebbets Field during the 1930s. I kicked back, a ridiculous mini-Mungo in the long-ago white hall, kept my footing and rolled my wrist as I released the gray rubber ball. The ball I thought I was hurling toward my father, my first curve, jumped out of my hand as I snapped my wrist, sailed sideways into the wall on my left with a certain amount of force. It caromed into the wall on the right. Then back to the wall on the left. *Boom blap. Boom. Blap.* Oh, nuts.

My mother, who had been reading Melville or Whitman on the blue crushed-velvet sofa in the living room, called out what would become a war cry: "No ball playing in the house!"

"It takes a while to get the hang of it," my father said. But we were finished for the night. Sometimes in later years the war cry could be ignored, but this evening my mother wanted to talk literature with my father. Further experiments with the curve had to be called off on account of Melville.

By the time I was eleven, playing six months of baseball a year at summer camp and prep school, I consistently could make a baseball bend. The school, named Froebel Academy after the nineteenth-century German philosopher Friedrich Froebel—supposedly the inventor of the kindergarten—was housed in a sprawling four-story mansion on a capacious flat site. Behind the mansion stretched a gravelly field, fenced in left and right, and in straightaway centerfield a high brick wall, the side of an old horse barn. This was the ball yard for myself and Donald Kennedy and Bobby Denzau and Fats Scott and Sanford Shumway and Gabby Fakir and the rest of us who comprised the Froebel baseball team. My father coached. On rare occasions, the headmaster, Carlton M. Saunders, MA, joined our workouts. We were disciplined and diligent young people. Each school day began with the reading of a psalm, and after closing our psalters, we had to sing a hymn. A favorite of our battle-ax kappelmeister began:

Come to my heart, Lord Jesus
There is room in my heart for Thee . . .

Froebel boys wore jackets and neckties to chapel and to class. Froebel girls wore long skirts and silk stockings. Like atheism, alternative costume was not allowed. The devotional formality of chapel and classroom, of windblown autumn mornings and chilly winter dusks, loosened with spring. Now crocuses erupted along the flagstone walks, and privet hedges, bordering the property, showed buds of green. The girls in choir practice sang a livelier tune:

April's in the air again,
Who can pause for sighing?
All the birds on feath'ry wing
Northward bound are flying.

And we boys entered most of what we knew of paradise. We ripped off our neckties and put on white-and-blue jerseys and pulled on our baseball knickers. Practice began at 3:05. After a few minutes of calisthenics, we loosened up by playing catch. My partner was lean, large-browed, athletic Bobby Denzau, and as we warmed up, we fired breaking stuff at one another, or what we hoped was breaking stuff. We had to be careful. We were just supposed to catch, throw nothing fancy. Wild fast balls tend to sail high. A wild curve most often scuffs down into the dirt. If a lot of throws went into the dirt, skipping off the pebbly field and past the boy trying to make the scoop, my father's assistant, Red Dohlon, barked, "Stop that. Just throw straight stuff. Okay?"

The practice baseballs at Froebel—I have never seen others like them—were gray, with a rough suedelike cover and raised seams. They looked like shrunken versions of a softball popular at the time, but in those days at a private school, boys shunned softball as they shunned soccer. Girls played softball and soccer. Boys played baseball and football. The raised stitches on the gray suede baseballs proved irresistible as curve-ball "handles." Denzau and I threw breaking stuff back and forth and communicated by looks. I'd throw hard, gripping the seams, roll my wrist and stare. When the ball curved, which it did not do every throw, Denzau confirmed the break with a quick nod.

Bobby threw a decent wrinkle. Mine was fair. Francis Ryan couldn't make the ball bend at all. In the priesthood of our youth, Denzau and I and Kennedy and Gabby Fakir knew important things—that a baseball curves, that Ryan's arm was rotten—beyond doubt or question. We were rough and sharp with one another, but deferential to adults. We grew and studied and played with a common obeisance to adult authority. It was the way of our generation.

The pervasive formality that ruled our relationship with elders wavered and all but disappeared one cloudy April afternoon when the Froebel headmaster, Mr. Saunders, told my father that he would like to throw a little batting practice to the boys. Mr. Saunders, a gangling North Carolinian, had been engaged to modernize the hidebound Froebel curriculum, bring the sports programs closer in line with those of the nearby rival prep, Adelphi Academy, and, most important, as the Great Depression lingered, to recruit students. Mr. Saunders had a fine classical education and a soft persuasive manner. Since he was quite tall and black-haired with thick, daunting brows he also could be intimidating. During one fire drill, Mr. Saunders caught one of my classmates looking up through the fire-escape grillwork, hoping for a glimpse of the undergarments worn by a pretty lower-school teacher called Miss Wright. Mr. Saunders suspended the student for three days and lectured us at chapel on the evils of lewd behavior and unseemly thoughts. As I remember it, during his sermon, Miss Wright blushed, arousing, also as I remember it, further unseemly thoughts.

Now, on the ball field, we saw another Saunders. He and my father threw back and forth, and as the headmaster's arm and shoulder unlimbered, he began winding up in a style lifted, I believe, from Dizzy Dean. He raised both arms, brought his hands together over his head, concealing the gray baseball within a small tan glove. Then he reared back and let go. Bob Denzau and I watched uneasily from our own catch.

"Gordon," Mr. Saunders said, "did ah evah show you mah Ol' Dipsy Do?"

"Keep it low, Carl."

I had not known that the headmaster and my father were on a first-name basis. For some reason, for *every* reason, that rang alarms. A boy needs separation between home and school, as a democracy needs separation between church and state.

"Is your father's name Gordon?" Fats Scott said, in a needling way. "What kind of a first name is that? *Gawdon?*" He was trying to be irreverent but kept his voice very low.

Bob Denzau stage-whispered intently, "The old man"—Saunders was perhaps forty—"is going to try to throw a curve." Carl Saunders bounced his first Ol' Dipsy Do. My father scooped it. Saunders bounced some more. Then he began to throw strikes.

When my turn came in batting practice, I had a difficult time. As a sixth grader I was becoming a decent fast-ball hitter, or anyway a decent hitter of sixth-grade fast balls. Mr. Saunders didn't throw me fast balls. He threw medium-speed curves that broke wide and down, bending underneath the plane on which I swung. I saw the ball breaking, and on my third turn at bat I tried to swing under the ball, to anticipate its arcing break. I was disrupting my normal swing. The headmaster's curve made me lurch and lunge. I fouled one pitch back, high over the backstop. In the school-yard term, a loud foul. I concentrated. The gray suede baseball started toward my face, then, on some crazy gyroscopic course, it bent and dipped gently away from me and under another lurching swing. The loud foul was my day's batting output. None of the other boys was able to do much better.

At home my father mentioned that Mr. Saunders had played college ball down in North Carolina. "That explains it, Dad. I'm eleven years old. How am I supposed to hit a college curve?"

"He wasn't throwing you a college curve. That was his easiest curve ball, his roundhouse. He throws several with a much quicker break. Don't be impatient. It takes a long time to learn how to hit breaking stuff. Follow the ball. Follow it all the way. Keep your head down when you swing. Try to see the baseball hit your bat."

I never was able to do that. I knew one major leaguer, Bobby Morgan, who said he could actually see the impact, speeding pitch against lashing bat. He was a career .233 hitter, and I knew scores of other major leaguers who scoffed at his claim. Practically, my father's advice was sound. Keeping your head still, as one does when looking down, improves your chances of hitting the ball. And if you try to see the ball hit the bat, you'll follow its flight as close to impact as your vision allows. That also improves the likelihood of staying with a curve.

Over the next few summers, I experimented among country friends. Playing table tennis, we noticed we could make the ball dip by rolling the paddle over it at impact, applying top spin. A slam that would sail long when smashed flat, dropped, hit the table, and often won the point when you rolled your racket sharply as you drove the ball. We tried side spins and bending cuts, and after a while we began throwing Ping-Pong balls to one another. I threw a nice hopping Ping-Pong fast ball. Holding it with the knuckles gave me a sinker. After a while I mastered three or four Ping-Pong–ball curves and the reverse curve that Christy Mathewson named the fadeaway. That is where my pitching career peaked. Firing the Ping-Pong ball, I threw stuff that hopped and sank and hooked. But this was a terminal skill. The commercial demand for Ping-Pong–ball right-handers was not only un-cluttered by agents, but nonexistent.

Games with tennis balls followed. We threw them hard, snapping our wrists. A right-handed sidearm pitcher named Jerry Solovey shaved the nap off one of the tennis balls. The shaved ball broke more sharply than the others; no one knew why. It was harder to make a baseball break than it was to make a tennis ball break, but we could do it. Not as well as Jerry, who was graced with a splendid arm and a strong hand and strong wrist. But we could break off baseball curves, or anyway wrinkles, and so in the mercy of high summer afternoons, that is what we did until, after many hours, hunger sent us wandering toward home.

When I went forth to cover the Brooklyn Dodgers in 1952, the most cerebral Brooklyn pitcher was a tall, skinny hillbilly named Elwin Charles "Preacher" Roe, who the season before won twenty-two games and lost three. That winning percentage, .880, stands today as seventh best in major league annals. Roe was a college graduate, a high school math teacher winters, but he grew up in a tiny Arkansas Ozark village called Viola, and affected the manner of a bumpkin. He was a country boy, but country slick. He had, he said, only three pitches: "Mah change, mah change off'n mah change, and mah change off'n mah change off'n mah change." Slow, slower, slowest. Actually, Roe had a fair fast ball—he led the National League in strikeouts as a young lefthander. In later years he spotted the fast ball to upset the timing of batters and once in a while used it for a strikeout by surprise. Roe's fast ball was the Stealth bomber of pitches. I took a Spalding National League ball one day—today's major league baseballs are made in the Caribbean by Rawlings—and showed Roe my father's old roll-the-wrist release. "I know that's how you throw a curve, Preach," I said. "Now how do you throw a slider?"

"Actually," Roe said, "what you just did—that's how I throw my slider. I throw the curve like this." Instead of rolling his wrist sideways, he snapped it forward, rolling it sharply over the ball just before the release. "You get a good curve-ball break that way. Why don't you come out some morning and maybe we can see what you can do?" I never had the audacity to throw my schoolboy breaking stuff to Preacher Roe. But from that day in 1952 onward, I recognized that the baseball I had played and the baseball my father played and coached was primitive stuff. From that day also, I could throw, on a modest level, two distinct breaking balls: a slider and a curve.

I never told my father what Roe taught me; my father had a generally fine knowledge of the game and great pride in the knowledge that he possessed, and I had no desire to embarrass him. Besides, batters—and my father's forte was hitting—do not have to know specific pitching mechanics for success. "I honestly think the best way to hit," says the Hall of Fame slugger Duke Snider, "is to swing without thinking. Follow the ball out of the pitcher's hand. See the ball. Hit the ball. Slider, curve, whatever. Just see it and hit it."

Besides that, there are any number of other ways to throw a slider, any number of other ways to throw a curve. The late Murry Dickson, a slim righthander who pitched for eighteen major league seasons, threw eleven different breaking balls. Overhand. Three-quarter overhand. Sidearm. A variety of speeds. A variety of spins. "He had so many pitches," Joe Garagiola, the catcher-humorist, has remarked, "that I couldn't call what I wanted with my fingers. Murry had more pitches than I had fingers. Sometimes I had to take off my shoes and call pitches with my toes." Despite his variety, Dickson was just a journeyman. For three straight seasons he led the National League in losses. How could a man with eleven different breaking balls lose sixty games in three years? Dickson insisted on throwing every one of his eleven pitches at least once in every game. Not all breaking balls are created equal; big-league hitters clobbered Dickson's lesser hooks.

Robert Adair, a physicist at Yale, has written, "Interest in the left–right curvature of balls sailing through the air is probably as old as ball games themselves." In the *Odyssey,* Homer describes an attractive princess named Nausicaa, daughter of the king of the Phaeacians, throwing a ball to her handmaidens. That was roughly thirty-two hundred years ago. Games of ball and with them Adair's "left–right curvature" run back into the fogs of prehistory. At the age of twenty-three,

Isaac Newton discussed the curve of tennis balls in terms of air pressure and rotation. A nineteenth-century Scottish physicist named P. G. Tait wrote on the hooks and slices of golfballs. Researchers at the Baseball Hall of Fame in Cooperstown, New York, credit William Arthur "Candy" Cummings with "inventing" the curve ball during the 1860s. A plaque to Cummings has hung in the hall since 1939, fifteen years after he died, at the age of seventy-five.

The origins of baseball itself are murky, but Candy Cummings painted an absolutely clear picture of the origin of the curve ball in an article he composed for the September 1908 issue of *Baseball Magazine*. Cummings called his story "How I Curved the First Ball." Reading it one thinks of another title: "Present at the Creation."

I have often been asked how I first got the idea of making a ball curve. I will now explain. It is such a simple matter, though, that there is not much explanation. In the summer of 1863 a number of boys and myself were amusing ourselves by throwing clam shells (the hard shell variety) and watching them sail along through the air, turning now to the right, and now to the left. We became interested in the mechanics of it and experimented for an hour or more.

All of a sudden it came to me that it would be a good joke on the boys if I could make a baseball curve the same way. We had been playing "three-old-cat" and town-ball, and I had been doing the pitching. The joke seemed so good that I made a firm decision that I would try to play it. I set to work on my theory and practiced every spare moment that I had out of school. I had no one to help me and had to fight it out alone. Time after time I would throw the ball, doubling up into all manner of positions, for I thought that my pose had something to do with it; and then I tried holding the ball in different shapes. Sometimes I thought I had it, and then maybe again in twenty-five tries I could not get the slightest curve. My visionary successes were just enough to tantalize me. Month after month I kept pegging away at my theory.

In 1864 I went to Fulton, New York, to a boarding school, and remained there a year and a half. All that time I kept experimenting with my curved ball. My boy friends began to laugh at me, and to throw jokes at my theory of making a ball go sideways. I fear that some of them thought it was so preposterous that it was no joke, and that I should be carefully watched over. I don't know what made me stick at it. The great wonder to me now is that I did not give up in disgust, for I had not one single word of encouragement in all that time, while my attempts were a standing joke among my friends.

After graduating I went back to my home in Brooklyn, New York, and joined the "Star Juniors," an amateur team. We were very successful. Next I was solicited to join as a junior member the Excelsior club, and I accepted the proposition. In 1867 I, with the Excelsior club, went to Boston, where we played the Lowells, the Tri-Mountains, and Harvard clubs. During these games I kept trying to make the ball curve. It was during the Harvard game that I became fully convinced that I had succeeded in doing what all these years I had been striving to do. The batters were missing a lot of balls; I began to watch the flight of the ball through the air, and distinctly saw it curve. A surge of joy flooded over me that I shall never forget. I felt like shouting out that I had made a ball curve; I wanted to tell everybody; it was too good to keep to myself. But I said not a word, and saw many a batter at that game throw down his stick in disgust. Every time I was successful I could scarcely keep from dancing from pure joy. The secret was mine.

There was trouble though, for I could not make it curve when I wanted to. I would grasp it the same, but the ball seemed to do just as it pleased. It would curve all right, but it was very erratic in its choices of places to do so. But still it curved! The baseball came to have a new meaning to me; it almost seemed to have life. It took time and hard work for me to master it, but I kept on pegging

away until I had fairly good control.

It was customary to swing the arm perpendicularly and to deliver the ball at the height of the knee. I still threw this way, but brought in wrist action. I found that the wind had a whole lot to do with the ball curving. With a wind against me I could get all kinds of a curve, but the trouble lay in the fact that the ball was apt not to break until it was past the batter. This was a sore trouble; I learned not to try to curve a ball very much when the wind was unfavorable.

I have often been asked to give my theory of why a ball curves. Here it is: I give the ball a sharp twist with the middle finger, which causes it to revolve with a swift rotary motion. The air also, for a limited space around it, begins to revolve making a great swirl until there is enough pressure to force the ball out of true line. I get a great deal of pleasure now in my old age [Cummings was fifty-nine] out of going to games and watching the curves, thinking that it was through my blind efforts that all this was made possible.

Cummings' major league record was brief. He pitched for the Hartford Dark Blues in 1876, the first season of the National League, won sixteen games, and recorded the new league's third-best earned run average, 1.67. Cummings stood 5 feet 9 inches and weighed 120 pounds. A contemporary commented: "God didn't give him much of a body for a pitcher, but Candy made up for that with his fighting spirit." The next season Cummings pitched for the Cincinnati Red Stockings, who won only fifteen games and finished a faraway last. Cummings' record was 5-and-14; his earned run average jumped to 4.34. This was ten years after he had startled Harvard ball players with his revolutionary pitch, and by now the curve was no longer Cummings' alone. It was swept into the basic repertoire, along with a number of other spin pitches, including the "inshoot" and the "riser." Cummings dropped out of the major leagues in 1878. He made an appearance at an old-timers' game in Boston during the summer of 1910, when he was sixty-two. A Boston newspaperman reported, Cummings still could throw "a wide and pretty curve."

A popular story in Cummings' day concerned a giraffe brought to a zoo in Ohio. A dirt farmer, who had ridden his wagon for hours to see the creature, stood in front of the cage and considered at length. Finally the farmer announced, "There ain't no sech animal." As soon as the curve ball became popular, ball-park doubters talked like the farmer. "There ain't no sech pitch." More than a century of argument was begun.

One Tommy Bond, a Hartford teammate of Cummings' and a thirty-one-game winner in 1876, demonstrated his curve ball to a crowd of fans and newspapermen in Cincinnati that season. Fred Goldsmith, later a star in Chicago, showed his curve for Henry Chadwick of the *Brooklyn Eagle* at the Capitoline Baseball Grounds. Both demonstrations employed wooden stakes, about eight feet tall, planted along a parallel line. The pitchers, who were right-handed, released the ball to the left of the first stake. The ball then carried to the right of the middle stake and curved back, so that it passed to the left of stake number three. Left, right, left. The ball was moving. The wooden stakes were no optical illusion. Throw after throw the pitchers showed that they could make a baseball describe a horizontal arc. The curve was real.

Scientists found explanations in classic studies by the physicists Daniel Bernoulli (1700–1782) of Basel, Switzerland, and Heinrich Magnus (1802–1870) of Berlin. Their work is still familiar to academics in the discipline called fluid mechanics. (From the point of view of the physicist, air is a fluid.) The most recent and probably most precise scholarly testimony on the curve comes from Yale's Adair, formally Robert Kemp Adair of Hamden, Connecticut, Sterling Professor of Physics and former Little League parent who in 1990 published a slim volume called *The Physics of Baseball*. Adair writes: "In the summer of 1987, [the late] Bart Giamatti, then President of the National League and later Commissioner of Baseball, an old friend and colleague from his days as Professor of English and then President of Yale, asked me to advise him on the elements of baseball that might best be addressed by a physicist. I told Bart I expected I would have so much fun that I would find it incorrect to accept payment. Bart responded by appointing me 'Physicist to the National League'—a title that absolutely thrilled the ten-year-old boy who I hope will always be a part of me."

Adair described his principal field as investigation of "the elementary particles and fundamental forces that define our universe." Compared to the big-bang physics of creation, a curve ball might be dismissed as simple stuff. But Adair, a devout ball fan, did not do so. "We don't have an absolutely precise understanding," he says, "of the effect of the airstream on the flight of a baseball with its curious yin-yang* pattern of red stitches." Working with carefully constructed models and devising more than fifty new equations, Adair advanced the state of baseball physics. "A baseball curves," he wrote, "as a consequence of asymmetries in the resistance of the air through which it passes. If the air resistance is greater on the third base side than on the first base side of a pitch, the ball will be forced—curve—toward first."

When a right-handed pitcher snaps his curve out of the common three-quarter overhand motion, the ball spins—broadly clockwise

---

*In classic Chinese cosmology yin is "feminine and moist," while yang is "masculine and bright." Colloquially the phrase has come to suggest opposites and in that sense it is applicable to neuter elements, such as the pattern of stitches on a ball.

from the pitcher's point of view. Air pressure builds on the third-base side. Pressure diminishes on the first-base side. The ball curves from the third-base side toward first and in the last fifteen feet of flight, as pressures continue to build, it breaks sharply. A factor in the "break" is the baseball's constantly changing speed. Like a bullet, a thrown ball has "muzzle velocity": the speed at which it is traveling when it leaves the pitcher's hand. Coming up against air resistance on its path to home plate, the ball constantly slows.

Adair presents as a laboratory physics model a baseball thrown at seventy miles an hour and rotating from the third-base side toward the first-base side at sixteen hundred revolutions per minute. This approximates a standard curve. By the time the pitch reaches the batter it has slowed to sixty-one miles an hour and is hooking sharply toward first base. Adair calculates that his "standard" curve moves 14.4 inches from a straight path—about seven inches, *more than half a foot,* in the last fifteen feet of flight. Thus in the laboratory as on the ball field, a breaking curve ball does exactly what it appears to do. It curves and it breaks.

One uses third-to-first break for reasons of clarity, but the flat, sideways curve is not particularly effective. A slider is flatter and quicker than a curve, leaving the pitcher's hand at eighty miles an hour, or even more. Batters complain, "It looks like a fast ball, until it breaks." The overhand curve—Carl Erskine, Sandy Koufax, and the young Dwight Gooden threw beauties—breaks straight down. The rotation on the overhand curve, the spin, runs from heaven to earth.

Many believe that the overhand curve is the closest thing there is to a perfect pitch, but it seems to put a fierce strain on the arm. (Both Erskine and Koufax retired early.)

The successful modern major league fast ball ranges between ninety and one hundred miles an hour, although some pitchers with fine control and good ball movement have gotten by with fast balls of eighty-five or even less. Adair calculates that a fast ball gripped across the stitches and thrown at ninety plus miles an hour hops about five inches in the last fifteen feet of flight. The high hard one is not only hard, it hops almost half a foot. How can a baseball move upward against gravity? Another question suggests the answer to that one. How can an airplane fly? The fast ball leaves a pitcher's hand with very strong backspin, and the backspin imparted to the stitches creates lift. Broadly speaking, the stitches are the fast ball's wings. Further models show that sinkers truly sink and that split-finger fast balls drop abruptly.

What about the knuckleball, the notorious butterfly pitch that appears to flutter to and fro as it meanders between mound and plate? I remember years ago watching a Popeye cartoon in which the one-eyed sailor had to pitch to the villainous Bluto if he wanted the favor of his paramour, Olive Oyl. After downing a can of spinach, Popeye struck out Bluto with a pitch that broke two ways. First it moved right. Then it moved left. Bluto swung mightily and missed, and spun into the ground, turning into a corkscrew. Popeye and Miss Oyl danced into an orange sunset.

Off the cartoon screen, does anyone really make a baseball break two ways? Yes, a knuckleball pitcher does it all the time. The knuckler can be thrown off the knuckles, but in practice most pitchers grip it with their fingertips. You lock your wrist and release the ball so that it barely rotates—perhaps a half of one rotation for the sixty feet from pitcher to batter. Adair created a model of a knuckler in a wind tunnel. He reports with a certain humor: "Thrown toward the center of the plate, the ball moves 11 inches off course and seems to be heading for the visiting team's dugout, back of first. The catcher moves desperately to his right to avoid a wild pitch. The right-handed batter relaxes, knowing that the pitch will be two feet outside. Then, confounding both batter and catcher, the ball ducks over the center of the plate for a called strike and possibly a passed ball."

What *has* happened? Uneven air pressures—Adair's asymmetric forces—have built because the surface of a baseball, broken up by stitches, is itself uneven. Here, with a baseball that is not rotating the air around, the pitch becomes a particularly important factor. The movement of a knuckler varies with altitude, temperature, and humidity. Currents—wind—also affect the buildup of pressures, and as these air pressures change, not only Popeye, but Hoyt Wilhelm and Early Wynn, could and did make a baseball break two ways.

With their equations and technical notes, Adair's studies may eventually lose some of us, including some pitchers. Simply stated, Adair in essence says this. Forget *Life* magazine, high-speed cameras, Gjon Mili, and the rest. A breaking curve ball curves and breaks, a fast ball hops, a knuckler flutters. In short, according to the state-of-the-science physical experiments described in his 109-page monograph-book, *The Physics of Baseball,* everything we believed about throwing breaking stuff when we were very young turns out to have been true. To many who writhed in classrooms while grappling with laws laid down by Boyle and Newton, that may be the nicest thing yet written on the subject of physics.

2.

FROM CREAG

TO BASEBALL

I n his glory years at the old *New York Herald Tribune,* the late Walter "Red" Smith liked to hold forth on "the magic of ninety feet." With Scotch in hand and his eyes and mind starbright, Smith expanded along a darkwood bar, "Whoever first put the bases ninety feet apart qualifies as a genius, the Einstein of the baseball cosmos." Votaries gathered about Smith, who spoke as entertainingly as he wrote. "Why do you say that?" asked sad-faced Ed Sinclair, a burnt-out bomber pilot whose later career as a sportswriter Smith was encouraging with great generosity.

"Ninety feet," Smith said, "is what makes the game work. How many times do you see a runner out by half a step? How seldom does a man beat out an infield hit? Almost every ground ball is an 'out,' just as it should be. Ninety feet between home plate and first base; one of the few examples of perfection on earth." I am a bit reluctant to debate Red Smith now that his voice is stilled, beyond the spindrift pages of collections. One comes to miss civil disagreements with friends who can no longer sally and riposte or drink or breathe. But I have been thinking about this for a long time, surely since Smith died in 1982, and I have come to believe that the magic spark of baseball lies within, rather than along, the base paths. Ninety feet is simply an arrangement of convenience.

As Smith decreed, most ground balls do have to turn into routine outs, if baseball is to function. With a few exceptions—mostly place hitting—a ground ball represents a victory for the pitcher. The batter has swung over the ball, rather than hit it squarely, as with a line drive. (Of course some grounders bounce through the infield, and some line drives get caught. But across enough innings, the fortunes of baseball balance.) Suppose the distance to (and between) the bases had been fixed at eighty feet or at one hundred feet. I believe that the infielders would simply position themselves differently and, even at these other distances, the great legion of batters punching out ground balls would be retired by a step or two. No laboratory tests of my theory exist, but in a sense infield distances already have been changed by plastic grass. The turf surface is a rug above a rubber pad atop cement. In St. Louis once Joe Torre invited me to play catch and blandly tossed a baseball so that it bounced five feet in front of me. I moved to glove the ball hip high and watched in surprised annoyance as it bounded ten feet over my head. "Nice move," Torre said over a smirk. "I'd like you to show me how to make that play."

The equation of the routine ground out consists of several elements: the distance from home to first, the position of the fielder, the strength of the fielder's arm, the running ability of the batter, and the *speed at which the grounder moves*. A ball not only bounces higher on turf than on grass, it also moves a helluva lot faster. Grass slows grounders; the plastic stuff speeds them on their way.

What is the defensive response to a hyperquick turf surface? Fielders position themselves differently. Often the turf second baseman plays in short right field. By accelerating ground balls, turf has destroyed the old balance. Ninety turf feet differs from ninety feet on grass. While I can't say I like artificial grass, it has not seriously damaged the game.* The ninety-foot distance to first and between the bases—fine, but hardly magic—was established by fiat 150 years ago. It has never been subject to tinkering or controversy. Not much art or metaphysics here, just the sensible application of plane geometry. The real magic of baseball, it seems to me, spins in and about the amazing and ever-changing balance between the batter and the pitcher. Balls, strikes, plate, mound,

---

*Pending breakthroughs in agronomy, turf ball fields are here to stay. Cheap to maintain, turf is essential to the indoor big-league baseball played in Tampa and Minneapolis. No one has yet developed a breed of grass that grows indoors. At this writing, turf also survives in Cincinnati, Montreal, Philadelphia, and Pittsburgh. My least favorite aspect of turf is not the trampolining bouncer; it is the ground-ball triple, the sharp grounder that does not seem to slow a whit until it hits the wall in right center. That is an abomination, but so was the old Polo Grounds pop-fly home run.

cushioned cork center, flame-treated northern ash, powerized, back-door slider, circle change . . . how do they make up this stuff?

Without question, the rules are oddball. The pitcher's slab, that chunk of off-white rubber, one foot wide and four inches deep, is fixed so that its front edge is sixty feet six inches distant from the back point of home plate. The plate itself is an odd-looking pentagon, seventeen inches wide, until converging foul lines shave it to a possibly phallic point. In theory the pitcher's back foot must remain in contact with the rubber until he releases the ball, although in practice pitchers cheat a little. The measurements are curious. Seventeen inches across home plate. As Newhart might ask, why not fifteen? Why not twenty? Sixty feet *six inches* from rubber to plate. Not even a straight sixty feet. Football, like the metric system, is governed by even numbers: ten yards, four downs, a hundred yards. Baseball's single most important measurement includes a fraction. Why? Who put the inches into the specifications, and what was his or their thinking when these specifications were set down? Although a variety of hypotheses contend, nobody really knows.

Nor can anyone can trace the origin of the pitcher's mound to a point closer than "the last years of the nineteenth century." Tom Shieber, a historian at the Baseball Hall of Fame, says, "The common theory holds that soon after overhand pitching was allowed in 1884, it became apparent that a downward slope over the range of a pitcher's stride increased the speed he could put on a fast ball. Groundskeepers, trying to help the pitcher's footing after rainstorms, often added dirt to the pitcher's box. Apparently the mound developed out of that, the extra, drying dirt. But soon pitchers were requesting extra dirt even on dry days." The official rules did not mention a mound until 1903, when a regulation passed providing that "the pitcher's box shall be no more than fifteen inches higher than the baselines and home plate." Shieber comments, "That tells us that the pitcher's mound existed in 1903, but it does not tell us specifically when or where we got the pitcher's mound in the first place."

This relatively modern history is elusive. You cannot trace the early evolution of baseball with consistent precision, nor can you even follow the game far back through the centuries. It was never a sport of kings and bishops, as tennis was, and our knowledge of medieval times springs almost entirely from court and church.* (Ordinary medieval folk left no records behind; few could read or write.)

To be sure, baseball is related to rounders, an English game of ball played not on a diamond but on a pentagon, and to cricket, the "summer pastime of the English race." A British manuscript from 1250 delineates two male figures playing a game of bat and ball. The left-hand

---

*Tennis balls feature dramatically in Shakespeare's *Henry V*, c. 1599, "that first great blast of English patriotism in literature." When Henry lays claim to certain dukedoms in northwestern France, the dauphin responds with a mocking gift: tennis balls. Shakespeare's King Henry responds fiercely:

> When we have matched our rackets to these balls,
> We will in France, by God's grace, play a set,
> Shall strike his father's crown into the hazard.

The old version of tennis, court tennis, was familiar to Shakespeare and his audiences four hundred years ago. Baseball has no such royal, long-lined literary heritage.

figure is a batsman, who holds his weapon upright. The right-hand figure is a fielder, who waits with hands extended. Another manuscript, in the Bodleian Library at Oxford, entitled "The Romance of Good King Alexander," shows a bowler—cricket for *pitcher*—and defensive players in the field. All are monks. The date of this manuscript is April 18, 1344; one can dreamily imagine that spring afternoon on a greensward in the Thames Valley or on Salisbury Plain as the first opening day.

King Edward III (1327–1377) disparaged *creag,* as cricket was then called, and in 1477 Edward IV tried to interdict the sport entirely. Anyone allowing creag to be played on his premises was subject to three years' imprisonment and a fine of twenty pounds. This was to discourage entrepreneurs, the medieval Rickeys and Steinbrenners and Murdochs. The players themselves were subject to two years in jail and a ten-pound fine. All implements—the balls and bats—were to be burned. English kings wanted their yeomen to work at martial skills, particularly archery. In the royal view, games of bat and ball were useless to the developing empire. But bans against creag in the fifteenth century seem to have been no more successful than the prohibition against drinking whiskey in the United States 450 years later.

The word *cricket* appears first in a document written in 1593. Six years later a chronicler says that "balls are used by noblemen and gentlemen in tennis courts, and by people of the meaner sorts [playing a form of cricket] in open fields and streets." The first formal rules for cricket were drawn in 1744. They provided that the weight of the ball "must be between five and six ounces"—the approximate weight of a baseball today. A standard circumference of about nine inches was incorporated into "the laws of cricket" in 1839. Today's major league balls have about the same circumference: "no less than nine and no more than 9¼ inches."

Early cricket balls were formed about "a cube of cork," with "layers of twine, cork and a covering of leather sewn on with parallel seams." The game of baseball may well be as American as Arkansas, but the baseball itself is simply a modern evolution of the medieval creag ball. The oldest surviving cricket bats resemble broad, curved hockey sticks. The straight bat with handle appeared shortly before 1800. Cricket bats weigh about forty ounces; so did baseball bats for many years. The best cricket bats have been made of willow. So were early baseball bats. Although most bats today are machined from ash, people still describe a batter as "waving the willow."* Like the modern baseball, today's bat is an American adaption of a cricket artifact.

With the roots of ball and bat so vivid, and baseball's English origins clear, surely colonial ball players, as well as Englishmen, celebrated in 1748 when a British court decided at last that cricket was a legal pastime. "It is," the judges ruled, "a manly game, not bad in itself, but only in the ill use made of it, by betting more than ten pounds on it; that was bad and is against the law."

---

*Willow is a pliant wood; a whip effect develops with a hard swing. But willow proved too soft a wood for baseball bats. When players swung heavier bats, as weighty as fifty ounces, the preferred wood became hickory. Babe Ruth hit sixty home runs in 1927, swinging forty-seven-ounce bats hewn from hickory. Roger Maris hit sixty-one home runs in 1961, swinging thirty-three-ounce bats made of ash. Ash is less dense; an ash bat weighs about a third less than a hickory bat of identical size. But ash chips and splinters more easily. Old-time ball players could use the same bat for an entire season. "The only time I ever broke a [hickory] bat," Lefty Gomez said, "was when I backed my car over one in the driveway."

By 1800 it had become customary to open the cricket season on Good Friday. According to an English chronicler, "Games began to be played for very large stakes. Cricket ground proprietors and tavern keepers farmed [organized] and advertised matches. Wagering was heavy. The result of matches was not always above suspicion." Another parallel with early American baseball soon will become apparent.

Rounders is an English ball game, originally played on a pentagonal field marked by five bases. To people raised on baseball, it may be jolting to think of a rounders star sliding safely into fourth or, as an overworked sportswriter might put it, "slamming out a five-ply wallop, a home run." The rounders feeder [pitcher] stands in the middle of an infield and tosses the ball to a batsman, who must strike at anything that passes over the plate between head and knee. The batsman then runs toward first and beyond, much like a baseball player, except the rounders bases are wooden stakes. Ten players constitute a side. Each side comes to bat three times a game. The batsmen can hit the ball in any direction. That this is at least reasonably close to baseball—except for the absence of foul territory—is apparent. But to say that baseball derives from rounders is probably not accurate. Rounders dates from the eighteenth century; no formal code of rules existed until 1889. Baseball also dates from the eighteenth century. Its rules— or one version of its rules—were codified in 1845 and significantly revised in 1857. Baseball and rounders (and one-old cat and two-old cat) certainly influenced one another, but all of them, each of these games with pitcher or feeder or bowler and batsman or striker or hitter, proceed from the sinful medieval game, which encouraged gambling and troubled warlike monarchs—the game called *creag* and later *cricket*. Rounders and baseball, like simian and man, are disparate descendants of a common ancestor.

When the *Mayflower* sailed from Southampton in 1620, bearing 102 intrepid souls to an uncertain world, the vessel may not have stocked cricket bats and balls. Given the severe Puritan ethos, it probably did not. A year later the ship *Fortune* brought to the Plymouth Colony thirty-five more settlers, most of whom were "lusty young men and many of them wilde enough." These youths certainly did bring balls with them, and on Christmas Day, 1621, they refused to go to work. Governor William Bradford excused them, somewhat reluctantly, and allowed, he later recalled, "frolicking in the street at play openly, some at pitching ball and such like sport."

As other English colonies developed in Virginia, Maryland, New York State, and the Carolinas, each band of settlers brought some knowledge of England's classic game of bat and ball. People began to play New World versions. The American edition of *A Little Pretty Pocket Book,* a work for children published at Worcester, Massachusetts, in 1787, consists of poems, illustrations, and "virtuous morals." On page 23 one finds a woodcut of two young ball players, above the title "Base Ball." Below there is this rhyme:

The ball once struck off,
Away flies the boy
To the next destined post,
And then home with joy.

One Horatio Smith wrote *Festivals, Games and Amusements,* published as part of Harper's Family Library in 1833. In the section on New England, Smith writes: "Young men are expert in a variety of games of ball, such as cricket, base, etc." Smith was an Englishman; that he listed baseball immediately after cricket suggests that the game had achieved significant stature. If youngsters were "expert" by the time 1833 came round, surely baseball had been played for many years. New England "base ball" was similar to upstate New York "town ball." Since the game requires a group—the early number varied—rural youngsters had to gather in towns for baseball. (Frost writes in "Birches" of "some boy too far from town to learn baseball.") The usual field was the village green. In the 1830s, teams employed at least five infielders: first baseman, second baseman, and third baseman, all of whom positioned themselves close to their base, plus a left shortstop and a right shortstop filling the gaps. Outfield? How many athletic young people were available? The outfield of the 1830s was a thundering herd.

Alexander Cartwright, an amateur athlete and surveyor, prepared the first written baseball rules in New York City in 1845. Cartwright set the number of players at nine per side. He sketched a model of the playing area with bases approximately thirty strides apart. His diamond is recognizable today. But finding a modern balance between pitcher and batter was beyond Cartwright's formidable inventive skills. That balance was half a century away.*

---

*The first modern or reasonably modern baseball game is said to have matched Cartwright's New York Knickerbockers against a team called the New York Nine, a ferry-ride distant from Manhattan at a park called Elysian Fields, in Hoboken, New Jersey. Cartwright umpired, from a position between home and first. The New York Nine won, 23 to 1, in four innings.

In the Cartwright diamond, the pitcher released the ball behind a line forty-five feet distant from home plate, which was round, rather than the pentagon we know. One can understand the reasoning of Cartwright, the surveyor. Separate the bases by ninety feet; separate pitcher and batter by half that distance. For the rest of the nineteenth century, baseball people tinkered ceaselessly with just about every aspect of the pitcher's trade. By raising or lowering the mound, by redefining the strike zone and fine-tuning the interpretations of balks, baseball people still tinker today.

The Cartwright rules spread through the Northeast after 1846, and Union soldiers carried them throughout the country during the Civil War. In the eleven months of the siege of Vicksburg, baseball became a favorite leisure game of the besieging army. Just four years after the war, the first professional team, the Cincinnati Red Stockings, loaded with former cricket stars, appeared. According to historians at the National Baseball Library in Cooperstown, New York, the records of the 1869 Red Stockings are not entirely reliable. The best surviving information suggests that the Red Stockings played fifty-seven games that year, ranging as far as Sacramento on the newly finished transcontinental railway. The Red Stockings won fifty-six games and tied one. The one tie is no tale of glory, but it indicates the widespread popularity baseball had realized as long ago as the first presidential term of Ulysses S. Grant—and with popularity, the ability to stir passions.

The Haymakers of Troy, New York, visited Cincinnati on August 27 and took an early lead. The Red Stockings came back and by the sixth inning tied the score at 17. Calvin McVey, the Red Stockings' right fielder, foul-tipped a two-strike pitch. "Cherokee" Fisher, the Troy manager, insisted that McVey had missed the ball and struck out. The umpire stayed with his decision, foul tip. Fisher pulled the Haymakers off the field and left town. Nowadays, such soreheaded action would lead to a forfeit; and as the rules now decree, Cincinnati would have won the game, 9 to 0. But long after Cartwright set down his first principles, the rules still were incomplete.

The Red Stockings claimed victory. The Haymakers insisted that the umpire was a Cincinnati "homer" and that they had fairly earned a tie. The game is customarily listed in record books as a tie, but the story has an even murkier side. According to the late historian Lee Allen, a group of "New York gamblers" had made a large bet on the Haymakers at very favorable odds. When the Red Stockings came back, "the New York gamblers entered into collusion with the team from Troy to stop the contest, using any pretext." The *Cincinnati Gazette* published a strong editorial on August 29, two days after the tie:

"It was reported before the game was played that large sums had been wagered in the East upon the success of the Haymakers. It was said that John Morrissey alone had staked $17,000 upon the issue. It was said that an [unsuccessful] effort had been made to bribe one of the Red Stockings to lose the game. [The Haymakers'] conduct was a disgrace . . . but the circumstance is chiefly to be regretted because its tendency will be to lead the public to suppose that base ball, like some other sports, is under control of the gambling fraternity." All this now-forgotten passion erupted in the same river city where 120 years later, many were shocked and others outraged by another gambling contretemps: *Organized Baseball v. Peter Edward Rose*.[*]

By 1869 the game was securely established in a country that had not yet begun to play football or basketball or hockey. But the pitcher, the place and role of the pitcher, was still being defined. Cartwright specified in 1845 that "the ball must be pitched, not thrown, for the bat." This meant, first, that the ball had to be delivered underhand with the stiff-wristed motion of a bowler. In Cartwright's terminology, "throwing" was overhand; "pitching" was underhand. Second, the pitcher was to throw "for the bat." His object was not to strike out the batter but rather to help the batter put the ball into play. In Cartwright's brand of baseball, the pitcher was an inconsequential performer, akin to the tee in golf.

A convention of baseball clubs gathered in 1857 and determined that a ball game should last nine innings. Previously many games were played to a fixed score, like tennis, where you win by capturing six games before your opponent has won more than four. Early baseball followed a twenty-one-run rule: First team to score twenty-one runs won. The rules convention of 1857 led to the formation of the National Association of Professional Base-ball Players in 1858, and that season,

---

[*]Civil libertarians found organized baseball's proceeding against Rose harsh, but historically an addictive gambler in the midst of baseball threatens the game's integrity more directly than do the convicted drug users, wife beaters, and other unappetizing characters who appear in the major leagues from time to time. At least, that was Commissioner Bart Giamatti's thinking when he expelled Rose from baseball. Subsequently, the Internal Revenue Service sent Rose to prison for income tax evasion.

the very first season of the very first organized league (it was named the National Association), the called strike appeared. Previously nothing counted unless a batter swung. That may sound odd until one realizes that modern equivalents persist. I remember hardball pickup games from the 1930s, which began with conversations like this:

"Are we gonna play balls and strikes?"

"We don't have an ump."

"The catcher can call 'em."

"Who's your team's catcher?"

"Me."

"Heck, let's just play two swings."

Even today, almost 150 years after the invention of the called strike, the two-swings game persists in that staple of corporate outings, slow-pitch softball. A great strength of baseball is its adaptability. No ump? No ump you *trust*? Two swings. Short a player? Okay, no right fielder and any ball hit on the fly into right is an out.

In the so-called Literary League, teams from publishing houses, magazines, and newspapers battled on softball diamonds in Central Park through the 1950s and 1960s. These teams were all male, often loaded with semipros and former minor leaguers. The pitchers threw hard and umpires called balls and strikes. Feminism arrived in the early 1970s, and the women of *Esquire* magazine, for whom I played third base, presented an ultimatum to management. At least four women had to be given positions in the starting lineup. A woman had to manage at least four and a half innings of every game. Unless these terms were met, every woman working at *Esquire* would go out on strike and trudge up and down Madison Avenue with a picket sign.

The women prevailed at *Esquire* and everywhere else. Few of these pioneers had played much ball before, and the idea of standing in against a windmilling underhand fast ball appalled them. The games were changed to two-swing, no-fast-pitch softball, and lots of people—although certainly not all—continued to enjoy them. Feminism is a point here, but not the main point. The main concern, neither feminist nor male chauvinist, is the amazing adaptability of baseball. I will confess to feeling shock one afternoon in August when a sinewy male editor from the Viking Press flattened our new *Esquire* second baseman, a graceful and attractive publicist named Phyllis Crawley, by way of breaking up a double play that we had no chance of making. Phyllis got up, brushed the dirt off her knees, and told me that she was all right in every sense. She knew, she said, that she was playing baseball, not croquet.

It was five years after the called strike arrived—1863—when a pitch outside the strike zone was first labeled a "ball." Early on a batter had four strikes. Nine balls gave him a walk. Clubs and committees were forever fiddling with the rules, and no wonder. The balance between pitcher and batter is delicate and fragile. Years of trial and error went into making the head game both interesting and reasonably fair. In a typical 1860s ball game, forty or fifty runs scored. The ball was hard. Infields were rocky, and pitchers, as we've noted, were not allowed to pitch. In the manner of cricket, early baseball games dragged on and on. (Cricket matches are not measured in hours, but in days.) The American temperament demands a quick pace, and at the end of the

1860s, by way of speeding up the games, a relatively dead ball was introduced. Scores immediately shrank. Although gloves did not come into general use until the 1880s, good fielding became a point of pride. And pitchers rebelled against throwing the ball "for the bat."

Contending forces worked against each other as rule makers tried to find a balance between the pitchers and the batters. Pitchers were given more and more freedom to deliver the baseball as they pleased. The stiff-armed bowling requirement disappeared in 1872; pitchers were allowed to throw three-quarter underhand. That same year, the restrictions against the wrist-snap—the root of breaking balls—were removed. Pitchers went from three-quarter underhand to sidearm. Finally, in 1884, all restrictions on the pitching motion were lifted, and on June 7 a wild twenty-one-year-old right-hander from San Francisco, Charlie Sweeney, struck out nineteen for the Providence Grays in a game against their archrival Boston Beaneaters. Still, as we shall see, the most effective pitcher overall that year was another Providence right-hander, Charles "Ol Hoss" Radbourn, who threw sidearm and underarm. In all, Radbourn won close to sixty regular-season games for the Grays, who captured the National League pennant by a wide margin. (I have not been able to find another sixty-game winner in the annals. The twentieth century's best total is the forty-one victories that Jack Chesboro of the New York Highlanders, the early Yankees, posted in 1904. Still, those Highlanders finished second to the Boston Pilgrims, the primordial Red Sox.)

Nineteenth-century pitchers began their assault against passivity by taking a running start toward the batter, charging up at the forty-five-foot pitcher's line to get more velocity on their stuff. Others threw from a sharp angle, say, toward the third-base foul line, delivering hard crossfire pitches. By way of curbing these tactics, a "pitcher's box" was instituted in 1865. Pitchers had to throw from inside the box. The standard dimension evolved into a rectangle, five and a half feet long. Some have suggested that the distance between the pitching rubber and the plate, 60 feet 6 inches, is the result of an error by a nineteenth-century surveyor. Actually, the odd six inches proceeds from the dimensions of the old pitcher's box. At first, the front edge of the box—and the pitcher had to work behind that line—was 45 feet 6 inches from the plate. In the continuing quest for balance, the box was moved back, in five-foot increments, finally to 60 feet 6 inches in 1893. When the present rubber slab replaced the box, its position in the earth, 60 feet 6 inches distant from the plate, was chosen not by accident or error but by design. (Curiously, the term "the pitcher's box" persists in the language, more than a hundred years after the box itself vanished.)

As the twentieth century dawned, pitching had become, in general outline, what we see at ballparks and on television screens today. Pitchers increasingly threw trick pitches: the spitball, the shine ball, the emery ball, a whole array in which a baseball, deliberately scuffed or nicked or moistened, could be made to break erratically—usually dipping—as it approached home plate. After these were outlawed, at least formally, pitchers devised knucklers, fork balls, sinkers, sliders, and splitters and continued to bedevil batters.

The cushioned cork center, core of the modern baseball, appeared in 1910. This made the ball somewhat more lively, but the single greatest

change came in 1920, when the A.S. Reach Company, which manufac-
tured the American League baseball, switched to a yarn loomed in
Australia. The Australian stuff was stronger and wound more tightly
than American yarn. Perhaps by accident, the cork-center tight-yarn
lively ball came to birth in 1920. Babe Ruth celebrated by hitting the
phenomenal total of fifty-four home runs. Never before had anyone hit
as many as thirty. Historians at the baseball library in Cooperstown cite
the new ball *and* the fact that Ruth figured out before anyone else
how to swing at it. As we shall see, there would now be less poking,
stabbing, or tapping. Swing from the toes—the balls of the feet, actually—and uppercut that swing. Common enough today with Mark
McGwire, Sammy Sosa, and the rest. Common even in the 1930s,
when Hank Greenberg and Jimmy Foxx both had fifty-eight-home-run
seasons. But Ruth, semiliterate, overweight, and a boor, was an unal-
loyed genius in the batter's box.

Like Jack Dempsey's thunderous knockouts, the home run capti-
vated the country. Spalding juiced the National League baseball at its
Massachusetts factory in 1922, and Rogers Hornsby hit forty-two
home runs. A year before, the last National League dead-ball year,
Hornsby had hit half as many. Baseball officials, and executives at the
manufacturers, insisted that nothing had changed. The lively ball—
the so-called rabbit ball—was only a myth, they said. About that time,
John Lardner recalled, his father, Ring Lardner, put his right hand into
a sack of the new baseballs, then withdrew it suddenly as though in
pain. "What happened, Ring?" someone asked.

"The rabbit bit me," Lardner said.

3.

THE PRINCE

OF TWIRLERS

Any delivery without control is no delivery at all.

CHARLES "OL HOSS" RADBOURN, c. 1884

lowering down at us from a variety of nineteenth-century prints, the first great pitcher looks serious and fierce. We know from the testimony of contemporaries that Charles "Ol Hoss" Radbourn liked drinking whiskey and the company of "ladies of easy virtue," often simultaneously. But what we see in the old line drawings is an intimidating sobersides, wearing a spiked mustache that suggests a weapon of war. Hoss would be pleased with that. He had an intimidating manner, as well we might expect from an oakhard character who once won more than sixty games in a single major league season.

HOSS RADBOURN

During the mid-1880s, when Radbourn had been pitching a complete nine-inning game every other day for three weeks or so, a reporter from the *New York Clipper* asked if he were not, perhaps, feeling a bit tired. "Tire out tossing a little five-ounce baseball for two hours?" Radbourn said. One can imagine the spikes of his mustache twitching with contempt. "Man, I used to be a butcher. From four in the morning until eight at night I knocked down steers with a twenty-five-pound sledge. Tired from playing two hours a day for ten times the money I used to get for sixteen hours a day?" Radbourn stopped right there. The *Clipper,* an intriguing nineteenth-century newspaper that covered vaudeville, burlesque, theater, and sports (but nothing else) played the quote prominently in a half-page feature on the most successful pitcher of the time.

He worked hard, lived hard, and died hard, when he was barely older than forty. Syphilis killed him. Henry Chadwick, the staunch journalist who invented the box score and was an imperious figure about the time someone was inventing the press box, wrote in 1889, "The two great obstacles in the way of success of the majority of professional ball players are wine and women. The saloon and the brothel are evils of the baseball world at the present day; and we see it practically exemplified in the failure of noted players to play up to the standard they are capable of, were they to avoid these evils." The plague of AIDS gives us a sense of how the devastating venereal diseases syphilis and gonorrhea laid waste to life in the centuries before the discovery of antibiotics.

By reputation Ol Hoss was a hell-raiser, or in the old phrase, "a hooray boy." When Radbourn was emerging as a star, pitching his way up from the sandlots of central Illinois, he spent some off-season days and nights whooping it up with an early baseball fan named Jesse Woodson James. Remembered now as a bank robber and murderer, James once enjoyed a Robin Hood reputation throughout his native Midwest. In time, while still a fugitive, he took a sabbatical from crime and tried to live obscurely as "Mr. Howard." But one of his felonious colleagues, Robert Ford, shot him from behind to collect a $5,000 reward from the state of Missouri. That was how James died, on April 3, 1882.

Having left the earth so abruptly, James missed Radbourn's great efforts over the next three seasons when the hooray-boy pitcher won more than 140 games for the Providence Grays in a National League that even then stretched from New England to Chicago. After the 1884 season, during which Radbourn won about sixty-three championship (as opposed to exhibition) games, counting victories in the first and forgotten World Series, his name was said to be more widely known than that of tall, handsome Chester A. Arthur, who had become president following the assassination of James A. Garfield.

If Radbourn was a "hooray boy" after hours, and there is no doubt that he was, the pitcher brought to the ball field a work ethic that touched fanaticism. He wanted to pitch every game, throw a complete game every time he pitched, and for a considerable stretch of the long-ago National League season of 1884, that is exactly what Charles Gardner Radbourn did. Despite what he said to the *Clipper,* he pitched through pain so intense that after ball games he was unable to comb his hair right-handed. Massage and hotpacks offered some relief, but in 1884, at the age of twenty-nine, Hoss Radbourn peaked. After that season, in which he pitched 678 innings, his arm was never the same. No wonder. A hardworking contemporary pitcher, say, David Cone, a twenty-game winner, pitched 207 innings for the triumphant 1998 Yankees, less than a third of Radbourn's total. Sometimes a sturdy modern will approach or even pass 300 innings. But 678 innings in a single season . . . for many moderns 678 innings is not a major league season but a career.

During 1884 Mark Twain published *Huckleberry Finn,* Louis Waterman invented the fountain pen, and a woman lawyer named Belva

Ann Lockwood ran for the presidency on the ticket of the National Equal Rights party. She finished fifth, after the victorious Democrat, Grover Cleveland; the Republican, James G. Blaine; the Greenback Party's Benjamin Butler; and the echoic representative of the Prohibition party, John P. St. John, who drew 150,369 dry votes. (Cleveland's winning total: 4,911,017.) To be sure, the dice were loaded against Belva Lockwood. Her so-called core constituency, women, would not gain the right to vote for another thirty-six years.

We know a great deal about Grover Cleveland, Mark Twain, fountain pens, women's rights, the prohibitionist movement, and other totems of the late nineteenth century, but what we know of Radbourn, though vivid, is episodic and sometimes contradictory. His last name is spelled differently in different sources—Radbourn or Radbourne, with a final "e"—and his regular-season victory total in 1884 is variously reported as fifty-nine and sixty. Sometimes his full name is recorded as Charles Gardner Radbourn, sometimes as Charles Radbourn, Jr. There is, however, no doubt about his pitching. All contemporary testimony agrees: Hoss was a master. He could throw varieties of curves, called inshoots and outshoots. He had a knuckleball that dropped and was known, even back then, as "a dry spitter." He spotted his fast ball—he led the National League in strikeouts—and he balanced his speed with a change of pace that seems to have been maddening.

He could do so much with a baseball that once, when he was pitching a minor league game for Dubuque against Prairie du Chien in southwestern Wisconsin, the local ball players stopped the game and insisted that the umpire examine the ball. "It's a crooked base-ball," someone claimed. "There's no way an honest ball could jump around like that." One can sympathize with the hometown sluggers who had been lunging, missing, and being made to look ridiculous before a crowd of fans and friends. The leading Prairie du Chien hitter, who comes down to us as "Home Run Hal," was particularly mortified and angry. "Radbourn," reported Ted Sullivan, an old baseball man who was there, "brought about the downfall of Home Run Hal with his breaking stuff and Hal led the charges that the ball was crooked." The ball was standard issue. Dead, to be sure. By current standards all the early baseballs were dead. But there was nothing crooked about the baseball; nothing magic. The magic lay in Hoss Radbourn's arm.

Sam Newhall Crane, an infielder and briefly a National League manager, wrote a newspaper series in 1912 on the men he regarded as "the fifty greatest baseball stars." Holding forth on Radbourn, "the sixteenth greatest ball player of all time," Crane recalled a conversation about that Wisconsin day. After the crooked-baseball interruption, Radbourn told Crane, fans and Prairie du Chien players, particularly Home Run Hal, kept looking at him hard, to see if somehow he was switching baseballs. With nothing up his sleeve but a stout right arm, Hoss pitched a shutout. He remembered the final score as 46 to 0. He was a very young pitcher that afternoon. He later learned, he said, to pitch only as hard as the game situation demanded, saving some strength for another day. Like all great pitchers he thought hard about the craft. At length he concluded that control—location, in today's argot—was the *sine qua non* of pitching. "Any delivery without control," Radbourn said, "is no delivery at all." Without much education—I doubt that he understood the term *sine qua non*—Radbourn was a very smart pitcher; he possessed an inborn sense of the art.

Three generations of the working-class Radbourn family emigrated from England in a great rush during the 1850s, first settling in Rochester, New York, where Charles was born on December 11, 1854, then moving en masse to Bloomington, the seat of McLean County in fertile Illinois farming country. Hoss' father opened a meat market at 511 East Jefferson Street in Bloomington, and with his wife, Caroline, raised eight children. One of Hoss' younger relatives, George Radbourn, called Dordy, pitched for the Detroit Wolverines of the National League in 1883. After posting an earned run average of 6.55, Dordy Radbourn dropped back into the minors and the family meat business.

Many early baseball players came out of a cricket background. Was Hoss descended from a line of outstanding cricket bowlers? The short and simple annals of English working-class families are not well documented. No one knows. Bloomington village records show Radbourns working as paperhangers, gunsmiths, clerks, and butchers. By 1889 one William Radbourn of 117 North Main was listed in the town register as "capitalist." That same year Hoss, who lived in an apartment above a store at 202 East Front Street, appeared as "baseball pitcher."

Normal, Illinois, is the twin city to Bloomington. (The town was the site of a teachers' college, then widely known as "normal schools.")

Clark Griffith, once a solid right-hander and later the shrewd but notoriously parsimonious executive who ran the old Washington Senators, grew up in Normal, where his mother ran a rooming house for students at the college. Griffith, fifteen years younger than Radbourn, became an enthusiastic apprentice. "Back home in Illinois I learned so much pitching from Rad, it's hard to single out particulars," Griffith said when Radbourn was posthumously inducted into the Hall of Fame, during the summer of 1939. Griffith was reaching back sixty years in memory. "I'd say the two greatest things he showed me were the curve ball, how to throw it, how to use it, and the importance of grit."

Radbourn was ten years old when the Civil War ended and baseball entered its first period of explosive growth. As the Cincinnati Red Stockings' tour through Indian country all the way to California in 1869 suggests, baseball was becoming a national obsession. It swept from New York and New England through the Midwest and rolled out across the high prairies toward the Pacific. In the South confederate veterans brought the game back to rural hollows, in one of which resided the forebears of Ty Cobb. The game's appeal cut across boundaries and overrode ethnic differences. Immigrants from England, Scotland, Ireland, and later, Germany took up baseball in country fields and city lots. As far back as 1877 the Cincinnati Reds signed a German-Jewish outfielder, one Lipman Emanuel Pike, to manage. (He was fired after managing fourteen games, of which the Reds lost eleven.) In 1884 Toledo of the then major league American Association signed two African American brothers, Moses Fleetwood (Fleet) Walker, a catcher, and Welday Wilberforce Walker, an outfielder. Tragically for hundreds of athletes, and for the country at large, a cotton curtain barring blacks from organized baseball fell the following year, and it would be six decades before Branch Rickey signed Jackie Robinson. But the 1870s and the 1880s were a free and wondrous time for the new pastime. Almost anywhere that leisure existed in America during the second half of the nineteenth century, you found a ball game.

Baseball-mad Charlie Radbourn of Bloomington was an indifferent student. At one point he attended Illinois Wesleyan College, but he found schoolwork confining. He worked long days for his father "hammering steers," then found a job as a railroad brakeman. All the while pitching preoccupied him. He played in pickup games and he practiced tirelessly. In one of his favorite drills, he put a small empty whiskey bottle on a tree stump and threw fast balls and breaking pitches at it. His hard stuff was said to have shattered bottles (formerly containing hard stuff) by the case.

Town teams were springing up everywhere, and Radbourn pitched for the Bloomington townies, picking up spare change. By the age of twenty-three, in 1878, he was good enough to join a prominent Illinois barnstorming troupe called the Peoria Reds. Sandlot baseball was the movie house, the television set, the vaudeville show of those distant summers on the middle border. Sandlot ball was entertainment. The Peoria Reds shuttled about, challenging all comers, and even managed to book an exhibition against the National League champion Boston Red Caps, later the Beaneaters and still later the Braves. A story in the *New York Clipper* reported that Peoria defeated "the champion Bostons" by a score of 3 to 1. Details are sparse, but the ball game must have been something to behold, a band of ragtags out of Peoria upending the big-league champions and their manager, Harry Wright, previously the captain of the storied Cincinnati Red Stockings. It was as if on an off day in the summer of 1999, the Blue Sox of Utica, New York, defeated the world champion New York Yankees.

Radbourn was right fielder and "change pitcher" for Peoria. The prevailing rules barred substitutions, except after somebody was hurt. "No player shall be allowed a substitute, except for illness or injury incurred in the game being played and then such substitute shall take the player's place only after the latter has reached first base." Suppose a fast ball to the skull rendered a batter unconscious? The rule makers overlooked that possibility. It was not until 1889 that a substitution rule approaching today's appeared. "One player, whose name shall be printed in the scorecard as an extra player, may be substituted at the end of any complete inning by either club, but the player retired shall not thereafter participate. In addition a substitute may be allowed at any time in place of a player who has been disabled." Beaned batters no longer had to make their way to first, heaving and groaning as concussion settled in.

During the Spartan no-substitute days, managers adjusted by working their relief pitcher into the starting lineup, usually assigning him to right field. In modern days, such great defensive players as Roberto Clemente and Carl Furillo graced right field, and their throws to nail reckless runners became the stuff of legend. But most batters hit right-handed, often pulling the ball to left. There tends to be less activity in right than anywhere else on the field. It was the defensive position where the "change pitcher" probably would do the least harm to his own cause. If the starter was hit hard in those long-ago games, the right fielder came in, became a pitcher, and relieved. To keep nine men on the field, however, the manager had to have the starting pitcher remain in the game. This led to many long and grumpy trudges from the glory of the pitcher's box out to the Siberia of right field.

Surviving records have Radbourn batting .289 in twenty-eight games at Peoria, but the Peoria pitching statistics for 1878 are lost. Radbourn did throw well enough to catch the attention of Ted Sullivan, who was organizing the Northwest League, the first minor league in the Midwest, where baseball was a preeminent growth industry. (By 1880 there would be major league teams in Cincinnati, Cleveland, and Chicago; soon after that big-league clubs appeared in St. Louis, Detroit, Toledo, Indianapolis, and Louisville. It was a booming market, but a risky one, with the weaker franchises frequently folding, to the fury of their creditors.)

Sullivan signed Radbourn to pitch for Dubuque in 1879. "From the time I met Rad," Sullivan later told an interviewer, "he was continually inventing a new delivery and trying to get it under control. He had a jump to a high fast ball, an inshoot to a left-handed batter, a drop ball that he did not have to spit on, and a perplexing slow ball that has never since been duplicated on the ball field. When he let fly with the high fast ball, he threw it so hard he actually leaped off the ground." Others confirm that Radbourn threw "a leaping fast ball." That is, he threw with such force—out of a three-quarter underhand motion—that the follow-through lifted his spikes, and the rest of him, off the ground. For a period during the 1870s and 1880s, the rules permitted pitchers to take a running start toward home plate. A few actually turned their backs as they moved in, delivering the baseball out of what someone called "a cyclonic gyration." In those days the pitcher's box was six feet by four, and the ball could be thrown from any part of it; one foot could be at the forward edge of the box, while the other could be stretched back as far as the pitcher liked; but both feet had to be on the ground until the ball was delivered. It is surprising how much speed old-time pitchers generated under those rules.

Sullivan is telling us that the young Radbourn could throw four pitches for strikes. This 1910 newspaper article is unsigned; the interviewer remains anonymous. He next asked Sullivan to compare Radbourn's "deliveries" with "the new pitches" of the early 1900s, by which he meant the spitter and Mathewson's "fadeaway," the screwball.

"He had all your new pitches and then some," Sullivan said. "Of course these deliveries have new names today or they would not be considered new. It's the same principle as at a French restaurant, where you get the same dish every day but with a new name. Vanity is a great thing in baseball! One generation does not want you to tell of the mighty deeds nor of the merits of that which preceded. The present generation insists upon being regarded as the pioneer in all the inventive and strategical features of the game."

One can sympathize generally with Sullivan, but he may have been getting ahead of himself on details, confusing Radbourn the polished major leaguer with the still-developing young athlete who was a "change pitcher," a reliever, at Peoria and Dubuque. In those days the only pitch he could throw with good certainty of getting it over the plate was a fast ball. An early scout who saw Radbourn at Peoria reported that "he has the makings of a pitcher if he can control a slow ball to back up his fast one." Radbourn did not become the prince of twirlers until he was thirty, which says a great deal about Radbourn and underscores the difficulty of mastering the craft of pitching during the nineteenth century, today, and, for that matter, in the future. Speed alone is not enough. It never has been.

John P. Sage, president of the Buffalo Bisons in the National League, signed Radbourn to a big-league contract in 1881 as an outfielder, second baseman, and change pitcher. Radbourn played a little second base and outfield for Buffalo but never pitched an inning. Here, in the fastest company of his life, Radbourn practiced his deliveries constantly and managed to strain his right shoulder. A disabled list for injured players did not yet exist. A sorearm pitcher was dead weight, and Sage released the rookie. Radbourn had played in six games and batted .143. He went home and then traveled to Eureka Springs, Arkansas, near the Quachita National Forest, where warm mineral springs bubbled with supposed healing powers. That was sports medicine as it existed in the 1880s. Shoulder killing you, son? Try a hot soak. One dollar, please.

But warm mineral water actually is soothing, like a hot Epsom salts bath, and Radbourn began to feel better. His shoulder still hurt a bit, but he was a warrior and later that summer he went back to the sandlots. The Bloomington semipro team managed to book a game against the Providence Grays of the National League and two more against the Chicago White Stockings, the lineal ancestor of the Cubs. The Grays won their game easily. Next, according to a contemporary account, the White Stockings "mopped up the outfield with Radbourn's change-up." They hit it hard, often, and deep. He pleaded for a rematch and this time went five innings and "held the Chicago professionals to three or four stray hits." Bloomington's backup pitcher that day was less effective. The White Stockings won, 29 to 2, which is about what would happen today if major leaguers played even a very fine town team. The critical element is now what it was then—the factor the writer John McPhee called "levels of the game."

Harry Wright, the old Cincinnati Red Stocking, saw Radbourn in his second effort against Chicago and liked what he saw. Here was a young pitcher not relying simply on power but working to fool the hitters by changing speeds. William Henry Wright appreciated that. He was a native of Sheffield, England, a boyhood cricket player, who took up baseball and won renown as a student of the game. During the nineteenth century he managed National League teams for eighteen seasons. Wright began managing the Boston Nationals, known over the years as the Red Caps and the Beaneaters, in 1876, and he was still there in 1881 when Radbourn signed on with the Providence Grays after another exhibition pitting a semipro team against major leaguers. The date is uncertain and details vary with the chronicler, but early in the season of 1881 Providence played against the Bloomington town team, supplemented on this occasion by a number of "extra railroad hands." These would have been ringers, itinerant professionals hired for the day to beef up the Bloomington squad.* Radbourn pitched for the locals, showing a good fast ball, a change of pace and fine control. He so impressed everybody that the Grays signed him on the spot. Harry Wright was an old hand in 1881, a forty-six-year-old baseball pro, and it isn't clear why he let Radbourn go to Providence. Radbourn himself was twenty-six by this time and he had certainly learned how to pitch. It is easy to fault Wright, but that is harsh. The baseball scouting process then, now, and always is rife with mistakes. The St. Louis Cardinals knew about Mickey Mantle before anybody else. While Cardinals people cogitated, Mantle became a Yankee. That languor cost the Cardinals the chance to field a fabulous outfield: Mantle, Enos Slaughter, and Stan Musial. It also surely cost them several pennants. The Red Sox turned down Willie Mays "because the kid can't hit a curve," missing a chance to have Mays and Williams in the same Fenway outfield

---

*My father had a friend named "Skater" Sayer who played semipro ball in Springfield, Massachusetts, around 1920. He recalled a Sunday game in which he went hitless against a ringer who called himself Pete Smith and who threw "the damnedest sinker I ever saw." Later Sayer learned that Mr. Smith was really Grover Cleveland Alexander, who would win twenty-seven that year for the Chicago Cubs. Alexander was moonlighting and picking up a bit of extra cash.

and batting order. The Brooklyn Dodgers signed the great right fielder Roberto Clemente but gave up on him and let him move on to Pittsburgh. As a Pirate, Clemente led the National League in batting four times. Missing out on Ol Hoss Radbourn, Harry Wright would find himself eventually with much company in the lodge of baseball scouts who missed a beauty.

Providence signed Radbourn for the summer of 1881 at a salary variously reported at $1,100 and $1,400, decent money for a ball player, or anyone else, at the time. This was the year in which "Rad" became a very good performer on a very good National League team. Often it happens that way with pitchers, a sudden flowering. Branch Rickey made an analogy to a rosebush. "It's all green today," he said, "and three days later it's all in color. I wish I could control a pitcher's development the way nature controls a rosebush."

The Grays of '81 won forty-seven games and lost thirty-seven, a winning percentage of .560, and finished second, fifteen games behind the mighty Chicago White Stockings, who collectively batted .279. Radbourn worked hard for his salary, $1,100 or $1,400. He played twenty-five games in the outfield and thirteen games at shortstop, started thirty-six games, completed thirty-four, and relieved in five others. By the time the season wound down, Radbourn had won twenty-five games (against twelve losses). His winning percentage, .694, was the best in the National League. He had become a star.

When Radbourn won thirty-three the next year, 1882, he demanded and got a raise to $2,000. Harry Wright reappeared in 1883 as the manager of Providence and signed a young righthander named

Charlie Sweeney, who possessed an overpowering fast ball and a brash, abrasive manner. Radbourn and Sweeney did not become friendly rivals. Radbourn, now twenty-eight, was the ace. Sweeney, just twenty, still learning how to pitch but possessed of daunting speed, was the contender. Radbourn did not appreciate being crowded; his relationship with Sweeney was a case of dislike at first sight.

Harry Wright sent Radbourn out to start sixty-eight times that season. Hoss completed sixty-six. The Grays played a total of ninety-eight games. Radbourn won forty-eight and lost twenty-five. Across the entire season of 1883, the Providence Grays won fifty-eight games and Hoss Radbourn won forty-eight of them. He pitched 632 innings, allowed less than one walk a game, and left behind an earned run average of 2.05. Despite a workload that taxes contemporary credulity as it once taxed the great pitcher's arm, Radbourn played twenty games in right field between starts and two more at first base. He batted .283 and hit three home runs. The Grays finished third, behind Boston and Chicago. Radbourn drew a raise to $2,500.

Hoss was not a large man, 5 foot 9 and about 165 pounds, and to survive he developed careful training routines. He had his right arm massaged before every start with one of the oils, snake and otherwise, then popular. He began his warmup by throwing easily from the mound. As his muscles loosened, he backed up, a few steps at a time, until he was pitching all the way from second base. (The distinguished Atlanta Braves pitching coach, Leo Mazzone, uses this device, "long tossing," in a somewhat different manner today.) After the game Radbourn had another massage and then proceeded to drink a little whiskey. He liked the company of women; indeed, his indiscriminate taste in women is probably what killed him before his time. But fundamentally, during the season, Radbourn was a disciplined athlete, not a night crawler. He saved most of his hooray-boy antics for the off season. No one ever, not even Babe Ruth, who may have tried, could drink all night and pitch all day across the length of a full season.

When Providence failed to win the pennant in 1883, Harry Wright lost his job. He had twice won pennants for Boston, and he was hired at Providence to win, not finish third. Providence and Boston were situated close enough to each other for the fans and players of one city to dislike the fans and players of the other, with expressions of contempt bred in the classic way by familiarity. Boston, of course, was the hub, claiming Paul Revere's house, Faneuil Hall, Emerson and Longfellow (both surviving until 1882), diverse Cabots, Lodges, Lowells, and all that assorted New England aristocracy. Providence, fifty-one miles off, at the head of Narragansett Bay, was smaller stuff, the capital of the first colony to declare independence, but still the tiniest state in the union. As John McGraw's swaggering New York Giants later looked at the Brooklyn Dodgers with contempt, so the Boston Beaneaters of the 1880s scorned the Providence Grays. In addition to everything else, ball players with the Beaneaters earned higher salaries than the Grays.

By the end of the 1883 season, the Providence franchise had become shaky. One hears today how "big market teams" (the Yankees) dominate small market teams (the Kansas City Royals) and threaten their survival. The scale of big-league baseball was entirely different in the nineteenth century when grandstands were wooden sheds and a ball club's annual payroll could promptly be worked out on an abacus. But economic fundamentals seldom change. As today, a poorly capitalized small-market franchise existed in chronic critical condition, even when it possessed, as Providence did, the greatest pitcher in the game. For 1884 the Providence owners brought in a baseball-wise thirty-eight-year-old New Englander named Frank Carter Bancroft to manage, and at the outset made his position plain: Win the pennant or the Providence Grays would be disbanded. Stars like Radbourn could sign on elsewhere, but with the Grays gone, manager Bancroft would likely find himself reduced to buck private in the rear ranks of the army of the unemployed.

In later years Bancroft wrote and spoke extensively about the season of 1884 and the episodes that drove Radbourn to pitch as no one has before or since. And well he might. That season was the sunburst of both men's careers. As Bancroft told the story, Radbourn became an irritable character during 1884, the year in which he would reach thirty, that threshold of senility for so many ball players. Bancroft suggested three causes for the irascibility. Pitching as often as Radbourn did kept him in pain much of the time. His right arm was a knifing toothache that would not go away. Second, Charlie Sweeney had improved significantly, and Radbourn felt the heat of the youngster's fireballs branding his neck. Finally, Radbourn had fallen passionately for a Providence belle—the lady's name is lost—and the rocky course of romance also played on his moods.

On June 7 cocky Charlie Sweeney shut out the Boston Beaneaters and struck out nineteen batters. (Roger Clemens shares the current major league record: twenty strikeouts in a game. He did that twice.) After this victory, Bancroft reported, Sweeney walked up to Radbourn and said with a smirk, "Howja like that for pitchin', Rad?" Radbourn glowered but stayed silent.

Historians regard three working 1884 baseball organizations as major leagues: the National League; the American Association, pretty much the lineal ancestor of the American League; and the brand-new Union Association, which raided the other two leagues for talent, shone brightly, and went bankrupt, all before the spring of 1885. Exactly one month after Sweeney struck out nineteen Boston Beaneaters, one Hugh Ignatius Daily of the Chicago Union Association team struck out nineteen Boston Unions. Daily threw right-handed, although not necessarily by choice. A childhood accident had cost him his left arm.

Now Radbourn spoke to his teammate. "Hey, Sweeney. What kind of trick is it to strike out nineteen men? Even a one-armed guy can do it."

Sweeney exploded. Two or three other players had to restrain him. Both Bancroft and Ned Allen, the Grays' general manager, faulted Radbourn. He was older; he should know better than to needle a short-tempered youngster; he was supposed to be a team leader. Up-braided by Bancroft, Radbourn left the Messer Street Park in Providence to brood and drink.

He had a wretched outing against Boston on July 16. He bickered constantly with the umpire, Stewart Decker. Fielders made errors behind him and he glared at them. His catcher, Barney Gilligan, missed a third strike. Radbourn retrieved the baseball and threw it so hard into Gilligan's body that the catcher, who weighed 130 pounds, fell over backwards. Then, with equal measures of anger and disgust, Radbourn began to lob the ball to the plate. No curves. No sinkers. No hard stuff. Just soft-toss lobs of the sort that office controllers throw today at the annual barbecue cum softball outing on Labor Day. Boston defeated Providence, 5 to 2. Frank Bancroft suspended Radbourn without pay.

"I'm gonna jump," Radbourn told Bancroft. "The St. Louis club [of the Union Association] has offered me three thousand dollars to play out the rest of the season with them." Bancroft told Radbourn to suit himself. It was a risk, he thought, but not a great one. Bancroft was aware of Radbourn's infatuation with the girl. He knew Rhode Island had a lock on a significant portion of the pitcher's heart.

With Radbourn still suspended on July 22, Charlie Sweeney staggered through an even worse outing against the Philadelphia Phillies. According to Bancroft, Sweeney had been drinking hard that morning and after the ball game began he kept his buzz by swigging on a flask between innings. P. W. I. Pitching While Intoxicated. For those who take major league baseball seriously, a group that included Frank Bancroft (and includes this author), that is a capital offense. Fast, wild, and plastered, Sweeney somehow made it to the seventh inning with a lead of 6 to 2. At that point Bancroft ordered him to give way to the change pitcher, Joe "Cyclone" Miller, who had been playing right field.

"Nothing doing," Sweeney said. "I finish what I start." He cursed Bancroft for a bit, then walked off the field and out of the park. The substitution rule then in force meant that Providence had to complete the game fielding an eight-man lineup. Bancroft tried to win it with only two Grays playing outfield, but the Phillies punched Miller's pitches into the gaps and won the ball game, 10 to 6.

That night, Ned Allen released Sweeney, who shrugged and moved on to St. Louis in the Union Association. There the owner, Henry Lucas, quickly agreed to pay Sweeney the same $3,000 he had offered Radbourn. (Hard by the Mississippi, Sweeney became St. Louis' ace, winning twenty-four games and pitching the team to a pennant. With his seventeen victories for Providence, he became a forty-one-game winner in 1884. Two leagues, true, but still forty-one victories. He had not yet reached the age of twenty-two, but this season climaxed Charlie Sweeney's fiery career and indeed his life.)

But in July at the old Messer Street Park in Providence, gloom was the order of the evening. "We might as well disband," Allen told Bancroft as players and officials mingled in uncertainty. Henry L. Root, the president of the Grays, agreed. By suspending Radbourn and releasing Sweeney, the Grays had maintained discipline. But at what cost? They had destroyed the pitching staff and demoralized the team.

As Bancroft remembered it, Old Charlie Radbourn stepped out of the shadows and said to him, "Do you want to win the pennant? Yes or no?"

"Of course I want to win the pennant."

"Then forget about disbanding. You and Mr. Allen and Mr. Root, here, give me a little raise. Enough to cover what I lost in the suspension. Maybe a little more. And exempt me from reserve. [Let me be a free agent for next season.] You gentlemen do those things and I'll start every game for the rest of the year. I'll win the pennant for you or pitch my right arm off."

"You're exempt from reserve," Henry Root called.

"You've got the raise," Ned Allen said. His voice was a shout.

Frank Bancroft pumped Radbourn's right hand up and down, and the old wooden clubhouse rang with cheers. The Hoss was back.

Bancroft recorded some of what happened after that, faces in a dusty picture, in an article he composed for *Baseball Magazine* twenty-four years later, in the summer of 1908. Between the date of the dramatic reinstatement, technically July 23, and September 24, when the pennant was clinched, the Providence Grays played forty-three games. Radbourn started forty of them. He won thirty-six.

During this streak it took the most heroic effort on Radbourn's part to keep going. Understand in those days we played about four games a week, so it wasn't as if Rad pitched a complete game every day. But he did pitch a complete game—almost always a fine one—every other day, and that's one reason I think Rad was the greatest pitcher who ever lived. As the season went on, his neck and shoulder muscles became all knotted up and he was so charley-horsed that even rolling out of bed was painful. There were days when his arm was so sore he couldn't raise it high enough to brush his hair or his mustache. Sometimes I had to send someone over to help him get dressed.

Instead of grunting, Rad stuck to his task and went out to the ball park hours before he had to be there. He began his warm up by throwing just a few feet, increasing the distance very gradually, until he was pitching from second base and finally from short center field. All the other players stopped what they were doing and watched Rad. When he at last was able to make the throws from the outfield, they would look at each other and say, "Ol Hoss is ready and we can't be beat." Nine out of ten, this proved to be the case. He was so good and so smart that he knew the weakness of every batter in the league. When he pitched, he gave the signals to the catcher, instead of the receiver giving signals, which was ordinarily the case. I consider him the greatest pitcher baseball has ever had.

When the season wound down in autumn, the Grays stood ten and a half games ahead of the Boston Beaneaters. Their record, 84 and 28, worked out to a winning percentage of .750. (In the recent memorable 1998 season, when the Yankees won 114 games, their winning percentage was .704.) Charlie Radbourn's 1884 record stands in the books forever: fifty-nine or sixty victories against only twelve defeats. A winning streak of eighteen straight games, during which he permitted only thirty-two runs. The Hoss in '84 was a record book all by himself.

He was not quite through for the year. The operators of the Union Association were busy dodging creditors, but the American Association seemed vigorous enough, with twelve competing teams. The New York Metropolitans, the original Mets, won the American Association pennant by four games. Then their manager, James J. "Truthful Jim" Mutrie, issued a historic challenge: The Metropolitans would take on Providence and Hoss Radbourn in a three-out-of-five-game set, a World Championship Series, playing the first three games at the Polo

Grounds in New York and the remainder at the Messer Street Park in Providence. The series never made it to New England. Radbourn won all three at the Polo Grounds, 6–0, 3–1, and 12–2. Major league record keepers today have the World Series beginning in 1903. But when the 1885 season began, two flags fluttered above the old ball field in Providence. One was the National League pennant. On the other banner, spun from silk, appeared two words: WORLD'S CHAMPIONS.

The world would never again be as sweet for Ol Hoss Radbourn, or for Charlie Sweeney, either. The Union Association went out of business, and Sweeney pitched for the St. Louis Maroons in the National League during 1885. He was still young, only twenty-two, but the strain of the forty-one-victory season damaged his arm. He finished 11 and 21. By 1888 he was out of baseball. Back in his native San Francisco, Sweeney shot and killed one "Con" McManus at 2:30 in the afternoon on Sunday, July 15, 1894. The men had been drinking heavily in a saloon called the Grand Central Wine Room. Sweeney told police, "Con just wouldn't let me alone. We started fighting and he rolled me on the floor. He tore my tie off. He ripped my collar. He was bigger than me. I had to defend myself." Forgotten Charlie Sweeney, the first great master of the overhand fast ball, died in prison on April 4, 1902, one week before he would have reached his thirty-nineth birthday.

The Providence Grays fell to fourth place in 1885 and then disbanded. Radbourn had stayed with the Grays, who paid him $4,000, "mostly," Bancroft said, "because he was still stuck on the girl from Providence." With the Grays history, Radbourn joined the Beaneaters in Boston, where in 1887, abandoning the Providence romance, he married a widow named Carrie Clark Stanhope. His major league career ended with the Cincinnati Reds in 1891, when he was thirty-six. With his spinning sidearm and underhand slants and drops, he was always a good pitcher, but he never again approached the form of his sixty-victory season.

After retiring, he opened "Radbourn's Place—Base Ball Headquarters" on West Washington Street in Bloomington. He advertised "billiards and pool; best of everything in wet goods and cigars; polite attention, pleasant associates." On a spring hunting trip in 1894, he moved out from behind a tree and walked into his hunting partner's line of fire. He took a bullet or a shotgun blast to the face—accounts differ—and the accident left him blind in one eye and disfigured. He became reclusive and depressed. At some point Carrie left him and returned to Boston. Radbourn sought solace in prostitutes and one gave him syphilis. The disease wasted his body, crippled him, and on February 5, 1897, killed him. Hoss Radbourn was forty-two.

Reporting his death, a reporter wrote in the *Bloomington Daily Pantagraph,* "He was the greatest baseball pitcher of his day. . . . He was the first to make [the curve] effective and thereby saved the game's prestige and revolutionized methods of play. Not many men in American history faced so many people and received so many plaudits.

"His name was used as frequently as was the President's."

Radbourn's name is not used frequently today, nor is the name of Chester Alan Arthur—except, perhaps, when people try to list all the presidents and find they have to look up number twenty-one.

4.

CY YOUNG,

TICKET SALESMAN

B y the time the modern World Series began matching the National League against the American League in a clash of pennant winners, the broad outlines of battle between pitcher and batter were set, along the lines that Mr. Newhart/Doubleday outlined fruitlessly to the Olympic Game Company. *Three strikes, yer out. Four balls, take yer base.* Some fine-tuning lay ahead, notably in discarding baseballs that became scuffed. As late as 1908 the St. Louis Cardinals and the Brooklyn Superbas—forerunners of the Dodgers—played a nine-inning game using a single ball. These days most games consume three or four dozen. Still, the rules and practices at the first "modern" Series were reasonably close to what obtains now on four to seven nights every October.

Since baseball was then limited to the United States, "World" Series was hype, from the beginning. Some newspapermen wrote anonymously that the first modern Series would determine "the champion of champions." Accurate but cumbersome. The catchy term "World Series" stands as an early triumph of American sports marketing. It survives and flourishes in our era, when sports marketing has evolved into a multibillion-dollar industry, for good or ill or something in between. About the only people who ever had trouble with it were the wonderfully oafish ball players in Ring Lardner's fiction. To them, baseball's climactic annual event was the World Serious.

....

Baseball—Organized Baseball—rough-tough, tobacco-chewing, whiskey-drinking, waitress-grabbing, spitting, kicking, spiking, cursing Professional Baseball seized the attention of the country in the autumn of 1903. That October, two months before Orville and Wilbur Wright made their first brief flight over a beach in the North Carolina Outer Banks, the Boston Pilgrims of the American League took on the Pittsburg (as it was then spelled) Pirates of the National League, in another "World Championship Series."

Honus Wagner, "The Flying Dutchman," the famous Pirate shortstop and slugger, made six errors in eight games and batted only .222. Denton True "Cy" Young, a great Red Sox righthander, won the fifth game and the seventh for Boston. When the crowd for game eight exceeded expectations, Young went to work in a booth on Huntington Avenue, outside the ballpark. Cy Young, who won 511 major league games—94 more victories than any other pitcher in history—sold tickets on October 13, before his Pilgrims went out to play the Pirates. Baseball owners, having created the classic October denouement to their long season, fell to squabbling among themselves with such intensity and churlishness that the 1904 World Series that would have matched the Pilgrims against John McGraw's feisty New York Giants had to be called off.

CY YOUNG

From 1892 through 1899 the National League operated as a twelve-team league, a major league, the *only* major league, a prosperous monopoly. It was not just the only game in town, but the only game in twelve different cities: Brooklyn, Boston, Philadelphia, Baltimore,

St. Louis, Cincinnati, Pittsburgh, Chicago, Louisville, New York, Washington, and Cleveland. Various rival major leagues appeared during the nineteenth century, but even the most significant challenger, the American Association (1882–91), had to fold. With the field to themselves, National League owners traded, released, and farmed out players on whim. In a monopoly situation the players became chattel. The league adopted a salary scale that fixed an absolute ceiling at $2,400 a year. Cy Young won thirty-five games for the Cleveland Spiders in 1895, at an annual wage of forty-six dollars a week.

Byron Bancroft "Ban" Johnson, a former collegiate catcher and Cincinnati newspaperman, became president of the minor Western League during the 1890s. At the turn of the century, Johnson expanded his circuit into eastern cities and renamed it the American League. He organized "raids" that brought 111 National League players into his new operation. Salaries doubled. By 1902, its second year, the American League, with such stars as Young and Rube Waddell and the tragic alcoholic slugger Ed Delehanty, outdrew the National League, 2.2 million to 1.7 million. Seriously threatened, the National Leaguers sought peace, recognized the American League, and concluded agreements making possible the 1903 World Series.*

---

*Ban Johnson attributed his quick success to "clean baseball, solid financing, and honest umpires." That he outbid the older league in salary wars was not something Johnson liked to mention. For with the major league agreements of 1903, competitive bidding for players once again ceased. What had been a one-league monopoly now became a two-league monopoly. Real bidding—which led to the phenomenal baseball salaries of today—did not resume until 1974, when the arbitrator, Peter Seitz, set aside the series of clauses which "reserved" a player for a single club

The last game of the very first World Series survived vividly in the memory of John R. Tunis, an author who alternated between romantic sports fiction and some clear, hard-eyed sports nonfiction. In his own phrase Tunis was "a nipper" at the Huntington Avenue Grounds in Boston for that game on October 13, 1903. Indeed, he was handed his ticket by the great Cy Young. The loudest Boston fans, Tunis recalled merrily, were known as the Loyal Rooters, a band led by a rugged Roxbury saloon-keeper named Michael T. "'Nuf Said" McGreevey.

"'Nuf Said was a huge Irishman," Tunis remembered, "and his place, on Columbia Avenue, was lined with signed photos of stars. Players and the umpires drank there after, and sometimes before, the games. His nickname originated from a habit he had of stepping around his bar whenever clients became boisterous, tapping them firmly on the shoulder, and adding two words: ''Nuff said.' If they refused to calm down, they found themselves bouncing off the beer drays and trolleys along the avenue. McGreevey was one powerful Irishman."

On October 13 the Loyal Rooters, clad in black suits and high white collars, marched to the Huntington Grounds, in military style, each man with a blue rosette pinned to his lapel and his ticket stuck in the band of his black derby. 'Nuf Said McGreevey led the Loyal Rooters. "Most, but not all, walked resolutely," Tunis remembered. "Many of the brethren had already visited McGreevey's that morning."

in perpetuity. Denying a ball player the right to free agency, Seitz argued, would be like denying the right of an immigrant to obtain U. S. citizenship. Federal courts upheld Seitz's decision.

A brightly uniformed marching band preceded 'Nuf Said and the Rooters, blaring out a hit song of 1903, "Tessie," from a musical comedy called *The Silver Slipper*. As Tunis recalled it, the marching Loyal Rooters sang out in full voice, with whiskey bassos predominating:

> *Tessie, you make me feel so badly,*
> *Why don't you turn around?*
> *Tessie, you know I love you madly.*
> *Babe, my heart weighs about a pound.*

Tunis and I were sitting in a New York restaurant, the luncheon guests of one of the editors of the *New York Times Magazine*. At seventy-five, Tunis had left his native New England to live in Florida. He quickly came to hate the state. "No hills," he grumbled, "and no vitality. The state flag ought to show an arthritic hand." Now he had moved back to a colonial house in Essex, Connecticut, and he was still winning doubles tennis matches against thirty-five-year-old opponents at the Old Lyme Country Club. Tunis wanted to talk baseball with a younger writer—myself—but he also wanted to sell the *Times Magazine* an unusual article: "I Retired *from* Florida." The *Times* editor rebuffed Tunis courteously but firmly. "Not the sort of thing we're looking for. Aiming for younger readers." Since the idea of retiring from Florida struck me as funny and pointed—and a good article will always find a life and an audience of its own—I felt pained for Tunis and embarrassed as well, a third party on a date that was not working out.

"I don't need for you to buy this," Tunis told the editor in a dignified way. "I have a large box at home full of stocks and bonds. I don't need for you to buy this, but I think you should." The editor said he would take it up with his superiors but couldn't offer much hope. I stirred the lemon twist in my drink. Suddenly Tunis said to me, "When was your first World Series?"

"October 1952."

"What do you remember most?"

"Joe Black starting three games for Brooklyn. Allie Reynolds throwing like hell for the Yankees."

"The Series," Tunis said, "has been a pitcher's show from the beginning." Under the gentlest urging, he began a remarkable reminiscence of his own first World Series game, when the twentieth century was fresh and new. John R. Tunis wrote more than twenty sports books that were marketed as juveniles and sold well. Probably the best known is *The Kid from Tompkinsville*. He had also published a variety of essays decrying commercialism in college sports. He possessed the sensitivity of a novelist and the discernment of a social critic. The son of a liberal Protestant minister who died young, Tunis was raised by his mother, a New England schoolteacher, and attended Cambridge Latin, an outstanding public school, before entering Harvard. He was a thirteen-year-old high school freshman in 1903.

"My brother and I were pretty good schoolboy athletes," Tunis said, "and we became terrific fans of the Boston Pilgrims. The National League team, the Boston Beaneaters, who became the Braves, were a good club, but the new Pilgrims—they started up in 1901—who signed Cy Young, just caught our fancy. Late in the 1903 season, with the pennant race pretty much over, Barney Dreyfuss, who owned the Pirates, recognized that the two leagues had better live together. As soon as his Pittsburgh club won, he issued a challenge to Henry J. Killilea, who owned the Pilgrims. Killilea accepted. Until that time, National League fans were laughing at nippers like my brother and myself, who rooted for the American League. Well, that 1903 Series stopped the laughter."

Tunis recalled October 13, 1903 as a gray, cool day. New England summer was past. You could feel the first forebodings of winter. "I remember in 1903 the despicable bigot Henry Ford was just getting started in the auto business and everyone was excited about the Panama Canal that was finally being built. A shirt cost a dollar. The first moving picture, *The Great Train Robbery,* came out. I remember 1903 very well." Tunis was spare and white-haired, but when he talked sports, even at seventy-five, youth stirred him.

"Were ball players heroes to children back then?" I asked.

"Some," Tunis said, "but Cambridge always had a kind of upper-class snobbery. The boys looked up to Sir Thomas Lipton, the yachts-man, and William A. Larned, the lawn tennis player. You wouldn't have found that in Hell's Kitchen down in New York or near Atlantic Avenue in Boston where the new Irish immigrants were growing up. But some of us Cambridge snobs, we knew our baseball. The biggest names were Honus Wagner, the Pittsburgh shortstop, and Nap Lajoie, who had headed out to Cleveland, in the wilds of the Middle West, and Jimmy Collins, the third baseman and the captain of the Pilgrims. And ol' Cy Young." Young was thirty-six in the season of 1903 and won twenty-eight games for the Pilgrims. He would pitch another eight years before retiring with 511 victories and 449 complete games, two records that have not been approached.*

"Cy's picture was in the Boston papers all the time in 1903," Tunis said, "the *Record* and the *Evening Transcript* and the rest. His real name, you know, wasn't Cy. It was Denton—Denton True Young—and he came out of a little country town in Ohio that was called Gilmore. In those days the newspaper sportswriters loved nicknames. John McGraw was Little Napoleon. Honus Wagner was The Flying Dutchman. So what do the Boston writers come up with for Cy Young? The Ohio Farmer." Tunis laughed. "The Ohio Farmer. How's that for flat?"

Young started the first game of the first World Series and took a four-run pounding in the first inning. The Pirates defeated the Pilgrims, 7 to 3. Boston won the second game, squaring the Series. Pittsburg won game three, despite Young's seven strong innings of relief pitching, and won game four, moving out to a large lead, three games to one. But Young won game five for Boston, 11 to 2; Bill Dinneen won game six for the Pilgrims; and on October 10 Young won the seventh game, leading all the way, 7 to 3.

"Then there was a pause," Tunis said. "We had some rainy weather. On the morning of October 13, my mother gave my younger brother and myself trolley fare, plus twenty-five cents each, which she said would buy us standing-room tickets. We didn't care about having

---

*Nolan Ryan, pitching across twenty-seven seasons—five more than Young—won 324 games and completed 222, less than a third of the record total.

to stand. We just wanted to get inside the Huntington Avenue Grounds and see the series.

"We were there before eleven o'clock, but others came even earlier. Special trains run by three separate railroad lines brought in fans from all over New England. The trains and the trolleys just poured fans into the long narrow passageway that led up to the gates. After a while, we heard a band approaching. They were playing 'Tessie.' Now here came the Loyal Rooters, marching in their black suits, behind the band and 'Nuf Said McGreevey, roaring out:

Tessie, you make me feel so badly . . .

"There were bankers and brokers from State Street and politicians from Martin Lomasney's Eighth Ward and longshoremen from Atlantic Avenue. They were all devoted fans who followed the Pilgrims faithfully, and they'd even hired day coaches and traveled west to watch the Series games out at Exposition Park in Pittsburgh. The Loyal Rooters expected favored treatment from the Pilgrim management and they got it. The crowd shoved up against the walls of the passageway to let the Loyal Rooters pass. Even to my youthful eyes, it was clear that, as I said, many of the brethren had already visited McGreevey's saloon; they were in excellent spirits.

"As the Rooters reached the ticket booths, the windows slammed up. The Rooters came first. Long lines formed behind them. When my kid brother and I finally got to a ticket booth, we were amazed to see behind the window the face of the great Cy Young. Cy Young himself. The crowd had come so fast and was so large that extra booths had to be set up quickly. Players who reached the clubhouse early were sent out to sell seats."

"Two twenty-five-cent tickets, please," Tunis said in high excitement to Cy Young.

"No standing room left," Young said. "The cheapest we have now are fifty-cent seats."

The Tunis boys debated. Should one go in? The other could climb a telephone pole on Huntington Avenue and see the game, if he wasn't grabbed by the police. The crowd behind the boys made impatient noises. Then, as in a miracle, the man behind Tunis leaned over and slapped a dollar bill in front of Young. "Give 'em both seats, Cy," he said. "Both seats" turned out to be behind first base. "That could well be as much of heaven as I shall ever know," Tunis remembered.

The *Times* editor stirred. "What differences were there," he said, "between the World Series then and now?"

"About as many differences as similarities," Tunis said. "First, there were no women present. Not a one. And every man in the stands was wearing his Sunday-go-to-meeting clothes. Black suits. Black derbies. Then all these people were fans. Nobody was there on an expense account. These people had followed the Pilgrims every day all summer. They knew every player. They recognized them. They called down to players by name. There were no uniform numbers, but none was needed. The spectators knew the players by sight and the stands were so close to the field that you could make out the players' faces. When we took our seats, the Pirates were working out. The strong fellow near shortstop, with gorilla arms and a jutting jaw, that was Hans Wagner. He moved around scooping grounders and throwing over to Kitty Bransfield at first. God, Wagner had an arm. Shagging flies in left was Fred Clarke, the Pirate manager and captain. There must have been some glare out of the clouds, because Clarke was wearing sunglasses. He was the first ball player ever to do that.

"Gradually, the Pilgrims appeared. They wore the white uniforms and red stockings. There was Buck Freeman, the right fielder who led the league in homers, and George LaChance, the first baseman, and Pat Dougherty, the left fielder and the best all around batter on the Boston club. Charles Deacon Phillippe started for the Pirates. He was a big feller, six feet two, and he threw sinking stuff. But he was going with only forty-eight hours' rest; the Pilgrims could get to him.

"The crisis of the game came in the fourth inning. Bill Dineen was pitching for the Pilgrims with four days' rest. He was throwing hard but he was a little wild. Tommy Leach hit a single. Now Wagner came up, and a band from Pittsburgh, out behind the outfield ropes, began to play his favorite song. Ol' Honus didn't smoke, but he loved a glass of beer. The Pittsburgh band played 'Down Where the Wurzburger Flows.'

"The Loyal Rooters were ready with a musical counterattack. To the tune of 'Tessie,' they sang lyrics they had just made up that morning:

> *Honus, why do you hit so badly,*
> *Take a back seat and sit down.*
> *Honus, at bat you look so sadly,*
> *Hey, why don't you get out of town?*

"The singing didn't rattle Wagner. He singled to right. After a pop up, Claude Ritchey beat out an infield hit and Tommy Leach made it to third. Word spread through the stands; out back of the seats Cy Young was warming up. Then Lou Criger, the Boston catcher, picked Tommy Leach off third, and an infield out ended the threat. I remember Cy Young—I guess his arm was ready—pushing through standing-room spectators behind the outfield ropes to watch the end of the inning.

"In the seventh Bill Dinneen knocked down Fred Clarke with a fast ball at the head. Clarke bunted to make Dinneen cover first, intending to spike him. Clarke was famous for that trick. But Candy LaChance, the Pilgrims' first baseman, was ready. He let the bunt roll past, and as Clarke ran by he picked up the baseball and fired it into Clarke's back. Players just came roaring off the benches. Fans broke through the ropes around the outfield. Soon a mob ten feet deep surrounded the diamond. My brother and I were small for this kind of thing. We stayed right where we were. It was a half hour before the umpires, Hank O'Day and Tommy Connolly, forced the fans back of the ropes and calmed the ball players and got the game resumed.

"Cy Young was still throwing, just in case, in the ninth inning, with the Pilgrims ahead, three to nothing. But he wasn't needed. Bill Dinneen struck out Wagner for the final out. The fans cheered and shrieked and hoisted up the Pilgrim players, Cy Young, Dinneen, just everybody, and paraded round and round, with the Loyal Rooters in the lead. The parade didn't stop. It was more than an hour before the Pittsburgh players could make their way to their carriages out on Huntingdon Avenue." Tunis looked at the *Times* editor. "You don't have scenes like that today," he said. "Fans who tried to hoist players onto their shoulders after a World Series victory would be arrested for assault and battery. And, at least as far as I know, Mickey Mantle doesn't sell Series tickets in one of those cement booths outside of Yankee Stadium."

The *Times Magazine* never would buy Tunis' account of his retirement from Florida. He died in 1975, at the age of eighty-five, leaving behind forty-one books, a shimmering memory of the first modern World Series, and one unsold magazine article. As for Young, he stayed with Boston through 1908, by which time the team had assumed the name of Red Sox. In 1908, the year of his forty-first birthday, Young won twenty-one and posted an earned run average of 1.26. He pitched through the 1911 season, which ended a few months after he turned forty-five. No one has since come close to his victory total, 511.

When the Hall of Fame was organized in 1936, the only five-hundred-game winner in the annals failed to make the premiere group. Along with Ty Cobb and Babe Ruth, the first-year inductees were Honus Wagner, Christy Mathewson, and Walter Johnson. But a year later Young made it, along with Tris Speaker and Napoleon Lajoie. Durable as he was, Young became a regular visitor at annual induction ceremonies at Cooperstown until he died, in 1955, at the age of eighty-eight.

As far as I can ascertain he threw hard, low sinking stuff, with an easy motion and great control. "I hit against him," Casey Stengel told me one day. "I went up to bat against him in spring training and I wondered who that fat old guy was, which shows what a dumb young punk I was, and you could look that up." An incomplete scouting report by modern standards, but all this was very long ago. Besides, Young's total of 511 major league victories is probably a thorough scouting report, all by itself.

5.

That first World Series finished baseball
as a sport. Afterwards the owners and later
the ball players became big-time businessmen.

JOHN R. TUNIS

To one glancing backward from the twenty-first century, the year 1905 lives on as a period of extremely nasty foreplay. Blood, gunfire, and tumult marked the year. The Russians were blundering through a war with the Japanese, and when black-coated workers swarmed to protest in St. Petersburg, the czar ordered his hussars to shoot them down. Imperial horsemen then rode wildly among survivors, swinging sabers. That date, January 9, 1905, is remembered as Bloody Sunday. In Geneva, Lenin plotted revolution.

Pogroms raged in eastern Europe. Everywhere seeds were sown for World War I and, a generation after that, Pearl Harbor, Auschwitz, and Hiroshima.

But if 1905 was a prelude for great and terrible events, and it was, in a small, exquisite area—Robert Frost's "pitching a baseball with distinction"—1905 was also something more. Quite simply, it was a benchmark. If you were to ask, *When did great modern pitching begin?* an excellent answer would be this: across six autumn afternoons in October 1905.* It was then, in the second World Series ever played, that Christy Mathewson, a strong and cultured right-handed pitcher for John McGraw's New York Giants, possessed of a fine fast ball and an Apollonian mien, shut out Connie Mack's Philadelphia Athletics three times. Three shutouts in six days. On the seventh day the Lord of Pitching rested. Mathewson, who had recently passed his twenty-fifth birthday, stood almost 6 foot 2, large for a ball player at the time, but the three shutouts did not proceed simply from physical strength. Mathewson was a quick, calculating fellow who believed, he said, "in observing, remembering, and cataloguing the weaknesses of every batter I have to face." His work ethic was towering, and by 1905 Mathewson had developed at least six different pitches that he could throw

---

*I mean to take nothing away from Radbourn, who deserves more recognition than has lately come his way. But modern baseball generally is regarded as beginning in the twentieth century, by which time the rules of today obtained, at least in general outline. Radbourn was retired before the distance from mound to plate was finally established as sixty feet six inches [1893–94]. Before the major league baseball universally adopted the pentagonal home plate [1900–1902] Ol Hoss was dead.

for a strike on any occasion. "I always try," he wrote in later years, "to give that batter exactly the pitch he least expects to get."

CHRISTY MATHEWSON

In his twenty-seven scoreless innings during the 1905 World Series, Mathewson limited the slugging Athletics to fourteen hits, mostly singles. He struck out eighteen. Dead ball? Of course, the 1905 major league baseball was dead, particularly when contrasted to the hyper-active baseball used today, with its patented plutonium core. But in those twenty-seven scoreless innings, Mathewson walked only one batter. Lively ball, dead ball, or beanbag, pitching with that sort of accuracy approaches the sublime.

"Back at my father's farm in Pennsylvania," Mathewson said, "I used to practice throwing baseballs through a slit in the barn door. The slit was four inches wide. I got so I could do it quite regularly." Mathewson knew the uses of understatement. He did not add that the baseball he threw through the four-inch slit measured three inches in diameter. He had a margin on either side of half an inch.

Mathewson's pitching and Mathewson's mind fascinated Ring Lardner, the greatest early chronicler of baseball. Indeed, Mathewson was probably Lardner's favorite ball player. "I remember my father telling me about Mathewson's intellectual makeup," the late John Lardner said over a tall Scotch and soda early in 1960. "Matty had a working knowledge of Latin and was decently read, unusual for ball players in his era. But where he was absolutely extraordinary was at playing games. Cards, billiards, checkers, baseball. My father said Matty was the most brilliant master of games he ever encountered." Mathewson could play eight games of checkers simultaneously while blindfolded, moving from board to board armed only with one of the most formidable gamesman's memories in the annals.

His pride was his arm, and this pride was fierce and magical. In interviews and in articles and books, notably *Pitching in a Pinch,* which he wrote with John N. Wheeler in 1912, he gives an unforgettable portrait of pitching as practiced ninety years ago by a grand master. He had close to a dozen pitches—varieties of curves, fast balls, screwballs and change-ups—that he could throw for a strike or, for that matter, throw right through a pinhole. As a teenager he taught himself the roundhouse curve, a big, wide, slow-breaking bender that deceives schoolboys and fat men batting between beers at company picnics. He tried the roundhouse in six games for the 1900 Giants and lost three times. After that he never again threw a roundhouse to a big-league batter. The slow break fooled none of the professionals.

By 1905 he had learned a fast, sharp curve (the modern slider) and another, wider hook that also broke down and away. He called the second pitch his "outdrop." By changing the grip on his fast ball, he could make the pitch veer upward, or to the right or left. In addition he threw a fast "straight drop" that he named his "dry spitter"; possibly the sinking split-finger fast ball of today. Finally, by rotating his wrist counterclockwise as he released the ball, he threw a "reverse curve." He called this pitch, which hooked down and into a right-handed batter—the curve and slider broke down and *away*—his "fadeaway." Today it is known as the screwball. Mathewson said that he did not throw his fadeaway more than five or six times a game because snapping his wrist counterclockwise to impart fadeaway spin strained his arm. One has to wonder whether this was so. For what the artful gamesman Mathewson said he could do and what he actually did often were not the same. Disinformation played a major role in his pitching.

"In most ball games," Mathewson wrote, "there comes an inning on which hangs victory or defeat. Certain intellectual fans call it the 'crisis.' College professors have named it the 'psychological moment.' Big league managers mention it as the 'break.' Pitchers speak of the 'pinch.' This is the time when each team is straining every nerve, either to win or to prevent defeat. In most of these 'pinches' the real burden falls on the pitcher. He must be able to live through these squalls."

Before Mathewson's pitching illuminated the autumn of 1905, the seething idiocy of one businessman–club owner had to be suppressed. There have been drunken owners, duplicitous owners, and avaricious owners by the truck load, but this one, a character named John Tomlinson Brush, survives as leader of a category identified by the columnist Red Smith as "fatheaded owners." ("Baseball," Smith liked to remark half a century later, "is such a marvelous game that it survives even the fatheads who run it.") All by himself, Brush succeeded in getting the 1904 World Series canceled.

Barney Dreyfuss of Pittsburgh was one of the good-hearted old sportsman-owners whose sense of values won admiration from such sensible observers as Tunis and Smith. Both these writers were secret sports romantics; venal baseball executives jarred them, where, say, venal securities salesmen did not.* They felt that baseball, unlike the floor of the stock market, was an arena that demanded nobility.

*Late in his life, when he had accumulated some money, Smith told me that following the suggestions of a securities dealer he had rapidly lost $150,000. He made no fuss other than to dub his broker "the Wolf of Wall Street." But ill-considered actions by a baseball commissioner, A. B. "Happy" Chandler or Bowie Kuhn, or the fatuous posturing of a buccaneer like Walter O'Malley, drove Smith out of his customary demeanor of amused detachment and moved him to rage.

At the end of the 1903 World Series, Dreyfuss decided to add some of his ball club's share of the gate receipts to the players' pool. As a result each Pittsburg Pirate received an extra $1,316 for his work across the eight games. Henry Killilea of the Pilgrims kept the team's share for himself; each champion Pilgrim drew $1,182. The 1903 World Series was the only one in which the losing players earned more than the winners. But as Dreyfuss showed himself a generous sporting man, and Killilea was characteristically greedy, Brush, who bought the New York Giants during the winter of 1902–1903, turned out to be a royal sorehead. Tall, gaunt, hard-faced, John Brush made his fortune in the men's clothing business, then strove to increase his wealth through baseball. He bought and sold franchises in Indianapolis and Cincinnati, and he paid heavily for the New York Giants. The price, $200,000, was a record for the time, but it gave Brush the franchise with the greatest potential in baseball. Playing under Coogan's Bluff—at what would become 155th Street and Eighth Avenue—the Giants had Manhattan, the country's prime sports market, essentially to themselves. The Superbas in Brooklyn played a world away, and there was not yet a New York ball club in the American League.

At first the potential fell short of expectations; the 1902 Giants were chaos in knickers. A second baseman named George Smith managed the team and so did one Horace Fogel, a sometime sportswriter whose background was buried in the minor leagues. According to the journalist and baseball historian Frank Graham, "Fogel's status wasn't clearly defined. He wandered in and out of the Giant clubhouse, sat on the bench when he chose, was free with his advice to one and all, and caused the players to wonder who was managing the team, 'Heinie' Smith or Horace Fogel? Possibly it didn't make any difference, since it was a very bad team." The 1902 Giants finished last, fifty-three games behind Dreyfuss' champion Pirates. Young Christy Mathewson looked like a major problem on this incompetent and possibly corrupt ball club. He seemed a misfit.

In later years sportswriters created a Mathewson so saintly that his wife, Jane Stoughton, a well-born and social Pennsylvania woman, issued a blanket correction. "If Christy had been the way these people say," Mrs. Mathewson remarked, "I don't believe I would have married him. He would have been too boring." The mythic Mathewson never smoked or drank or gambled. The real Mathewson smoked cigarettes and a pipe. He wasn't a hard drinker but, Graham said, "Matty knew the difference between Scotch and rye." As a master gamesman, he shot billiards and played poker for moderate stakes. Graham said he never encountered anyone who knew better when, and when not, to draw to an inside straight.

Betting on ball games by managers, owners, and players was rife when Mathewson broke in, and he sensed very quickly that gambling by baseball people was dangerous. As we shall see, he was one of the first to recognize that the Chicago White Sox were throwing the infamous World Series of 1919. To expand Mathewson's aversion to ball players betting with bookmakers into a sweeping, starchy distaste for gambling at large is to turn Mathewson from a prudent character, which he was, into a bluenose, which he was not.

Mathewson could be nasty, and in time he held himself aloof. Graham remembered an episode in a Pullman club car, after Mathewson had become a national hero, when a conductor walked up to the pitcher Art Nehf and said, "Can I have your autograph, Mr. Mathewson?" Nehf signed Mathewson's name. When the conductor moved on, Nehf said to Graham, "It's a good thing that feller didn't ask Matty. Matty would have told him to go to hell."

Mathewson was a sensitive man—he was known to weep after losses—and his character was surely affected by the coarse and essentially insensitive surroundings of the early big leagues. His genteel rearing hardly prepared him for the rowdy world of professional ball players, where many, like poor Charlie Radbourn, were addicted to going to bed with whores. Reserve and bouts of sharp-tongued sarcasm became his trustworthy defenses. "Matty," Graham remembered, "had hundreds of acquaintances, but he didn't like anybody getting really close, except for his wife and John McGraw and a sourpuss rockhead of a catcher named Frank Bowerman. That I guess was kind of classic. The upper-class gentleman picks for his friend a dead-end character."

As a twenty-one-year-old Giants pitcher at the Polo Grounds, Mathewson seemed a visitor from another world, possibly the Court of St. James. It is not true that he was the first college man to reach the major leagues. Bill Lauder came out of Brown to play third base for the Phillies in 1898, and for the Giants in 1902. Roy Thomas went from the University of Pennsylvania to the Phillie outfield in 1899. Eddie Plank pitched for Gettysburg College before Connie Mack brought him to the Athletics in 1901. Even Radbourn, as we've noted, briefly attended Illinois Wesleyan. In 1905 the *New York Times* ran a rapturous headline: COLLEGE MEN RANK HIGH IN PROFESSIONAL BASE-BALL. But in truth the great majority of early-twentieth-century major leaguers were ill schooled. Some were illiterate. Many of the greatest players—like Rube Waddell and Ed Delehanty—were drunks. Ball players seemed always to be brawling on the field or getting into bar fights or screaming obscenities at one another and at the umpires and at the fans.

I once asked Branch Rickey to describe the typical major leaguer when he broke in as a catcher with the St. Louis Browns in 1905. Rickey refused, saying that "to speak the truth in this instance" would offend us both. "The players," reported one early chronicler, "were, to say the least, a rough and ready lot. First-class hotels turned away baseball teams. The players got drunk and broke chandeliers. In the dining room, they complained about food in barbaric ways. If an old-time ball player thought a steak was tough, he'd get a hammer and nail it to the wall. Even second-rate hotels had special rules for ball players. They were not to congregate in the lobby. Under no circumstances could they mingle with other guests. When a ball club arrived at a hotel, no waitress under the age of sixty was safe from pinching and lewd and taunting remarks. Ironically, Mathewson, so uncomfortable in this world of rowdies, was the man who did more than anyone else to change it."

Mathewson was raised in a comfortable and devout Presbyterian household in Factoryville, near Scranton, fifty miles from the larger college town of Lewisburg, Pennsylvania. He attended a private secondary school, Keystone Academy, and Bucknell in Lewisburg. His parents, particularly his mother, wanted him to study for the ministry. "I preferred pitching of a different sort," Mathewson commented in his wry way. His father, Gilbert Bailey Mathewson, of Scottish stock, made money as a mill owner and real estate investor. He became at length a gentleman farmer. Gilbert Mathewson survived into his eightieth year, outliving his wife, Minerva Capwell Mathewson, by several months. Christy, the oldest of five children, remembered his childhood as happy and privileged. He always played baseball, he said. By the time he was four, he was strong enough to throw a ball clean over his father's barn. He couldn't remember *not* playing baseball.

Imbued with a strong work ethic, he performed well on athletic fields and equally well, he was proud to say, in classrooms, particularly in literature and English composition. When he published books and articles in later years, he insisted that he wrote his own stuff. John N. Wheeler, a journalist and businessman who subsequently honed and syndicated articles by Winston Churchill, helped Mathewson polish his work. But Wheeler told me at his home in Ridgefield, Connecticut, "I was at most Matty's editor, or rewrite man. He knew how to write, and his reading was voracious. He liked the essays of Charles Lamb and studies of psychology. The psychology of pitching? Sure. But more than that. Matty liked to read William James. His favorite novelist was Victor Hugo. I think Matty was the only major leaguer of his era who had read all of *Les Misérables*. He read it two or three times."

His first ambition, Mathewson maintained, had not been to pitch. "I wanted to be a slip-horn [trombone] player. I used to follow the Factoryville Brass Band and I'd just started blowing the slip-horn

myself when the band got a good job and the leader needed extra mu-
sicians. He hired me for eighty-five cents. Then he found out I couldn't
play very well. He told me to 'string along' and 'stall.' Keep sliding the
horn and pretending to blow. That's what I did. I was fourteen years
old. Afterwards many people complimented me on my performance. I
hadn't played a note. Then several things happened. I went home and
practiced. After a while the leader told me I'd become the best slip-
horn player in Factoryville. But my salary stayed the same: eighty-five
cents a concert. I earned the same for playing as for 'stalling.' That
started me thinking. Fooling the other fellow was just as valuable com-
mercially as playing well. In time I related that to pitching. Fooling the
other fellow was just as valuable as throwing hard—and a darn sight
easier on the arm." Mathewson could overpower hitters, but this slip-
horn-playing, Hugo-reading righthander prospered most gloriously,
fooling major league batters across the length of sixteen summers long
ago, summers kept green and golden by the memory of Matty.

At Bucknell University he starred in football as fullback and drop-
kicker, centered the basketball team, and was elected president of the
junior class. He sang in the glee club and joined Euepia, the campus
literary society. But, he told Wheeler, "the first game of baseball I ever
played where the result was really important was down in Scranton. I
always played to win. I mean something more when I say *really* important. I got together thirty-five cents and I went down to see a game between the Scranton YMCA and the Pittston Reds. I was seventeen,
but I had no thought of playing ball that day. I just wanted to see a
game. While I was sitting in the stands, a friend came by and told me

the Scranton Y needed a pitcher. They would use me if I cared to go in. I jumped at the chance. They rigged me up a uniform and I went in to work against Mike O'Neill from Minooka, near Scranton, who went on and pitched in the National League for five years. I had the roundhouse curve and a fast one. I kept the curve down and away and the fast ball high and inside and I struck out fourteen.

"We won with ease. The manager was so pleased that he asked me to come back next week and make a trip with the team to Easton. Sixty miles by train. I'd never been sixty miles away from home. But I went and I won again and when the college term ended I signed to play in the Wayne and Orange County semipro league. My salary was twenty dollars a month. After my sophomore year, when I was eighteen, I got an offer to go clear up to Massachusetts and pitch for Taunton in the New England League. They promised to more than quadruple my pay. Ninety dollars a month." Mathewson grinned at Wheeler. "I learned more about practical economics than pitching up there. I learned that twenty dollars a month, paid regularly, is a greater sum than ninety dollars a month, promised but not paid at all."

The season of 1899 was unrelieved tumult for minor league baseball in New England. The league began with eight teams: Brockton, Cambridge, Fitchburg, Manchester, Newport, Pawtucket, Portland, and Taunton, a circuit running from Rhode Island up to southern New Hampshire. In May Fitchburg moved to Lawrence and Cambridge moved to Lowell. In June Lawrence and Lowell dropped out of the league. In August Brockton and Pawtucket folded. When the season ended in September, only four teams were left. Newport won the pennant. Taunton finished last. One old record book gives Mathewson a record of 5 and 2. Another has him winning only two. More significant, it was at Taunton that Mathewson started throwing his most famous pitch, the fadeaway, that reverse curve now called a screwball or, in modern-day aggressive informality, "the scroogie."

It was a summer of maturation, rather than triumph, for a big blond kid with scholarly airs and a cowlick. "The owners said they just couldn't pay us, so we Taunton players decided to keep going on our own and play a doubleheader on Labor Day. We lost both games to Newport, but my share of the gate was forty dollars. That was more than enough for what I needed most. Train fare home."

Mathewson returned to Bucknell but his future now was baseball. He took another ninety-dollar contract the next season and pitched for Norfolk in the Virginia League. ("They really paid me this time.") He was strong and fast, and for the first time his remarkable control came clear. In twenty-two games at Norfolk, the nineteen-year-old Mathewson walked only twenty-seven. He won twenty games and pitched a no-hitter, which a local reporter recorded with high enthusiasm:

The game played yesterday was beyond a doubt the greatest exhibition of ball playing ever seen on a Norfolk diamond. For eight innings both teams tried hard to score, but all efforts were proven futile. Mathewson, for the home team, was in good form and pitched one of the greatest games that ever went down in the annals of baseball history. For nine innings not a hit was made off his chain lightning delivery, and the consequence was that nine Hampton sluggers fanned the atmosphere with vain attempts to find the ball. Norfolk scored in the ninth.

Mathewson won his Virginia League no-hitter, 1 to 0. In mid-July the Norfolk club sold Mathewson's contract to the New York Giants for two thousand dollars, not a particularly large sum even then. Eight years later, the Giants would pay Indianapolis of the American Association $11,500 for Rube Marquard, a fireballing lefthander. (When Marquard failed to win across his first two New York seasons, he became "the $11,500 lemon.")

Mathewson made his major league debut at the Washington Park, the lineal ancestor of Ebbets Field, situated in the Red Hook section of Brooklyn, hard by the docks. Washington Park was built in a hollow, and topography sealed its doom. My father recalled watching games there when he was eight or nine without having to buy a ticket. He simply dropped on a hillside with some chums and they looked over the grandstands and into the playing field. Joe McGinnity, later famous as Iron Man McGinnity—he pitched both games of a doubleheader on five occasions—started for the Brooklyn Superbas, a strong team that would go on and win the pennant. This day the Giants hit McGinnity early and moved to a 5-to-2 lead. In the bottom of the fifth inning, Ed Doheny, the Giant's starter, lost his control. After the Superbas tied the score at 5 to 5, Mathewson relieved. According to the Associated Press, "when the Giants substituted Mathewson late of the Norfolks, New York immediately went up in the air and Brooklyn won as it pleased, the score being 13 to 7." Welcome, as they say, to the big leagues. Mathewson was nineteen years old and nervous. He walked two and hit three more. Despite his Norfolk "chain-lightning delivery," he struck out only one Brooklyn batter. He lost two more games that season, without winning any. Mostly he worked batting practice.

What happened to Mathewson's superb Virginia League mastery? What became of the great Norfolk control specialist with no-hit stuff who made batters "fan the atmosphere"? A classic transition from the minors to the highest level of the game is what happened. A hard transition is more the rule than the exception. Bob Gibson was a .500 pitcher across his first four major league seasons. He threw hard, to be sure, but his record during that stretch with the St. Louis Cardinals was thirty-four victories and thirty-six defeats. Sandy Koufax joined the Dodgers in 1955. Seven years passed before this left-handed virtuoso was able to win as many as fifteen games in a season.

We are considering two Hall of Fame power pitchers. Three, really. The early Mathewson was a power pitcher, too. Clearly, as well-conditioned rookies, each man had achieved a peak of suppleness and strength. But the twenty-four-year-old Gibson won three and lost six for the Cardinals. The twenty-four-year-old Koufax won eight and lost thirteen for the Dodgers. Similarly, Mathewson, up from Norfolk at the age of nineteen, threw like chain lightning but couldn't win.

My father articulated the first principle here, long after we had advanced from indoor games of catch and prep school baseball and seriously considered the pitcher–batter balance in the major leagues. My father had extraordinary vision out of gray-green eyes, stout forearms, and excellent coordination. But he never advanced beyond college baseball. You could not consistently throw fast balls past my father; the first principle he espoused for pitching proceeded from that reality. "Speed alone," he said, "is not enough." A pitching machine, geared to gun baseballs at 200 miles an hour, would get everybody out. But in practice good fast balls cover a range from about 82 to 95 miles an hour. Occasionally, although not over a full game, a strong-armed pitcher gets his fast ball close to, or at, 100. (An electric eye clocked the great fireball pitcher Bob Feller at 106.) But if all a pitcher has is a string-straight 90-mile-an-hour blazer, he had better look for work driving an eighteen-wheeler. He won't stay in the major leagues.

After a few innings, batters time the fastest pitches human beings can throw. When I owned the Utica Blue Sox of the New York–Penn League, we signed a righthander named Willie Finnegan, who fired at 92. He didn't win. Willie couldn't control his fast ball. Often he threw high to high-ball hitters and low to low-ball hitters. Not intentionally, of course. You can't get away with that in the Penn League, single A, a very low minor league, let alone in the majors. Finnegan had to leave baseball. He became a broker, and the players joked that his market picks had better be more controlled than his fast ball, or his clients would have to go on welfare.

"Speed alone is not enough," my father told me again and again. "You want to throw hard but you also need control. They couldn't throw fast balls past me, but they got me out in other ways." He paused. "Lots of other ways," he said without cheer, sounding a bar from a common song of mourning.

Speed is uncomplicated. How fast does a pitch travel? That is measurable today with a hand-held radar gun and has been measurable for at least sixty years with cumbersome devices employing photoelectric cells. Control is more complicated. Walks are a good but incomplete measure. In 1913 Mathewson pitched sixty-eight consecutive innings for the Giants—the equivalent of more than seven full games—without issuing a single base on balls. That whole season, in forty games, Mathewson walked only twenty-one batters. In contrast, as a young fireball pitcher, Bobby Feller pitched in thirty-nine games during the 1938 season and walked 208. Can we conclude that Mathewson, 1913, was a great control pitcher and that Feller, 1938, was a wild man? We can, but what we have are extremes. In 1939 Feller cut his walks markedly and won twenty-four games.

The late north Georgia gentleman Whitlow Wyatt, an excellent pitching coach for years, said he had seen pitchers issue two bases on balls, or one or none, and yet be wild. "Walks only tell you about pitches outside the strike zone. You can be wild within the strike zone, too. The catcher wants a low outside fast ball. The pitcher throws a fast ball waist high down the middle. He's thrown a strike. He hasn't walked anybody. Still he's been wild. That's why his fast ball—wild and a strike—goes for a long ride into the left-field stands." The batter also interacts with a pitcher's control. In the minors, batters often are fooled by breaking balls that bounce around home plate, and fast balls that sail in chin high. They swing at bad pitches, and as they do, a ball becomes a strike. Batters can be fooled in the major leagues also, but that happens less frequently. Close to the field you hear managers and coaches reminding, bellowing, "Make him throw strikes."

Mathewson disliked talking about his failures, but we can reconstruct with a good probability of accuracy what befell him as a Giants rookie in 1900. His minor league roundhouse curve wasn't worth much. His fast ball—the chain-lightning delivery that overpowered weak hitters in Virginia—was less effective on its own. Hitters with slow bats don't linger in the major leagues. As a Giants rookie, Mathewson learned that his curve wasn't worth much and that he had better throw his fast ball to spots—up and in, or over the outside corner of the plate. Further, he had better hit those spots dead on, keep the ball on the corners but in the strike zone. Otherwise, the batters wouldn't swing. He pressed and as a rookie walked more men than he struck out: twenty bases on balls versus fifteen strikeouts in thirty-four innings. What about the vaunted fadeaway, the reverse curve he had learned at Taunton? Rattled and confused as a Giants rookie, he couldn't throw the fadeaway for a strike. Before the year was over, the Giants brain trust considered turning Mathewson into a first baseman. Few saw great pitching potential in the cowlicked college kid. He finished 0 and 3.

Mathewson had a highly developed sense of personal privacy and did not discuss or write extensively about his family's reaction to his wretched rookie season. He did mention to John Wheeler that his parents, particularly his mother, renewed a campaign for him to enter the Presbyterian ministry. Throughout his baseball career, Mathewson traveled with a Bible, which is still displayed in the National Baseball Museum at Cooperstown,* open to a passage from Isaiah that he annotated. After 1900, at family urging, he insisted that all his contracts include a clause that said: "No Sunday baseball."

Records from the Factoryville–Lewisburg area show Mathewson plunging himself into great activity during the winter of 1900-1901. He reentered Bucknell as a junior and became class president. He sang in the glee club, played trombone in the band, bucked the line as a football fullback, and joined a fraternity, Phi Gamma Delta. He also courted willowy Jane Stoughton, six months older than he, who was attending the Female Institute at Bucknell and resided with her parents in a comfortable home at 129 Market Street in Lewisburg.

When Mathewson returned to the Giants for the 1901 season, he went on a tear, won eleven straight, and beat the St. Louis Cardinals, 5 to 0, with a no-hitter on July 15. But then the team and Mathewson sank into a dreadful slump.

Looking at the 1901 record and Mathewson's losing mark in 1902 (14 and 17), some conclude that he was not an outstanding major league pitcher until he was supported by the hand, head, and affection of John McGraw, whose initial full season managing the Giants came in 1903, the year in which Mathewson first won thirty games. (He had three other thirty-victory seasons.) That view oversimplifies actual happenings. Once he got over rookie nervousness and replaced

---

*His glove is on display also, along with another Matty totem, his checkers set.

the roundhouse curve with a sharper hook, Mathewson became a splendid big-league pitcher. He was a splendid pitcher but neither a big winner nor a happy ball player for some time to come. The head game is ceaselessly complicated.

An outfielder named Jack Hendricks, who played for the 1902 Giants and managed the Cincinnati Reds for six seasons during the 1920s, told interviewers that the young Mathewson was the least popular man on the Giants. "He was a pinhead," Hendricks said. "He didn't care about anybody except himself. Why, one of his throws hit one of our best infielders in practice and knocked the poor guy out. Mathewson didn't even walk over to see how he was. What a conceited pinhead."

The word "pinhead," suggesting a small cranium, small brain, small intelligence, is inapplicable to Mathewson. But imagine coming from the Bucknell Glee Club and Phi Gamma Delta and the courtship of Miss Jane Stoughton to a society of drunken brawlers who hammered steaks into walls. According to Hendricks, Mathewson held himself aloof, and after a while the other Giants—Kip Selbach, Mike Grady, and Piano Legs Hickman—stopped speaking to him. Hickman said some Giants players went further than that. When the team fell out of the pennant race in 1901, "they threw down" Mathewson. That is to say, they deliberately missed ground balls, and "short-legged" flies. (An outfielder "short-legging" a fly runs hard but deliberately takes such small steps that the baseball bounces beyond his reach.) Betting by ball players was endemic, and although no one is recorded as charging the early Giants with fixing games Mathewson pitched, suspicion is, to say the least, appropriate. Possibly the 1901 Giants finished seventh, rather than third or fourth, because they threw a lot of ball games.

A season later, 1902, with the odd couple Heinie Smith and Horace Fogel in charge until mid-July, Mathewson's record continued to be perplexing. He pitched eight shutouts—among them the rest of the six-man staff pitched three. He averaged more than five strikeouts a game. His control, while not yet at its peak, was fine, fewer than two walks a game. But his won-and-lost record was only 14-and-17. The 1902 Giants made 330 errors, just about triple the minimum standard for a major league team today and a depressingly inept record even in a period of pebbly infields and undersized gloves. (As big gloves started to appear, an outstanding modern fielding team, the 1952 Dodgers, committed only 106 errors in 155 games. In 1999 the New York Mets played 163 games; they made only 68 errors.) The Giants finished last in the standings, as we've noted, and they also finished last in fielding percentage, at .943, well below the league average for the time. Whether Mathewson suspected his teammates of throwing games behind him is uncertain, but he took to complaining angrily after losses. "I can't win," he said, seething and despairing in the clubhouse. "I can't win the way you fellows are playing behind me."

"Go back to the woods," Piano Legs Hickman told him. "You ain't playin' with college boys no more."

"You're no good in the big city. You're just a big country stiff," someone else said.

Horace Fogel started Mathewson at first base for a few games. Hickman, who played second or third, and Joe Bean, the shortstop, delighted in sending throws into the dirt to make the college-kid first baseman look ridiculous. Fogel shifted Mathewson to the outfield, then had him play a game at shortstop. As a position player Mathewson batted .200.

In July 1902, John McGraw took over the New York Giants. The climate changed quickly. "I wasn't much of a hitter," the outfielder Jack Hendricks remarked to Frank Graham years afterward, "and there is a story that McGraw fired me off the club as soon as he saw me swing. Fired me off the Giants the first day. That is a lie. I hid in the clubhouse the first day. McGraw never fired me until the second day."

"Why the hell," McGraw stormed in the clubhouse, "have these dimwits been using Mathewson at first base or the outfield?"

"They think the kid can hit," catcher Frank Bowerman said, "and nobody's been doing any hitting on this club."

"He's got as fine a motion as any young pitcher I've ever seen," McGraw said.

"He can throw through a brick shithouse, Mr. McGraw," Bowerman said.

"Kid," McGraw said to Mathewson in July of 1902, "you're a starting pitcher, maybe my number one starting pitcher. Full time." McGraw later recalled, "I didn't ever tell Matty much of anything else." In 1921 McGraw told Frank Graham, "During my twenty-year connection with Christy Mathewson in baseball, he never asked me what to do, and I never had to tell him. I had the utmost confidence in his doing the right thing, on the mound or off. He never failed me. I consider what success I have attained in baseball is largely due to Matty." McGraw never expressed such admiration and affection for any other ball player, through a managing career that ran for almost thirty-three seasons.

On March 5, 1903, Mathewson married Jane Stoughton at the Presbyterian Church in Lewisburg. The wedding was described as "the most fashionable event of the Lewisburg social season." Jane had graduated from the Bucknell Female Institute with a baccalaureate degree. Mathewson, now totally dedicated to major league pitching, did not return to Bucknell for his senior year.

The newlyweds proceeded to New York by train and then embarked by boat for Savannah, Georgia, where the Giants gathered for spring training. "I confess," Jane Stoughton Mathewson said, "that I felt ill at ease at my first baseball camp. But Blanche McGraw, the manager's wife, understood and took me under her wing. Blanche and I got along so well, and so did my husband and John, that the four of us decided to take an apartment together in New York." McGraw, who won ten pennants in New York, pointedly maintained distance between himself and his players. He was the first man to announce, "Managing in the big leagues is not a popularity contest." He had the power to fine, suspend, or release any ball player who disobeyed him, and he was not reluctant to use all his authority. That was why sportwriters nicknamed McGraw, who stood 5 foot 7, "Little Napoleon." (Napoleon I, the Corsican, is said to have been three or four inches shorter than McGraw.)

McGraw had apprenticed as a third baseman with the Baltimore Orioles, the roughest and the nastiest of the nineteenth-century teams, and he quickly set about recasting the Giants out of a rough and nasty mold. He anchored his pitching staff with the former Brooklyn star

Iron Man McGinnity and Luther Haden Taylor, a mute from Os-
kaloosa, Kansas, who was saddled with the nickname of "Dummy."
"McGraw had Dummy Taylor teach us all the sign-language deaf
people use," Mathewson remembered. "Sometimes we gave our signals
in sign language. McGraw was just about our best sign-language expo-
nent," Mathewson added, with the faint smile, "until one afternoon
when, in a sparkling flash of repartee, he threw a finger out of joint."

Raiding and cajoling, McGraw brought in a veteran roustabout
shortstop, "Bad Bill" Dahlen; a big, brawling first baseman named
Dan McGann; and the hard-drinking and gifted catcher Roger Bresnahan, who split the work behind the plate with Frank Bowerman. He
drove his players hard and there could be no thought now of "throwing
down" behind Mathewson or anybody else. McGraw's 1903 Giants
were powerful and exciting. One game with Pittsburgh drew a crowd
of 32,000 to the Polo Grounds. About 18,000 sat in the grandstands;
the balance stood behind ropes in the outfield. Iron Man McGinnity,
in his prime at the age of thirty-two, won thirty-one games for the 1903
Giants. Mathewson, who was twenty-three, won thirty and led the
league in strikeouts. The Pittsburg Pirates won the pennant but Mc-
Graw's Giants were establishing themselves as the kings of New York.
"When I was a kid growing up," the columnist Jimmy Cannon said,
"real New Yorkers rooted for McGraw's Giants. The Yankees? They
played to tourists."

McGraw's Giants barked at umpires. They brawled with other
teams. Sometimes on the road extra police had to be called up to prevent fights between the Giants and the rival crowds. Mathewson is
said to have kept himself aloof from such violence. Usually, but not

always. One contemporary newspaper account describes an early Giants game in Philadelphia under the headline HOODLUM TACTICS:

Hoodlum [first baseman Dan] McGann lost his temper because he was thrown out at the plate by [outfielder Sherry] Magee, trying to score from second. He was so angry that he punched [catcher Frederick Harry "Faithful Fred"] Abbott. The latter threw the ball at the big tough and hit him hard in the back. McGann turned around and squared off at Abbott, who was there ready to defend himself. Umpire Joe Bausewine jumped between the pair and ordered both out of the game. McGraw helped to irritate the 22,000 spectators at Baker Bowl by running out to argue with Bausewine. Mathewson, just to show that his association with the old Baltimore crowd had also made a hoodlum out of him, hit and knocked down a little lemonade boy passing in front of the New York players' bench, splitting the boy's lips and loosening several teeth. All this was done in full view of the spectators, who became wildly excited over the ruffianly conduct of the visiting players. The result was that several thousand bleacherites mobbed the New York players in their carriages after the game was over, throwing stones and missiles at them and a hundred police officers had great difficulty in quelling the riot and rescuing McGraw and his team of ruffians.

How long will the National League continue to stand for the hoodlum tactics of this New York team? They are intolerable to all decent self respecting people. Even their supposed gentleman, Mathewson, strikes children in the face.

Onward, Christian soldier.

6.

THE RIGHTHANDER

FROM OLYMPUS

When John Tomlinson Brush refused to allow his Giants to play the Boston Pilgrims in the 1904 World Series, his baseball career touched an abysmal pit. Frank Graham, born in the then white and almost suburban outlying district of Harlem, in 1893, wrote long afterward: "But flinty and headstrong though he was, Brush became in many ways the perfect owner for New York. He gave McGraw all the money he wanted to buy players and never second-guessed. He poured a small fortune into repairing the Polo Grounds, which had tumbled into shocking decay. Brush's clothing-store money and his confidence in prickly John McGraw built the best ball club and the best ball park. But Brush had a blind spot as big as eight states. He could not see the American League."

For the 1903 season—Mathewson's fourth with the Giants and first as a husband—bride and groom shared an apartment with the McGraw family at Columbus Avenue and Eighty-fifth Street, on the

Upper West Side of Manhattan. "It was a roomy ground floor apartment," Blanche McGraw recalled, "and the rent was fifty dollars a
month. John paid that and he paid the gas bill for our lights. The
apartment wasn't electrified. Christy paid for the food. Since John
and Christy were on the road half the time, that came to about the
same amount. But we never worried if somebody was paying a few
dollars more. We were friends." McGraw called Mathewson "Christy"
or "Matty." Mathewson called McGraw "John." No other Giants
player was given that privilege. To all the rest, Bad Bill Dahlen, sullen
Frank Bowerman, "Turkey Mike" Donlin, and the Duke of Tralee, the
manager was "Mister McGraw."

For twelve consecutive years, from 1903 through 1914, Mathewson
won twenty games or more. No pitcher in this century has matched
that triumphant consistency. We have no clear record of specific
coaching that helped turn Mathewson from the losing pitcher of 1902
into the most consistent winner of all time. Some said that Rube Foster, an early black pitcher, worked with Mathewson on control, and
these same sources suggest that Foster taught Mathewson the fadeaway. Since Mathewson threw the fadeaway at Taunton in 1899, em-
phasizing Foster's role sounds fanciful, but he may well have helped
with final polish. McGraw had his pitchers experiment with different
finger pressures and grips, searching out exotic breaking stuff. But by
his own account, he left Mathewson alone.

Surely the two talked pitching after ball games as they rode by
carriage or elevated train down to the apartment on Eighty-fifth
Street. These were two of the best minds that ever considered win-

ning baseball.* We have tape recordings of Branch Rickey lecturing scouts and managers, during his glory days as baseball's most cerebral executive. We have no records of pitching talks between Mathewson and McGraw, only the word of both that the pitcher developed his craft as he pleased. Given Mathewson's competitive nature, intelligence, and gamesmanship, this seems believable. No Yankee batting coach instructed Babe Ruth. Not even Rickey presumed to give Jackie Robinson pointers on base running. I remember a Giants star flourishing generations after Mathewson, the matchless Willie Mays, telling me in his own way about ball playing. "Nobody can teach you nothing," Willie said. "You have to learn for yourself."

Mathewson taught himself to throw strikes, as he put it, "away from the center of the plate." He developed his variety of breaking balls on his own. He learned to change speeds on his own. What Mc-Graw appears to have supplied was confidence. He treated Mathewson like a young nobleman, the Prince of New York. If the other players resented Mathewson's special caste, his closeness to the manager, his aloof manner, his quiet arrogance, McGraw reasoned, they could go to hell, or play for Brooklyn. Unlettered but shrewd and bright, McGraw admired Mathewson's culture and quality and dignity. Before the term existed, McGraw was a blue-collar character; vastly successful and in time wealthy, but still a cursing, booming, gambling blue-collar guy. He cherished his friendship with an aristocrat. Besides, by building

---

*Casey Stengel possessed the best tactical baseball mind I have personally encountered. His great teacher, Stengel said, was McGraw.

Mathewson's confidence, and playing to Mathewson's ego, McGraw was present at the emergence of the greatest pitcher in the world.

John Brush wanted New York for himself, but in 1903 the Baltimore Orioles of the American League moved into upper Manhattan, where the new owners renamed the team the New York Highlanders. Brush raged at the invasion. Any team would have infuriated him, but the Orioles were a particular bête noir. They had formerly been the team of McGraw and certain key players McGraw lured to the Giants—Dan McGann, Roger Bresnahan, and the infielder Billy Gilbert. Now familiarity bred resentment. Worse yet, the Highlanders built their ball field, Hilltop Park, at 165th Street and Fort Washington Avenue, within a mile of the Polo Grounds. The Hilltoppers finished fourth in 1903; in 1904, with "Happy Jack" Chesbro winning 41, they made a serious run for the pennant, finishing only a game and a half behind Cy Young and the Boston Pilgrims. That October when Brush refused to let the Giants meet the Pilgrims in the expected "match to determine the champion of champions," he took advantage of loopholes in the agreements between the National League and the American League. Baseball fans and sportswriters wanted a second World Series. So did the ball players. They would earn more money. "Even John McGraw," Graham notes, "who had no love for the rival league, sought to persuade Brush to change his mind, but to no avail." Masking petulance, Brush issued a mild statement after the Giants clinched the pennant. "We are content to rest on our laurels."

A firestorm burst. *The Sporting News* published a cartoon in which Brush hid under home plate, cowering before a huge figure of Jimmy Collins, the Pilgrims' manager, who peered over a Polo Grounds fence and challenged him. "To a man down a hole," read the caption, "the American League champions look like the real Giants." The weekly, which advertised itself as "Baseball's Bible," followed through with an editorial. "Brush's refusal to permit his team to play a World's Series with the [defending] Champions of the World's team, has been condemned in the base ball department of every paper of prominence in the major league circuits and editorially in many of them. As between the major leagues there is [sic] more or less partisans in the representatives of the press, but this question is not one that concerns the leagues or individuals but the baseball public. There is a public demand for a World's series and the owner of one club stands between the game's patrons and their wishes."

Where McGraw had been unable to budge John Brush, the wide condemnation succeeded. That winter, he took the lead in devising a permanent arrangement for a championship play-off by proposing what became known as the Brush Rules. Best of seven series. Players get 60 percent of the receipts of the first four games, but nothing after, eliminating financial temptation for players to "throw down" early games. Each pennant-winning team had to post a bond, guaranteeing it would play in the World Championship Series. Brush transformed himself from sorehead to innovator. He had seen the abyss and decided he preferred the Grail. In broad outline, the Brush Rules of 1905 govern the World Series today.

McGraw later told Frank Graham, Heywood Broun, and other newspapermen with whom he liked to drink that the 1905 Giants were the greatest team he ever managed and the greatest team that ever played. It is hard, probably impossible, to quantify that opinion across generations. The 1905 Giants led the league in batting (.273), stolen bases (291), doubles (191), homers (39), and outdistanced the Pittsburg Pirates by nine games. The numbers, including that dead-ball home-run total, are very good but have been surpassed by many teams. The Giants won 105 games and played .686 ball, extremely healthy figures, and finished nine games ahead of the second-place Pirates. No Giants team has since won 105; only sixteen ball clubs in the major league records have matched or bettered that total. (One would be the 1906 Chicago Cubs. Another was the 1998 New York Highlanders, playing under another name, Yankees.)

Arguing with McGraw's judgment put one at peril. After the 1927 Yankees trampled the American League, won 110 games, and swept the World Series from the Pirates, Frank Graham asked Wilbert Robinson, then managing Brooklyn, how the slugging Yankees would have fared against the 1890s Orioles with McGraw and Robinson and Hughie Jennings and Wee Willie Keeler, who once batted .432. "They would have kicked the living hell out of us," Robinson said.

McGraw turned furious. "Is that what Robinson told you?" he asked Graham. "Well, I've known for a long time that he was getting daffy. Now he's blown his top. The old Orioles were a great team. They'd beat anybody, any time, anywhere. Except my 1905 Giants. They were the greatest." Graham wondered in his gentle way if the passing years had colored McGraw's judgment. "We're most impressionable when we're young," he said, "and in 1905 McGraw was a young manager, a young manager winning his first pennant." I then asked Graham if *he* could compare the 1905 Giants with the 1927 Yankees and some modern great teams as well. He declined, saying only, "Had the years colored McGraw's judgment? Perhaps."

Mathewson completed thirty-two of the thirty-seven games he started that year. He would have had difficulty recognizing contemporary major league pitching when, for example, in 1998, the Yankees' illustrious David Cone started thirty-one games, won twenty, but finished only three. Whether pandemic relief pitching, which has swept through major league baseball, is truly necessary or largely faddist is something to consider in later pages. To Mathewson long ago, failing to finish a start was deplorable and the cry bellowed at faltering starters, *Take him out,* was "the dirge of baseball."

Mathewson paced himself at work. As a rookie in 1900, he remembered, he had just about abandoned the roundhouse curve, and decided he would beat the Cincinnati Reds late in the season by throwing every pitch as hard as he could. He had the Reds, a seventh-place team, defeated, 2 to 0, in the ninth inning. "I'd been popping my fast ball, trying to strike out every hitter," he recalled to John Wheeler, "but in the ninth, the first man up singled. Then came a two-bagger. By the time they stopped hitting me, the scorer had credited Cincinnati with four runs, and they beat us, four to two." Afterward Mathewson, still wearing his full uniform, sat bleakly on a three-legged stool in the clubhouse, silent and depressed. George Davis, shortstop and manager for the 1900 Giants, walked over to the rookie. "Never mind, kid," Davis said. "What happened today was worthwhile, if you remember it. This game ought to teach you not to pitch your head off, every pitch, all afternoon, when you don't need to." Mathewson nodded and never forgot.

Part of the art, he said, was to work no harder than you had to. Some put up arguments against Mathewson's approach. "They suggest," he reported, "that if a pitcher worked as hard as he could, all of the time, instead of just in the pinches, he would not get into pinches in the first place. But there still would be pinches. They happen. An error. A bad pitch. You can't assume that you will totally control a game. If the pitcher has not conserved his energies, the pinches usually go against him. A pitcher should realize that there are eight other men on his team, drawing more or less salary, to stop balls hit at them, or, in the case of the catcher, balls bunted in front of him. You do best in the major leagues having confidence in your teammates. Further, when things get tight, you want to surprise hitters. If a pitcher displays his whole assortment early in the game, uses all his speed and his sharpest breaking curves, then when the crisis comes he, rather than the hitters, will end up with surprises, mostly unpleasant." *Finish what you start. Don't throw your arm out. Save your best stuff for your worst moments. Pitch only as hard as you have to for victory.* Commandments from the gospel of Christy Mathewson.

Hasn't the lively ball changed everything? In 1905 Jasper Davis of the Philadelphia Athletics led the American League by walloping eight home runs. In 1993, on the World Champion Toronto Blue Jays, eight of the nine regulars, all but shortstop Tony Fernandez, hit more than eight homers, and Toronto was not a notable long-ball team. Certainly it is more difficult for a pitcher to coast, particularly in a close game, since just about everyone he faces possesses home-run power. But it is usually safe to coast a bit when you have a four- or five-run lead.

Besides, certain factors in the dead-ball days favored hitters. Fielders' gloves were little larger than a hand, and pebbles littered the infields, leading to bad hops. The 1905 Giants, a strong defensive team, made 258 errors. (The 1905 Brooklyn Dodgers, a last-place team, kicked, bobbled, missed, or threw away baseballs no fewer than 408 times.) A competent defense ball club, playing with fishnet gloves on today's polished infields, will make no more than 125 errors. Improved fielding and improved fields counter some of the impact of the lively ball.

In his prime of youth and sinew, Mathewson pitched about ninety innings—ten full games—a season, more than anyone does today. Were he around, I suspect he would pitch less and also coast less, and still finish more of his starts than conventional wisdom suggests is possible. It took a brave manager to remove Mathewson from a ball game. His blue-eyed glare turned lesser men to custard.

The *New York Times* reported on Sunday, October 8, 1905, that the resumption of the World Series has excited patrons of the game to a greater extent than any other event in the history of baseball. That the coming contest will be fought out between the teams that are justly entitled to the distinction cannot be questioned. In a season that surpassed all others in brilliancy, the New York National League team, under the management of John J. McGraw, showed itself to be points stronger than any other. . . . The American League campaign was closer. It was not until the meeting of Connie Mack's Philadelphia club and Chicago, week before last, that the Athletics gained a clear lead.

That pitching will cut a big swath in the series is confidently believed by all competent judges. Philadelphians always believed that Waddell, their great lefthander, could outpitch any other man in the country. As against this contention, the supporters of the champion New Yorks point to the brilliant achievements of Mathewson this year and believe that he is without an equal as a pitcher. It is quite probable that these two successful boxmen will be pitted against each other tomorrow and, with both in form, rare pitching will be witnessed.

The *Times* covered most of a page with head shots of the competitors, Bowerman, Bresnahan, McGinnity, Dahlen, Mathewson, McGraw, Waddell, Eddie Plank, Lave Cross, and—in a wing collar— Connie Mack.

George Edward "Rube" Waddell, a left-handed fast-ball pitcher from the northwestern Pennsylvania community of Bradford, was a drunk. Sportswriters early in the century had no inclination to write about alcoholism in the major leagues. But baseball was a drinking business.* Ball players worked short hours, made a decent living, and spent half their working lives on the road. Drink filled their nights. Pitchers, who worked only one day in four or five, were particularly susceptible to boozing. They only had to be in shape to work one day a week, or at most two.

Some wrote of Rube Waddell as "a character, a real character." Fire engines obsessed him. On several occasions when he was not pitching, the lure of sirens proved irresistible and he burst from his dugout seat, past austere, wing-collared Connie Mack, and fled out into the street, in full uniform and spikes, to follow the wagon to the fire. "My father confirmed that something like that happened," John Lardner said, "and on more than one occasion. On none was Waddell sober." In Florida once Waddell saw a performer wrestling an alligator in a pond. Waddell had been drinking McMullen's White Label Rye and thought, in his haze, he saw not a performer but someone in trouble. Waddell jumped into the pond, pulled the performer to one side, and heaved the alligator to a far bank. Waddell was a courageous man and powerful, but confused. He thought he was saving a life. Actually, he was ruining an act.

At the height of his fame, he appeared on stage in a play called *The Stain of Guilt*. He was cast as the hero, and the script called for him to cuff the villain in the second act. On several occasions after Waddell had been drinking, he cuffed the villain so hard that an understudy had to be summoned to finish the play.

*Full disclosure seems in order. Sportswriting was a drinking business, too.

In his early drinking days, Waddell seemed able to shake off alcohol when it came time to pitch. He was a twenty-game winner every year from 1902 through 1905. But Waddell's late days in the season of 1905 were unhappy. He had been divorced and could not meet his alimony payments. Like many heavy drinkers, he had trouble holding on to money, although he was earning three thousand dollars, a decent salary in a period when a custom-tailored silk-lined wool overcoat sold for twenty-five dollars. He disappeared for days between starts. Connie Mack always said, in his serious way, "I've given Mr. Waddell a little time off to go fishing." That was all that found its way into print, but at least two nastier Waddell stories circulated orally.

Andy Coakley, a Holy Cross graduate who started thirty-one games for the Athletics, affected a certain elegance. He sported a boater, the stiff straw hat that stylish collegians liked to wear on summer afternoons. On September 1, Waddell told Coakley to take off his boater. Coakley ignored him. "You can't wear that kinda hat, except in July and August," Waddell said. "Take it off." Waddell had been drinking. He advanced on Coakley. Both were six-footers. They scuffled, and Coakley spun Waddell to the floor of the clubhouse. Waddell apparently twisted his left shoulder. He had just given himself a sore arm.

This story, in which Waddell appears as a bibulous bully—something other than the amusing drunk of legend—is the gentler of the two tales. The other proceeds from Waddell's chronic need for money. He was seen with gamblers and a rumor spread. Waddell was going to take a bribe and deliberately lose his World Series starts. Someone reported this to Connie Mack, who didn't want a pitcher "throwing down" games but didn't want a scandal, either. Mack simply benched Waddell. Whether the cause was a sore shoulder or shaky ethics, the big lefthander did not pitch an inning in the 1905 World Series. (Waddell was out of baseball by 1911. He died destitute in 1914, at the age of thirty-seven.)

Even without Waddell, Mack's Athletics had one of the finest pitching staffs in baseball. Primed and ready behind the uncertain Rube were "Gettysburg Eddie" Plank, who had won twenty-six; Coakley, who had won twenty; and the formidable Native American Charles Albert (and inevitably "Chief") Bender. Plank, who finished a seventeen-year career with 326 victories, was an intellectual pitcher like Mathewson, with a shade less speed and stuff. Coakley, a tall, thin righthander, had led the league in winning percentage (.741). Bender, of German, Dutch, but mostly Chippewa descent, was twenty-one and tall and smiling and very tough. He kept talcum powder in the back pocket of his uniform and applied the talcum to the baseball— then within the rules. Bender's powder pitch dropped sharply like a sinker. A soul of geniality off the field, Bender at work knocked down hitters impersonally and regularly. Behind Mathewson, McGraw had Iron Man McGinnity, Red Ames, Dummy Taylor; he would not have to go very far behind Mathewson.

On October 9, Charles Evans Hughes declined to run for mayor of New York, and President Theodore Roosevelt convened a luncheon meeting at the White House on the topic of "brutality in football."

Roosevelt told representatives of Yale, Harvard, and Princeton that violence in football had to be eliminated. His son, Theodore Jr., playing football for the Harvard frosh, had already suffered bruises and a black eye in scrimmages. That night, a physical culture show, in which young men and women wore sheer tights, created such a crush around Madison Square Garden that police reserves had to be summoned to control a disorderly and heavy-breathing crowd. These were the front-page stories. Back on page 4, the *New York Times* informed its readers about baseball.

Giants Triumph, 3–0

In Inter-League Game

Mathewson the Hero of the Day

In Defeating the Athletics

Never Gave Them a Chance

At the Columbia Grounds in Philadelphia, the Giants scored twice against Gettysburg Eddie Plank in the fifth inning. Mathewson lined a single to center. After Bresnahan forced Mathewson, Turkey Mike Donlin singled to left, scoring Bresnahan, and Sandow Mertes singled into the crowd in center, sending Donlin home with the second run. The Giants scored again, in the ninth, when second baseman Billy Gilbert singled, advanced on Mathewson's bunt, and scored when Bresnahan's bounding ball carried into center field for a fourteen-hop single. The story was not so much the Giants scoring as pitching, the

Giants pitching. "Mathewson's speed," the *Times* reported, "was terrific." (We have only anonymous stories. Bylined baseball writing was still a decade away.) The chain-lightning delivery was back. "He alternated slow and fast ones. He used the wet ball.* He curved them in, out, down, and over. Philadelphia was at his mercy. Not a single base on balls did he grant and only four hits were made from his delivery."

Among the crowd of 17,945 were five hundred Giants fans who had come down to Philadelphia in private railway cars. McGraw's friend Gentleman Jim Corbett, the retired boxing champion who had won the heavyweight title from John L. Sullivan thirteen years before, led this cheerful group. Some fans placed bets on the game. McGraw himself told reporters he had bet four hundred dollars on his team at even money. "Matty at even money," he said, "is too good a bet to turn down."

When Lafayette Napoleon "Lave" Cross, the Athletics' captain, grounded to short for the final out, McGraw sprang from the dugout, met Mathewson at the third-base line, and shook the pitcher's hand. Giants fans ran onto the field and surrounded the two. By the time reporters worked their way through the fans, McGraw was ready with a quote. "Mathewson is phenomenal. We'll win the Series. I'll pitch McGinnity at the Polo Grounds tomorrow."

So he did. Connie Mack started Bender, and the Chief with the talcum-powder sinker all but matched Mathewson's opening effort.

---

*Probably not. Mathewson had a sharp sinker, much like today's split-finger fast ball. That likely was the pitch the reporter called a spitter.

Although Bender walked three, he pitched a four-hit shutout. The Athletics won, 3 to 0, before, one newspaper reported, "30,000 leaden-hearted sad-eyed baseball enthusiasts at the Polo Grounds." The Series was tied.

It rained on Wednesday. When the Series resumed in Philadelphia on Thursday, McGraw started Mathewson again, this time with only two days' rest. Mathewson pitched his second four-hitter and the Giants won, 9 to 0. In the *New York Times* of October 13, 1905, alongside advertisements for Eade's Gout Pills and the Santa Fe Railroad, we find the work of a sportswriter so moved by Mathewson's pitching that he aspires toward poetry. "A eulogy of to-day's play," he began, "would point individually to that professor of occult speed and pretzel curve, Christy Mathewson. . . . In contrast to the work of Coakley [Mack's starter] that of Mathewson was as the rays of the midday sun to the flickerings of a frost-coated firefly." (The absence of a byline was a blessing for this newspaperman. Mathewson may indeed have been a sun god, but I knew Andy Coakley when he was head baseball coach at Columbia. He was definitely no frost-coated firefly.)

Given a two-run lead in the top of the first, Mathewson limited the Athletics to four singles. He struck out eight. No Philadelphia runner reached third. Still trying hard, the man from the *Times* informed New Yorkers that Mathewson was "the Factoryville Baseball Genius."

The next day, McGraw started Joe McGinnity, and the Giants defeated the Athletics and Eddie Plank, 1 to 0. Now the Giants led the World Series, 3 games to 1, and McGraw had a bench full of good, rested pitchers: Leon "Red" Ames, who had won twenty-two; Luther

"Dummy" Taylor and George "Hooks" Wiltse, each of whom had won sixteen. With a commanding 3-to-1 lead, McGraw might have started Ames or Wiltse. Both had winning percentages above .700. Start Ames, or Wiltse, or Taylor (16 and 9), and give Mathewson another day or two to gather his resources, to recoup.

McGraw would have none of that. His ace was pitching to perfection. The challengers were reeling. Don't let up. Give them Mathewson again. Always go with your best, if your best is able to go. "I can pitch, John, if you want," Mathewson said. "My arm feels all right."

A crowd of 24,187 filled the Polo Grounds on Saturday, October 14. The old ball park seated about twenty thousand. (Most seats were benches. Capacity varies with the hip size of the fans.) Now fans— called "cranks" in those days—stood ten deep behind ropes in the out- field. Men hung on the fences. Some found perches atop the grandstand roof. Others, on distant telephone poles and buildings, watched through binoculars. A band played before the game, and its rouser began:

We'll all get stone blind—
Johnnie go fill up the bowl.

As McGraw left the clubhouse in center and walked onto the field, a cheer arose. "Clinch it today, Mac," someone shouted, accord- ing to the *New York Tribune.* "Nothing but a championship will suit us." McGraw smiled and turned toward the crowd. "A championship is what you'll get." While McGraw went striding toward the dugout behind first base, the visiting Athletics appeared. "Back to the tepee," a fan yelled at Chief Bender. "Giants grab heap much wampum." Bender walked impassively toward the visitors' dugout. He had a job to do.

Gentleman Jim Corbett moved among the Giants as they loosened up. The glib boxer bantered with the players. After a while Corbett and Roger Bresnahan unfurled a green Irish flag and held it high while a blur of photographers swarmed toward them. The final Giant to leave the clubhouse was Mathewson. An ovation greeted him and ran on for more than a minute. At length fans began to call, "Doff your cap, Matty. Doff your cap." Mathewson walked over to Joe McGinnity, who had pitched the shutout the day before. He made a little bow and then lifted McGinnity's cap. The crowd cheered and cheered. Finally McGinnity, grinning over his large jowls, lifted Mathewson's baseball hat. Someone cried, "Shake 'em up, Matty. Go after 'em." Mathewson raised his right fist and nodded his head.

A newspaperman counted half a dozen men moving through the grandstand, offering to bet one hundred dollars against seventy-five dollars that Mathewson and the Giants would win. There were no takers. "Hey," someone said, "they got an Indian going against us, but we got an Indian sign going against them. Matty." Starting a third World Series game in six days, Mathewson was not as fast as he had been. He would strike out four, no more. But his control, the Mathewson touchstone, remained, as the *Times* would put it, a ray of the midday sun. He would not walk a man. His confidence, this long-ago day, was that of a divinity. *Oh, I may tease you with the luxury of hope, and let you dream a while of victory. But the outcome—and we understand this in our souls—is not in question.*

Tully Frederick Hartsel, who that season topped the major

leagues in bases on balls—he walked 121 times—led off for Philadelphia. Hartsel stood 5 feet 5 and crouched.* But against Mathewson, he had no real chance of walking. Hartsel swung at the third pitch and lifted a short slicing fly to left. Shortstop Bill Dahlen reached the ball but dropped it. Hartsel was credited with a single. Bristol Lord, the Philadelphia center fielder, squared around to bunt. Against Mathewson you played for one run at a time, for one run any time. Mathewson threw a hopping high fast ball, and Lord popped his bunt to catcher Roger Bresnahan. Harry "Jasper" Davis, a slugger who had led the American League in home runs, runs batted in, and doubles, grounded to third and forced Topsy Hartsel, just beating Billy Gilbert's throw at first. Then Lave Cross bounced to second, ending the miniature threat. Bender retired the Giants quickly and the game stayed scoreless through four innings. The *Times* baseball writer called both pitchers "magnificent." And so they were.

After Bender retired the Giants in the fourth, he drew respectful applause. A fan stood up and shouted, "You're the real thing, Injun. Kangaroo [jump] out of the American League and come play for us next season." Walking toward the Athletics dugout, Bender looked toward the grandstands and tipped his cap.

In the fifth, Bender walked the first two Giants batters, Sandow Mertes and Bad Bill Dahlen. Art Devlin, the Giant's third baseman, sacrificed. Mertes scored on Billy Gilbert's fly to left. The Giants and Mathewson had a run. Mathewson survived two Philadelphia singles

---

*His great rival in drawing walks was Miller Huggins, later famous as manager of great Yankee teams in the 1920s. Huggins, who weighed 140 pounds, was skinnier than Hartsel, but taller, 5 feet 6. He drew 103 walks for the 1905 Cincinnati Reds.

in the sixth. After working Bender for a walk in the eighth, he scored the Giants' second run. Mathewson retired the last ten Athletics batters in succession. None hit the ball hard. The Giants won the World Series, four games to one. Mathewson had pitched his third shutout in six days. He returned to the Giants clubhouse, in a stately, regal jog.

A crowd followed him and stood outside the clubhouse, cheering and chanting, "Matty." When Mathewson emerged, Roger Bresnahan placed a wreath of laurels on his brow. Mathewson responded with a bow and a smile. Mathewson walked onto a little platform outside the clubhouse at the old Polo Grounds and stood with his catcher, stout 5-foot-8-inch Roger Philip Bresnahan, inventor of the shin guard, whom romantics nicknamed "The Duke of Tralee." Bresnahan had a strong tenor voice and liked to sing the popular Irish rondelet "The Rose of Tralee." With a bit of O.F.C.-rye whiskey inside his round belly, Bresnahan was not above telling the newspapermen that he himself was sprung from the green sod of County Kerry, in the west country down by the roaring sea. (Bresnahan was born and died in Toledo, Ohio.)

With the squat Toledo Duke at his side, Mathewson smiled faintly, remotely, and unfurled a newly inked banner to the October breeze. Its inscription read:

THE GIANTS
WORLD'S CHAMPIONS, 1905

Bresnahan grinned broadly. Mathewson, laurel-wreathed and restrained, continued to smile his distant smile. He eyes sought the distant sky and, one imagines, he saw heaven.

As the championship banner opened, the *New York Times* reported, "ten thousand throats bellowed forth a tribute that would have drowned a broad-side of twelve-inch guns. As volcanoes assert themselves upon the earth's surface, surely must that deafening, reverberating roar have lifted Manhattan's soil from its base." Great pitching moves fans and sportswriters to their ganglia. Ever afterward men would wonder whether Christy Mathewson was mortal or divine.*

New Yorkers at large celebrated in a more restrained way. To establishment Manhattan, the biggest sports story that October was not Mathewson, McGraw, or the Giants. Rather, it was the Vanderbilt Cup Automobile Race, run over 283 miles of freshly oiled Long Island roads. (Racing cars were novel and exotic. The Giants had been around for almost thirty years.) A French driver named Victor Hemery won the Vanderbilt at the wheel of an eighty-horsepower open-cockpit car called a Darracq. "It was a race," reported another anonymous *Times* sportswriter, "of alternate exhilaration, of hope and depression, of hairbreadth escapes by the Guinea Road, of burst tires and lost pins and broken cranks and cracked cylinders, of upsets and perilous, dizzy shaving of dizzy spots—in short a day of coquetting with sudden death." M. Hemery averaged 61.5 miles an hour, a speed the newspaper described as "frightful," although it was almost twenty miles an hour slower than Mathewson's change-of-pace and a good thirty to forty miles an hour slower than his fast ball. The *Times* took pause to

*Although my father as a Brooklyn native became a Dodger enthusiast, Mathewson was the favorite of his youth. He left me his copy of *Pitching in a Pinch,* in the Every Boy's Library, Boy Scout Edition of 1912. The book is dog-eared now, and cherished.

note Mathewson's accomplishment in its secondary story, the so-called "off-lead," and paid him an unusual oblique tribute on its editorial page. The newspaper's editorial board proposed that baseball bats immediately be "flattened, in order to put the batsman on an equality with the pitcher." The published editorial complained that the "preponderance of the pitcher is injurious to the interests of the game. The pitcher is now too important and the other players too unimportant. The better pitcher wins in professional baseball. Whether flattening the bat be the device to put the two sides more nearly on equality is not important. The important thing is that some device to that end be sought and found." The flat-bat proposal was first ignored and then forgotten. Editorial writers commenting on sports usually make even less sense than sportswriters commenting on politics. A year later, facing hitters still required to hit a round ball with a cylindrical bat, Mathewson won twenty-two, but he was defeated twelve times.

That nameless *Times* sportswriter called Mathewson, 1905, "the pitching marvel of the century." (The century was only five years old.) Slightly misquoting Shakespeare on Julius Caesar, he added: "He doth bestride the field like a colossus."

Whatever its merits, the *Times* has never been a poetic newspaper. Journalists with lyric gifts chose to work elsewhere, at the *New York World* or the *Herald Tribune*. But when the straining *Times* man returned to earth and prose, his work improved. He concluded, "Mathewson's superhuman accomplishment [three World Series shutouts in six days] will stand as a mark for all pitchers in the future." As these lines are written, ninety-five years later in another century,

Mathewson's 1905 World Series accomplishment stands as the reporter forecast, beyond equal and beyond compare.

Life was never again quite so golden for cowlicked, laurel-wreathed Christy Mathewson. He would win 373 games, pitch seventy-eight shutouts, and gain the idolatry of fans, sportswriters, and colleagues. "What a pitcher," John "Chief" Meyers, who succeeded Bresnahan as the Giants catcher, told that splendid oral historian Lawrence S. Ritter. "The only time he might walk a man was because he was pitching too fine. I don't think he ever walked a man in his life because of wildness." But baseball is, in the end, a team sport. Following the 1905 season, no team with Mathewson pitching won a World Series again.

After a contentious race in 1908, the Giants met the Chicago Cubs in a one-game play-off for the pennant on October 8. "My part in the game was small," Mathewson wrote, not quite accurately, in *Pitching in a Pinch*. "I started and I didn't finish. The Cubs beat me, 4 to 2. I never had less on the ball in my life." He said that he had been overworked and that a short rest, rather than provide recuperation, "further deadened my arm." He was hurt badly when his center fielder, Cy Seymour, played Joe Tinker's high fly into a three-base hit.

Misfortune seemed to dog Mathewson in big games. It was not until 1911 that the Giants won another pennant. Mathewson beat the Philadelphia Athletics' Chief Bender, 2 to 1, in the first game of the World Series, but he found trouble and frustration in the third game. Mathewson carried a shutout and a one-run lead into the ninth inning when John Franklin Baker, the Athletics' best power hitter, came to bat. "I had carefully nursed my lead"—the Giants scored a run in the third—"and studied every batter's weakness, and pitched to it," Mathewson recalled. "It looked as if we were going to win the game. And then zing! And also zowie!"

Baker had led the American League in home runs. (He hit eleven, three more than Ty Cobb.) Now he crowded the plate, secure in the knowledge that Mathewson did not throw at batters. He then pulled an outside fast ball on a line into the right-field stands, tying the score. The Athletics beat Mathewson in the twelfth inning, 3 to 2. "When Baker homered," Mathewson said later, "I realized I had been pitching myself out, expecting to win in nine innings. My arm felt like so much lead hanging on my side, after Baker's hit."

Some, including Rube Marquard, the Giants' second-best pitcher, said Mathewson should have backed Baker from the plate with a fast ball close to the ribs. Mathewson disagreed, maintaining that Baker had hit an excellent pitch, and returned to the theme that he simply had not geared himself to go into extra innings.* After a week-long rain interruption, the Athletics beat Mathewson again, 4 to 2, and went on to win that Series, by the same numbers, four games to two.

A year later, in the World Series against Boston, Mathewson lost the deciding game, 2 to 1. In the tenth inning his center fielder, Fred Snodgrass, dropped a fly, and his first baseman, Fred Merkle, failed to

---

*Mathewson's ornate explanation for losses—the "deadened" arm of 1908, the "lead" arm of 1911—have led to speculation that he was the model for Ring Lardner's gifted, unconsciously comic baseball star, nicknamed in the famous short story "Alibi Ike."

catch a foul pop. Mathewson recorded an earned run average of 1.57 in the 1912 Series, but lost two games.

In 1913 it was the Giants against the Athletics once again. Mathewson pitched a ten-inning shutout in game two but lost the fifth and deciding game, 3 to 1. He did not pitch in a World Series after that.

From as far back as memory runs, I've read sportswriters who question the courage of pitchers. Tommy Holmes of the late *Brooklyn Eagle* considered a Dodger righthander named Red Evans who appeared in 1939. "At first," Holmes said, "Evans lost ball games one to zero and two to one. Later on it turned out that if he had to lose nine to eight, why, he could do that, too." Evans went 1-and-8 with a good third-place Brooklyn team, and Holmes was not only amusing but accurate. The pressure of big-league ball was too much for Russell Edison "Red" Evans. It clearly was not too much for Mathewson, and some may suggest that mentioning Red Evans and Christy Mathewson in the same paragraph is sacrilege. But it must be noted that Mathewson, the righthander from Olympus, lost a number of important games, by a run or two, and that after 1905, he lost more often than he won in the World Series. It should also be mentioned that in 1914, when he was thirty-four years old, he won twenty-four games and pitched five shutouts for the Giants.

By this time his demeanor had become forbidding. In a rough-house world full of drunks and gamblers, Mathewson held himself aloof from the hurly-burly and even, or especially, from idolatrous fans. "Who wants to be thought a hero all the time?" he asked Ring Lardner, by way of explaining his reserve. But he knew precisely who he was, and his own celebrity pleased the inner man. On days when he was scheduled to pitch at the Polo Grounds, Mathewson never left the clubhouse for the playing field until fifteen minutes before game time. He liked to wear a cape. Proceeding slowly down the long green stretch from centerfield to the warmup mound behind home plate provided an entrance for the caped and regal Mathewson that Sarah Bernhardt might have envied.

When a young pitcher asked in spring training to show him how he gripped his best curve, Mathewson obliged. "Do you think Hans Wagner is as good as Ty Cobb?" the rookie said. "Listen," Mathewson snapped. "Did you come down here to learn to play ball or with the idea that you are attending some sort of conversational soirée?" The rookie retreated. Spurned by veterans when he was a young major leaguer, Mathewson in turn spurned rookies as a Giants elder. "Many recruits [rookies]," he observed, "think that if they can get friendly with the veterans, they will be retained on account of their social standing. I cannot abide young ball players who attempt to become the bootblacks for the old ones."

McGraw traded Mathewson to the Cincinnati Reds in 1916 so that he could manage. Ring Lardner, the great baseball writer, responded with a remarkable exercise in verse.

> *My eyes grow very misty*
> *As I pen these lines to Christy;*
> *Oh, my heart is full of heaviness today.*
> *May the flowers ne'er wither, Matty,*
> *O'er the grave in Cincinnati*
> *Which you've chosen for your final fadeaway.*

In Ohio, Mathewson spurred a bad team from last place into the first division. Late in the 1918 season, he left baseball for what he regarded as a higher calling, service in World War I. At the age of thirty-eight, Mathewson was commissioned a captain in the Chemical Warfare Division of the American Expeditionary Force in France. At the front he took it upon himself to ascertain when the trenches were safe for infantrymen to occupy. In the course of this harrowing duty, he inhaled quantities of chlorine gas. "When he came back to me after the Armistice," Jane Stoughton Mathewson recalled, "he caught cold and that developed into a cough that he could not shake off."

He coached for McGraw, then became too ill to continue. The cough turned into tuberculosis and Mathewson retired to a sanitarium at Lake Saranac, New York. When he improved he purchased a modest house, the only home he ever owned. McGraw had to organize a charity exhibition game to pay Mathewson's medical bills.

Mathewson felt well enough to accept the presidency of the Boston Braves in 1923, and Burton Whitman of the *Boston Herald* celebrated: "Matty has come back. In the mind of every boy, young man and old fan, today there will be a little refrain of thankfulness that this most heroic and for a time most pathetic figure in baseball has recovered."

He had not. A relapse sent him back to Saranac, and he spent his last summer walking on a cane through upland meadows, classifying plants in English and in Latin. He found early goldenrod and Canadian thistle and yellow loosestrife, which he recorded in his notebook as *Lysimachia terristris*. He meant to live a useful life for all his days.

He died on October 7, 1925, two months after his forty-fifth birthday and almost exactly twenty years after his first World Series shutout. The Washington Senators were playing the World Series in Pittsburgh that day. Both teams donned black armbands in Mathewson's memory. At two o'clock, the ball players marched single file to the centerfield flagpole. The flag, at half staff, was raised, then lowered halfway again. The players and the umpires and the crowd at Forbes Field stood bareheaded. Quite spontaneously a woman spectator began to sing "Nearer My God to Thee." Her voice floated across the field. Slowly, unevenly, players and umpires and spectators joined in the hymn.

Mathewson was buried at the Lewisburg City Cemetery on October 10. The American Legion, in convention at Omaha, passed a resolution mourning his death from "wounds received in action overseas." Kenesaw Mountain Landis, the commissioner of baseball, put his grief into a question. "Why should God wish to take a thoroughbred like Matty so soon, and leave some others down here that could well be spared?"

Jane Stoughton Mathewson, who lived until 1967, presented many of Mathewson's letters, his notebooks on Adirondack plants, his glove, his checkers set, and his Bible to the Hall of Fame. She continued to follow baseball, Jane Mathewson said, but never returned to the Polo Grounds after her husband's death. "It would have been too much," she said, "looking at the pitcher's mound, looking at *his* pitcher's mound, with Christy gone."

BOOK TWO

MODERN

TIMES

Home plate is seventeen inches wide, but I

ignore the middle twelve inches. I pitch to

the two and a half inches on each side.

WARREN SPAHN

7.

PITCHING GOES

OUT TO LUNCH

For some twenty years—broadly the troubled intermezzo between the two twentieth-century world wars—major league pitching sank into appalling decline. "It was bad, all right," the sardonic baseball writer Tom Meany conceded to me once over his lunch, which consisted entirely of extremely dry martinis. "I covered ball games every day back then. I ought to know. But a lot of things went bad. They tried to shove Prohibition on us. The market crashed. The economy went to hell. Everything slid out of whack over a few years. Pitching was just one more damn thing that soured."

In the years following the World War I armistice, home runs exploded in length and height and number. "It's no secret," the great columnist Heywood Broun pointed out in the *New York Tribune*, "that baseballs who want to travel have a new saying: *Join Ruth and see the world.*"

On April 4, 1919, Babe Ruth, accelerating his transition from pitcher to outfielder at the age of twenty-three, hit a home run that traveled 525 feet. Or 579 feet. Or 587 feet. Or 625 feet. The site was Tampa, Florida. Ruth and his Red Sox teammates were playing an exhibition against the New York Giants. The assembled New York and Boston sporting press saw the home run and spent hours trying to calculate how far the baseball traveled. According to William Curran's interesting work *Big Sticks,* the playing field was set up within the infield of a racetrack, that is to say the portion inside the white rail that runs a full mile in an oval. Curran reports that Ruth's drive sailed "over a stand of coconut palms bordering the far side of the track in right center and landed in a plowed field where it finally rolled to a stop." The roll is important. By certain surviving testimony, Ruth's homer traveled farther than any ball can travel on a fly, following the calculations of baseball physics, as preached in New Haven by Professor Robert Adair. (He writes, as mentioned earlier, that the farthest a batted ball can travel on the fly is 545 feet.)

McGraw, managing the Giants, estimated the distance at 587 feet. As a lord of discipline, McGraw disliked Ruth and Ruth's mindless, muscular style, but he conceded that this was the longest home run he had seen. Ed Barrow, later the triumphant and flinty general manager of the Yankees, was the Red Sox field manager in 1919. He came up with 579 feet. Apparently these numbers include a certain amount of roll. Curran says that the most "conservative witness agreed that Babe's shot was airborne for about 525 feet."

After the game Ross Youngs, the Giants' right fielder, walked a group of reporters to the spot where he believed the ball had stopped. Using borrowed surveyor's equipment, the writers came up with the high number 625, an amazing 175 feet longer than an average well-paddled major league home run would travel today if the ball bounced and rolled unimpeded. No one knows with certainty, nor can anyone now determine, how far Ruth's home run really traveled. (McGraw traded the pitcher who threw it, "Columbia George" Smith, a month later, as if to banish the most obvious reminder of the wallop.) I content myself with the report of W. O. "Bill" McGeehan in the *New York Tribune*. McGeehan wrote that the baseball traveled so high "it came down coated with ice."

At his best Ruth played on a planet by himself, splitting molecules with a swing that is a wonder. My father, not notably inclined to exaggerate, remarked that it was more exciting to watch Ruth strike out than to see a mortal major leaguer hit a home run. (Actually, Willie Mays, Mickey Mantle, Henry Aaron, Duke Snider, and Reggie Jackson, among others, struck out more frequently than Ruth.) But as baseball revived between the wars, more and more mortals hit home runs, at an ever-increasing rate.

The 1917 Yankees, with Mathewson's nemesis John Franklin Baker playing third base, led the American League in home runs. Baker hit six. First baseman Wally Pipp hit nine. The Yankees' league-leading total was twenty-seven. That same year the entire Washington ball club hit four home runs. The Senators' power man, Joe Judge, hit, two. Ten years later the Yankees, led by Ruth and Gehrig, smacked out a total of 158 home runs, an increase of nearly 500 percent. The 1927 Senators managed to hit twenty-nine, not much by modern standards, but still an astounding increase, almost 700 percent, over their total ten years earlier. Today a good power-hitting major league club routinely hits more than two hundred homers.

A home run requires a lusty swing, and with more batters aiming for the fences, one would expect an upsurge in the number of strikeouts. (Ruth led the American League in strikeouts on five occasions without ever fanning more than ninety-three times in a season.) But curiously, as home-run totals increased, strikeouts actually decreased. Again proceeding from 1917 to 1927, we find the American League home-run total jumping from 133 to 439 and the strikeout total declining from 4,192 to 3,341. The National League decrease was similar.

Finally, amid all this assault on pitching, batting averages went orbital. In the season of 1930, the National League, all eight teams, collectively recorded a batting average of .303. The whole *league* was a .300 hitter. McGraw's Giants hit .319 as a team—and finished third. The St. Louis Cardinals, who won, batted .314. Along with the economy, pitching made a staggering sort of recovery during the 1930s, but even the final baseball season before Pearl Harbor, 1941, is set apart primarily by the accomplishments of batters. Joe DiMaggio hit safely in fifty-six consecutive games. Ted Williams led the majors with an average of .406.

The game had come about 180 degrees since the editorial board of the *New York Times* demanded that bats be flattened. There is no shortage of characters anxious to expound on factors that led to the post–World War I decline in pitching. There is no shortage of conflicting viewpoints, either. With minimal argument we can begin by considering rule 8.02. According to 8.02:

The pitcher shall not:

Apply a foreign substance of any kind to the ball;

Expectorate on the ball, either hand, or his glove.

The rule went into effect for the season of 1920 and outlawed the spitball.* It did not eliminate it. As someone once remarked, "The spitball and Scotch whiskey were outlawed at about the same time; the applicable edicts were equally ineffective." Rule 8.02 and its interpreters went on to outlaw trick pitches of all sorts, and scuffed baseballs as well, until all a pitcher could properly apply to a baseball was his hand. The very sweat of a pitcher's brow had become contraband. But 8.02 remained subsidiary to the greater overriding rule that governs professional sport: *You do what you have to do to win.* Grantland Rice, the most romantic of sportswriters, wrote a quatrain once that became famous, particularly in press boxes.

> *When the One Great Scorer comes*
> *To mark against your name,*
> *He writes not whether you won or lost*
> *But how you played the game.*

---

*Seventeen pitchers, certified spitballers, were allowed to continue throwing wet ones. In the National League these were Bill Doak of St. Louis, Shufflin' Phil Douglas of the Giants, Dana Fillingim of Boston, Ray Fisher of Cincinnati, Marvin Goodwin of St. Louis, Burleigh Grimes of the Dodgers, Clarence Mitchell of the Dodgers, and Dick Rudolph of Boston. The nine American Leaguers exempted were Yancy "Doc" Ayres of Detroit, Ray Caldwell and Stan Coveleski of Cleveland, Red Faber of the White Sox, Hubert "Dutch" Leonard of Detroit, Jack Quinn of the Yankees, Allan Russell of the Red Sox, and Urban Shocker and Allan Sothoron of the St. Louis Browns. Quinn pitched into the 1933 season with Cincinnati, the year in which he reached the age of fifty. Grimes threw legal spitballs through 1934, when he turned forty-one, and pitched in that one season for the Cardinals, the Pirates, and the Yankees. Coveleski, Faber, and Grimes have been selected for the Hall of Fame.

That is an excellent approach to propound when instructing little leaguers and also nuns who are starting a convent softball team. John Lardner, Ring Lardner's son, caught the reality of the major leagues with another, less familiar verse:

> *Right or wrong is all the same*
> *When baby needs new shoes.*
> *It isn't how you play the game.*
> *It's whether you win or lose.*

Breeches of 8.02 began just as soon as 8.02 went into effect. Ball players, managers, umpires, and even a few sportswriters knew that the spitball remained a staple of the major league game (as it is today). It was not until July 20, 1944, that an umpire enforced 8.02. On that day, Cal Hubbard ejected Nelson Potter, the ace righthander of the St. Louis Browns, for throwing a spitter at Yankee Stadium. One ejection in twenty-four years. That enforcement rate for 8.02 defines permissiveness.

Spitballs were prominent throughout the great New York pennant races and World Series of the 1950s. Roy Campanella, the Dodger catcher, insisted that Sal Maglie, the glowering Giants righthander, threw spitters every time he faced Brooklyn.

"You think so?" I said, a little thickly.

"I don't think so, buddy," Campanella said. "I *know* so. I know what they look like. Remember, I caught a million spitters myself in the colored leagues."

Maglie was getting out Campanella with great proficiency and I wondered if Campanella was using the spitter as an excuse. But some months later, I found myself at dinner with Sal Yvars, a genial and open New Yorker who was the Giants' backup catcher.

"Campy says Maglie throws a wet one," I said.

"If you put this in the paper I'll deny it," Yvars said, "but between us, Campanella is right. We've got a regular signal for Maglie's spitter, and everything."

"'Where does he get the moisture?" I asked the catcher. "And aren't the umpires looking at him?"

"The umpires don't give a shit," Yvars said. "Mostly they're in a hurry for the game to be over so they can get to their beer. Maglie puts a drop of olive oil down below the thumb of his pitching hand. There's a little hollow there where the sweat gathers. When he rubs up a ball, he'll touch the sweaty area with his left hand. Then he transfers the moisture to the ball."

"That doesn't seem like a lot of moisture," I said.

"You just want to wet a small patch of the ball," Yvars said. "You don't need the fucking Atlantic Ocean."

Campanella, three times chosen as the most valuable player in the National League, did not discourse on spitballs as extensively as he might have. He was not only swinging at spitters, he was calling them. Preacher Roe, the Dodger lefthander who twice led the league in winning percentage, celebrated his retirement, in 1955, by selling a confessional to the magazine *Sports Illustrated* that the editors titled, "The Outlawed Spitball Was My Money Pitch." Roe reported that Beech Nut gum, rather than Wrigley's Spearmint, provided ideal saliva. In the article, he neglected to tell the merry tale of how he and the Dodgers' infield outwitted a solid umpire named Larry Goetz.

Roe had wet the baseball and was about to wind up when Goetz, who was umpiring at second base, charged up to him from the rear, shouting, "The ball, Preacher. Gimme the fucking ball." Roe, a splendid control pitcher, tossed the ball toward Goetz, but somehow the toss carried high, over the umpire's head. Pee Wee Reese rushed over from shortstop, rubbed the ball, and tossed it to the second baseman, Jackie Robinson. Another rub. Robinson flipped the baseball to first baseman Gil Hodges. Then over to Billy Cox at third. Now back to Roe on the mound. With a look of sublime innocence Roe extended his left hand, palm up. "Here's what you wanted, Larry. Here's the fucking ball."

On the testimony of various batters, another skillful spitball artist was Whitey Ford, the Yankee lefthander who started a record twenty-five World Series games. Maglie, Roe, and Ford—three very fine pitchers, three masters of the illegal spitball.

In recent times Steve Carlton and Don Sutton have been cited as practitioners of another illegal pitch, the scuff ball. Nicks on the baseball's smooth service affect its flight at major league velocity. Scores of hitters who don't want to be quoted cite Carlton and Sutton as premier nickers and scuffers. Some attributed Carlton's extended silence—he would not talk to reporters about baseball—to a fear of questions about his wicked and possibly scuffed slider. Sutton was ejected by umpire Doug Harvey in 1978 after Harvey had collected three balls scuffed while Sutton was pitching for the Dodgers against the Cardinals. "In my term as National League president," the late Charles "Chub" Feeney told me in 1992, "I was sent dozens of balls that Sutton had supposedly scuffed with his belt buckle. I didn't feel that was good enough evidence. It was ex post facto. I told umpires, you have to catch him in the act of scuffing. Nobody did."

Rule 8.02 certainly helped batters, but in the checks and balances always at play, the resin bag, introduced in 1926, helped pitchers, who now maintain a firm grip on the baseball. Before that, on hot days pitchers had to reach down and grab dirt to dry their palms. For a time John McGraw impregnated dirt around the Polo Grounds mound with soap shavings. Visiting pitchers, reaching for dirt, came up slippery. The home side, knowing where soap-free patches lay, did not.

I first heard the intriguing history of the lively ball from a small, bespectacled Brooklynite named Hy Turkin, a second-line baseball writer at the *New York Daily News*. As far as I know, Turkin played no baseball. He was slight, pale, myopic. The editors at the *Daily News* did not let him cover a team on a regular basis; he was backup man, moving from ball park to ball park, filling in when the regular writers took days off. This small, pedantic, underappreciated reporter was one of the great researchers in baseball history. He invented *The Baseball Encyclopedia*.

Turkin's curiosity was measureless. At the old Polo Grounds, the right-field wall stood 257 feet 8 inches from home plate, at the foul line. Or so the Giants said. By fiat, no outfield fence could rise at a point less than 250 feet distant from the plate. One morning in 1950 Turkin appeared at the Polo Grounds with a yardstick and began measuring the distance to the right-field wall. As Turkin made his scrambling way past first base, Chub Feeney, then the Giants' general manager, dispatched two security men to stop him. Turkin was led off to a press room, where the Giants offered him food and drink.

"This is outrageous," Turkin said. "Simply outrageous."

"Hy," Feeney said, uneasily, "the sign on the right-field wall says 257 feet, and if that's good enough for me, it ought to be good enough for you."

These days baseball research is made easier by such technological innovations as a machine that can photocopy five hundred pages of ancient sports sections in an hour. In Turkin's day, one set down data by hand; recording information from five hundred pages in a month was an efficient research pace. Turkin's partner in early investigations was one S. C. "Tommy" Thompson, a horn player who worked in the pits of Broadway musicals. The idea of the first encyclopedia was to compile the names, dates, and records of everybody who had ever played in the major leagues. Turkin and Thompson researched in libraries, newspaper offices, and even, on occasion, graveyards, obtaining information from tombstones. When this prodigious effort was completed in 1951, the publisher, John Lowell Pratt of A. S. Barnes, offered a prize of fifty dollars to anyone who could find a major league player ever whom Turkin and Thompson had missed. Not even ten prizes were awarded. Turkin died of cancer at the age of forty, in 1955, after completing work on a revised edition.*

I mention Turkin because, to be sure, he deserves mention and also because he is my preferred source on the lively ball. In a book I

*My most recent copy of *The Baseball Encyclopedia,* published by Macmillan, indicates that newer is not necessarily better. The listed birth year of Christy Mathewson is incorrect and his batting record as first baseman and outfielder in 1902 has been neglected. (He hit .200.) Nowhere are Turkin and Thompson credited with their landmark idea.

wrote for Doubleday in 1954, I used information Turkin generously supplied: "[In 1920] the manufacturer of the American League baseballs decided to try Australian yarn instead of the American yarn that had been used [because it was cheaper]. The Australian product was stronger, wound tighter. The lively ball was born. In 1919, before the lively ball, Babe Ruth hit twenty-nine homers, a record total. In 1920 the Babe hit fifty-four."

In *Big Sticks* William Curran objects to Turkin's lively approach. Why, he asks, in effect, if a rabbit ball was sneaked into play was Ruth the only man to benefit from it so dramatically? He was not the only strongboy in the game. Curran believes the ball was not suddenly made more lively. The liveliness came over some years in modest increments. What changed the game, he believes, was Babe Ruth's colossal up-from-the-toenails swing.

Curran is an engaging writer. His chapter on the lively ball begins: "The baseball's frequently noted perfection of form is a Platonic conceit." One would be hard-hearted not to find Curran's prose pleasing. But I am just hardheaded enough to stay with Hy Turkin's position. The Lords of Baseball stumbled upon the lively ball by accident in 1920. Ruth, as the Hall of Fame historians point out, knew how to attack the lively ball before anyone else. Then, when home runs turned out to be more commercial than bunt singles, the club owners clutched lively baseballs as a vigorously as bankers today clutch ATM fees.

Of course, the lords denied that they had tampered with the game. Later lords praised plastic grass. You trust a baseball lord at your own risk. But the essential idea in 1920 was to make as many people as possible forget the crooked 1919 World Series. The craggy incorruptibility suggested by Commissioner Kenesaw Mountain Landis helped make that happen. But no fan ever paid a dollar to see Landis. What restored the game were lively baseballs, being whacked regularly into cheap seats by characters named Ruth and Hornsby and a forgotten slugger named Fred "Cy" Williams, who hit forty-one homers for the Phillies in 1923.

Hitters grew bigger and stronger. In the Mathewson era, the largest and strongest ball players became pitchers. Big strong athletes threw hard. Mathewson, Walter Johnson, Chief Bender, Grover Cleveland Alexander, all stood at least 6 foot 1. A stumpy gathering played behind them: 5-foot-5-inch center fielders, 5-foot-6-inch shortstops. After World War I scouts began looking for big young men, not merely to pitch but to play the new power game. The size and physical strength of major leaguers increased dramatically. Lefty Gomez's description of the slugger Jimmy Foxx: "He scares me in the batter's box. Those huge forearms; those big hands gripping the bat, all that sawdust oozing out between his fingers." Gary Cooper, who played Lou Gehrig in the popular movie "Pride of the Yankees," was tall and lean. The real Gehrig, slightly over six feet, had the huge shoulders and the biceps of a weight lifter. Lewis "Hack" Wilson, who hit fifty-six home runs for the Chicago Cubs, stood 5 foot 6, but Wilson weighed 195. With an eighteen-inch neck, Wilson was the most powerful 5-foot-6-inch ball player on earth.

The Yankees became baseball's dominant team between the wars, winning eleven pennants in twenty seasons. Ed Barrow, appointed general manager in 1921, directed his scouts to sign the biggest prospects they could find. Let the slick little finesse players go to the

St. Louis Browns. John McGraw's game of bunt and steal and hit and run fell into decline. Big muscles reigned.

Some fine pitchers flourished during the batting boom. Robert Moses "Lefty" Grove, the rangy, hot-tempered flame thrower, won three hundred games in the 1920s and '30s. Jay Hanna "Dizzy" Dean, almost as good as he said he was, won thirty in 1934. In July of that season, quiet Carl Hubbell amazed everyone at the All-Star game in the Polo Grounds. Hubbell threw a hard screwball and mystified batters unfamiliar with the peculiar break of his reverse curve, Mathewson's fadeaway redux. Pitching against mighty American League sluggers who had seen him seldom, if at all, Hubbell struck out Babe Ruth, Lou Gehrig, Jimmie Foxx, Al Simmons, and Joe Cronin in succession. Some regard this as the greatest short-burst pitching ever. But even on that day, July 10, batters dominated in the long run. The American League bruisers pounded other National League pitchers and went on to win 9 to 7, cracking out fourteen hits.

How bad could pitching have been in an era of Hubbell, Grove, and Dean? The first-line pitching was excellent, although not nearly as overwhelming as Bob Gibson in 1968, who recorded an earned run average of 1.12, or, in earlier times, Walter Johnson, whose earned run average in 1913 was 1.09. But second-line pitching was dreary, as it tends to be today and—unlike today—the use of relief specialists was neither widely attempted nor understood.* One Erv Brame, of the

---

*An exception appeared on the Yankee teams of the 1930s, now remembered for power. The Yankees used Johnny "Grandma" Murphy, their relief specialist, in thirty-five or forty games a season. Murphy saved nineteen in 1939.

Pittsburgh Pirates, led the National League in complete games in 1930, finishing twenty-two. Brame gave up more than a hit an inning. He walked more batters than he struck out. His earned run average was 4.70. He pitched no shutouts. Hardly a Hall of Famer. Behind each Dean, Grove, and Hubbell between the wars worked a dozen mediocre pitchers such as Erv Brame.

What turned things around as much as any single factor was the development and popularization of a pitch easy to master and hard to hit. It was a small, sharp curve ball, usually thrown for the low outside corner of the strike zone, that looked for all the world like a low fast ball. It looked like a low fast ball until it wrinkled. Then the ball slid in a small sharp break. This was the slider. A right-handed pitcher's slider breaks away from a right-handed batter—a few inches lower and a few inches wider. The slider is not as spectacular as the big breaking curve ball Koufax threw, nor as intimidating as a Bob Feller fast ball. But this undramatic little wrinkle is largely what restored balance to the game. Individuals may have thrown a slider of sorts as far back as the nineteenth century, so technocrats can argue with anyone calling the slider new. But its appearance in the mainstream during the late 1930s and 1940s was a breakthrough.

I asked Whitlow Wyatt, an early (c. 1940) master of the slider, if he felt the slider was the best pitch in baseball. Wyatt's brush backs in the 1941 World Series prompted the usually unflappable Joe DiMaggio to raise his fists. (Wyatt was willing. Umpires intervened.) Off the mound, Wyatt was unfailingly soft-voiced and scholarly. "I wouldn't say the slider is the best pitch in baseball, young man," he lectured me in a kindly way. He was working then as pitching coach for the Milwaukee Braves, who won pennants with the great staffs Wyatt tutored in 1957 and 1958. "I wouldn't say the curve is, or that the fast ball is, either, for that matter." Wyatt was holding forth in a Socratic manner, drawing a question.

"Then what is the best pitch in baseball?" I said.

"The best pitch in baseball is a strike." That speaks banners. What the slider became, and continues to be, is the pitch that many run-of-the-mill pitchers, without a great curve or a ferocious fast ball, can throw and get a strike when a strike is absolutely essential, say with the count 2-and-2, two men on base and Sammy Sosa kneeling on deck. One way to snap off a slider is relatively easy. Hold the ball along the seams. At the moment of release roll the wrist sharply clockwise. The wrist roll, as opposed to the curve ball's full wrist snap, won't take much velocity off the pitch. But the spin from the roll creates a sharp deceptive break, fifty-five feet or so down the chute. "I could always tell a curve ball from a fast ball in the first thirty feet of flight," Stan Musial, a lifetime .331 hitter, says. "I picked up the speed of the ball and I knew who was pitching and I put the two of them together and I'd know just what the ball was going to do. Break or hop. The slider was tougher. I got my share of hits off sliders. But during the years I played for the Cardinals [1941 through 1963] the slider changed the game."

Bucky Walters, who threw a small sharp curve and won twenty-seven games for the Cincinnati Reds in 1939, said he had learned the pitch from Mathewson's World Series rival, Chief Bender. The Chief said he had used it as far back as 1910. "I never called that pitch a slider," Walters told Martin Quigley. "I just didn't call it anything. I didn't have a name for it."

When the slider became widely known, some denigrated it as "a nickel curve." Not much of a pitch. Not worth a dime, let alone a silver dollar. Walters and Wyatt and Mel Harder at Cleveland slowly spread the gospel, beating against conventional baseball thought. Bob Lemon, not overpowering, lacking a great curve, won 207 games for Cleveland between 1946 and 1958. His favorite pitch: the slider, low and away. Steve Carlton probably threw the roughest slider of all time. Today every major league pitching coach, and every minor league coach as well, teaches the slider as basic, on a par with the curve and the fast one. It turns out that the slider is not a miserable nickel curve at all. It is the pitch that saved baseball from becoming something initially intriguing that wears badly. It saved major league baseball from becoming extended batting practice.

8.

SPAHNIE

He is Davy Crockett at the Alamo.
He is the river boat gambler going down to New Orleans.
He is Dan'l Boone in old Kaintuck. "Reckon we won't
be troubled by no more Redskins," said Dan'l as he spat
a fresh ball down the barrel of his long rifle.
He stares contemptuously at the smile curling
Casey's lip and at the bat in Casey's hand.
He flicks one terrible glance at the men on base.
He shifts his cud.
He throws.
"Steee-rike!" cries the umpire,
and the westward course of empire flows unchecked.

PAUL O'NEIL,
IN *Sports Illustrated*, ON WARREN SPAHN

Warren Spahn was born in 1921, during the lifetime of Christy Mathewson, and he survived to pitch for the New York Mets and Casey Stengel, forty-four years later. When they told him he was too old for the major leagues, Spahn went south and signed with the Mexico City Tigers. He was old for a ball player in Mexico, too, but a season after that he put on a uniform and pitched for Tulsa of the Pacific Coast League. He didn't leave the mound for good until he approached his forty-seventh birthday. "I enjoyed my work," he reminded me quietly at Cooperstown a few years ago. "That's one reason I wanted to pitch forever. I never did retire from pitching. It was baseball that retired me."

More than one observer has suggested that the latter-day Christy Mathewson is George Thomas Seaver, who shared Mathewson's All-American good looks, fine competitive intelligence, and great seasons with a New York ball club. Seaver, who won twenty games on five different occasions, is certainly a remarkable modern pitcher. But my own candidate for Mathewson II did not, at first sight, resemble Mathewson at all. In his prime, Warren Spahn had a receding hairline, a long narrow jaw, and a big, bold nose. No one suggested that Spahn appeared Apollonian. Someone said he looked like a railroad brakeman. He threw left-handed—"every pitch," he says—and his one stint with a New York ball club proved disquieting.

Mathewson, it is said, taught the country that ball players could be legitimate heroes. Fifty years later Spahn reminded a country that had largely forgotten that pitchers, as well as home-run hitters, could be enduring icons. Although World War II stole three seasons from his pitching career, Spahn won 363 games, only ten fewer than

Mathewson. Until Spahn won his three hundredth game, in 1961, the idea of winning three hundred had become dubious. Up to that moment in Milwaukee County Stadium, twelve men had won three hundred major league games but just six—Cy Young, Mathewson, Eddie Plank, Walter Johnson, Grover Cleveland Alexander, and Lefty Grove—pitched in the twentieth century. Grove won his three hundredth and last game in 1941. That, some concluded, was that. The three-hundred-game winner, like the legal spitter and the New Deal, was history.

WARREN SPAHN

Such great pitchers as Carl Hubbell, Dizzy Dean, Bob Feller, and Robin Roberts had grown old or gone lame far short of three hundred. Paul O'Neill, one of *Sports Illustrated*'s early gifted contributors, wrote during the 1950s: "They're pulling in fences everywhere to create more home runs. More and more late-inning tie ball games are put in the hands of relief pitchers. A pitcher winning 300 looks less and less likely with each passing season." Then Spahn broke through.

"I grew up like any other kid, hearing about pitching immortals," he said to reporters afterward, and sounded both contemplative and droll. He recited the honor roll of three-hundred-game winners slowly, with great respect. Walter Johnson. Christy Mathewson. The names came back out of the past like a locomotive whistle on a prairie night. "Walter Johnson," Spahn repeated. "Christy Mathewson. Now me." He grinned, mostly to himself. "It seems almost immoral."

Once Spahn won three hundred, the dam, psychological, physical, a bit of both, crumbled; three hundred game winners flooded into sight. A small flood actually. Since Spahn's three hundred, seven others have reached or passed that point: Early Wynn, Seaver, Gaylord Perry, Phil Niekro, Don Sutton, Steve Carlton, Nolan Ryan. All are in Cooperstown. As with Roger Bannister and the 3:59.4 mile he ran in 1954, Spahn broke a barrier that had begun to appear unbreakable. Then, once he did, the barrier faded, so that now few remember it existed. I remember the barrier, and I remember quite wonderful pitchers who not only did not win three hundred but never won two hundred: Bob Friend (197), Allie Reynolds (182), Camilo Pascual (174), Ron Guidry (170), Sandy Koufax (165), Don Newcombe (149), Carl Erskine (122), Sal Maglie (119).

I watched Spahn work across three decades, and he stands out as the most enduring great pitcher I have seen. He won twenty-one games in 1947, when he was twenty-six years old. He won twenty-three games in 1963, when he was forty-two. He was not flawless. For three years during the 1950s, he did not start at Ebbets Field. The combination of powerful right-handed Dodger hitters and a short left-field fence was too much for him. But at the least Warren Spahn was the Chateau Margaux of major league pitchers. He aged splendidly.

During the 1950s, I wrote stories about Spahn for the *New York Herald Tribune, Newsweek, SPORT,* and the *New York Times Magazine,* and an editor at the *Times* (the same fellow who would not buy John Tunis' article on retirement) commissioned an illustrator to draw a robotic pitcher, based broadly on my descriptions. The robot is left-handed, like Spahn; its controls and sensor make what the *Times* editors regarded as an amusing list.

An antenna labeled "signal receiver"
Cathode tubes labeled "strike-zone calculator"
A batter-data computer
A glower meter
A change-up switch
A pitch-out cable
A slider lever
A fast-ball pulley
A curve-ball activator
A pick-off joint that swivels

The accompanying story recalled a conversation with Spahn. "Do you go to ballet?" Spahn asked one spring evening in a home he had rented on San Marco Island, near the Milwaukee Braves' training base at Bradenton, Florida.

"Not if I can avoid it," I said.

"But you know ballet."

"A bit."

"I wonder," Spahn said, "why a dancer can pirouette exactly the same way five hundred consecutive times. If she can do that, why can't I throw my slider so it moves exactly the same way five hundred times in a row? Doing a pirouette and throwing a slider are both physical activities. I can't understand why what goes for one doesn't go for the other."

Spahn was not, like Mathewson, a college man. "I had a scholarship offer from Cornell," he says, "but times were tough. The Depression. You've heard of the Depression." A slight grin. "The Braves were offering eighty dollars a month. I passed on college." But much like Mathewson, Spahn was a student of pitching, which he considered in fresh and original ways, studying, always studying, and remembering. He played the memory game as brilliantly as he pitched. At the end of a tough nine innings Spahn could retrace his efforts, pitch by pitch, recalling every one of the 125 pitches he had thrown, what each was, where it was, how the ball moved, how the batter reacted. This feat of memory suggests not only intelligence but also the phenomenal concentration Spahn brought to every game.

We were talking education in his Florida house long ago, and he wondered why I thought that he had gone to college.

"Your vocabulary," I said. "You don't speak like most ball players."

"Well, to be honest," Spahn said, "I've always thought about my speaking. Words are terrifically important. How else do people know you? Where I grew up (Buffalo, New York) everybody had the double-negative habit. 'I don't know nothing about that.' I knew it was wrong, but I couldn't help but pick it up. After I married, I asked my wife, LoRene, to tell me every time she heard me using a double negative. As you've noticed, I don't use double negatives anymore."

Spahn could be difficult—usually he was congenial—but at his best a moving humility radiated from him. In Cooperstown, when he was seventy-two, he walked up to me and in a droll, youthful way, said, "Didn't you used to be Roger Kahn?" We were standing on a terrace overlooking the unspoiled waters of Lake Otsego. I introduced him to my wife. "After a ball game," I said, "Mr. Spahn remembered each one of the hundred and twenty-five pitches he threw." Spahn looked embarrassed and made a small bow. "Nothing special, Mrs. Kahn. Pitching is what I did." Why all the fuss about a feller just working his craft? this astonishing craftsman wanted to know.

For Warren Edward Spahn, learning the pitcher's trade began in boyhood. He was granted a sturdy arm, a limber body, and a nimble mind. To this he added monolithic intensity, disguised by humor to be sure, but the same intensity one finds in a violin virtuoso or, for that matter, in a prima ballerina. He was named for President Warren Gamaliel Harding, a Republican who played excellent bridge, and for his father, Edward Peter Spahn, who played semipro third base in Buffalo and who, for a living, sold wallpaper. "There were six children," Spahn says, "and all of us had plenty. My folks took care of that. What they had left for themselves was something else."

His early baseball memories would be unexceptional to hear, except that he is Warren Spahn. Playing games of catch with his father in soft summer dusks. "I loved to play catch and play ball and I played every chance I could. I played on street teams and in the Buffalo Twilight League, the American Legion, city municipal. I was always playing ball and always thinking about playing ball. I never excelled in the classroom. Baseball was my focus. In the beginning, I wanted to be an outfielder or a first baseman. I wanted to get into every game every day. I could always throw well, but I loved action. I didn't care for sitting on the bench. After a while, it dawned on me that pitching was where the action really was, really is. I don't mean this to sound superficial, but when you're the pitcher, you're the one most intensely involved with every pitch. Oh, the catcher calls it, and the fielders pay attention, but there isn't any ball game until you throw.

"I had excellent mechanics and a decent arm. We didn't have radar guns but I knew I could throw the ball by certain hitters. That is number one, when you're starting. Early on everything revolves around the fast ball. Can you throw it by hitters? Can you throw it over the plate? Can you throw it where you want to throw it over the plate? High, low, inside, outside. When you're starting out, if you have a good fast ball that you can throw over the plate, you're going to get a lot of people out. Later you go on from there."

Spahn's windup, he says, came naturally, although, to be sure, he would add refinements. No pitching motion in baseball these days resembles the Spahn delivery, which was ornate and smooth, easy to imitate in a broad way, and just about impossible to duplicate. He began alone, motionless on the mound. Each pitch begins with that, one man at the center of things, alone and motionless. Spahn pumped both arms behind him in a gentle swaying movement, and as he rocked his arms forward, he tipped far back, his right foot kicking skyward. His eyes focused on home plate. Then, in a fluid continuation of this astonishing motion, he rocked forward in a rolling movement as the right leg came cartwheeling down. He released the ball and finished with his pitching hand almost touching the ground. This unique delivery had the effect of transferring pitching shocks and stresses from arm to leg. Late in his career Spahn had to undergo knee surgery, but across 5,244 innings of major-league pitching, he never injured his arm.*

Most contemporary pitching coaches preach against elaborate windups. They reason that the more motion, the greater the chance for something to go out of whack. The tendency today is to teach economical delivery, along these lines: Bring hands together at the midsection. Rock backward very slightly and throw. Dick Bosman, pitching coach for the Texas Rangers at this writing, says, "The simpler the mechanics of a delivery, the easier it is for most pitchers to master it. Warren Spahn, of course, is not most pitchers. I grew up

---

*"The one time I hurt my left shoulder, I was batting," he says. "I decided it ought to be stretched. I jumped up and grabbed a pole in the shower room and hung on from both arms. Something popped in my left shoulder. The next day the pain was gone."

in Wisconsin and I saw him pitch often when I was a kid. He was awesome. But the thing I remember most is a night when Spahn tipped his hat to the crowd. It amazed me that a great pitcher was bald-headed."

At South Park High in Buffalo, Spahn had the wondrous motion and a fine fast ball and good control. He won every game he pitched as a junior and as a senior. He was strong and disciplined and hardworking and just about the best pitching prospect anyone had seen since Bob Feller was signed off the sandlots of Van Meter, Iowa, at the age of seventeen. Spahn passed on the offer from Cornell, leaving everyone, including himself, to wonder how a college education might have refined his extraordinary native intelligence. Bill Myer, the scout who signed him for the Boston Braves, told the men in his front office, "This kid is the real goods. With a little experience he'll go right to the big leagues."

In 1940 Spahn pitched for Bradford in the PONY League. (The initials stood for Pennsylvania, Ontario, New York.) His won-and-lost record was not imposing, 5-and-4, but he struck out sixty-two batters in sixty-six innings. He was learning how to be a professional pitcher. Spahn blossomed in 1941 at Evansville, Indiana, in the Three-Eye League. (The Three Eyes were Indiana, Illinois, Iowa.) "The greatest influence on me was my Dad, but after that I give thanks to Bob Coleman, who managed me at Evansville." Robert Hunter Coleman caught briefly in the major leagues during the Mathewson era and would manage the Boston Braves during World War II, when Spahn was in the army. At Evansville, Spahn says, Coleman was parent-uncle-teacher-manager all in one. "He would check with all of us to see if we had written home that week," Spahn says. "I was twenty. We were very young. If you hadn't written to your parents, Bob Coleman would not give you your meal money. That was the kind of fellow he was, stern when he had to be, and highly respected." Coleman knew immediately what he had in Spahn. This slope-shouldered kid was his one ball player with the potential to star in the big leagues.

"You have to think when you're pitching," Coleman told the young Spahn. "I know you can think, so I'm treating you as a special case. I don't believe the other fellers are going to the majors. You are, if you remember to think. So here's the rule. Everyone on this ball club is entitled to make the same mistake twice. Not you. If you make the same mistake twice, I fine you fifty bucks."

Spahn remembers how that threat helped him concentrate. "A fifty-buck fine would have been a disaster," he says. "My month's paycheck was only one hundred twenty-five dollars." Spahn did not repeat mistakes at Evansville. He led the Three-Eye League in victories (nineteen) and earned run average (1.83). Later the next season, 1942, at the age of twenty-one, he was pitching for the Boston Braves. Casey Stengel, who managed the Braves to a seventh-place finish, had a weak pitching staff. Still, he soon became disenchanted with Spahn. During a game against Brooklyn, Stengel directed Spahn to loose his wicked fast ball at the head of Pee Wee Reese, the young Dodger shortstop. Reese had been hospitalized by a beanball some time before, and Stengel wanted his young lefthander to traffic in terror.

Spahn would throw close to Reese, protecting the inside corner, but he refused to throw a fast ball at Reese's skull. "I remember that clearly," Spahn says. "I threw three straight inside fast balls. They never fazed Reese. He simply leaned back and took them. Stengel stormed out to the mound and pulled me out of the game because I hadn't decked Reese. In the dugout, Stengel told me to pick up my railroad ticket to Hartford. I wasn't staying with the Braves. 'Young man,' Stengel told me, 'you've got no guts.'"

Two years later, facing the *Wehrmacht,* Spahn received the Silver Star for gallantry. He had entered the army late in 1942, moved up to staff sergeant, and during the Battle of the Bulge was commissioned a second lieutenant. "They were running out of officers," he says, managing to be at the same time smiling and grim. During the First Army's assault over the Rhine, bombardment destroyed every bridge except the crossing at Remagen. Spahn's unit was to reinforce that structure so that Sherman tanks could rumble across. His unit was assigned to relieve another group at 4:00 P.M. Lieutenant Spahn walked to the center of the bridge and discussed the construction work with other officers. Then he walked off the bridge to ready his platoon. Twenty-seconds later he heard "what sounded like thunder." The bridge had collapsed. The soldiers working on it were killed. "Something like that," Spahn says, "tends to make you a fatalist." Spahn does not dwell on his wartime heroism. "Let me summarize it like this," he says. "After you've slept in frozen tank ruts, every day you spend playing baseball is a breeze."

When Spahn returned to the Braves, Stengel was gone; fired, to the sound of rejoicing in New England. Billy Southworth, managing Boston, used Spahn as a spot starter and a relief pitcher. The year 1946 is significant in that it was the season when Spahn, at the age of twenty-five, won his first major league game. Mathewson won his first when he was twenty; Walter Johnson was nineteen. Spahn won most of his 363 victories either at the doorway to baseball's middle age or as a downright geriatric pitcher.

At twenty-six in the postwar world, Spahn arrived in a hurry. He won twenty-one games in 1947 and led the league in innings pitched, shutouts (seven) and earned run average (2.33). That was the first of thirteen seasons, when he won twenty games or more. The last time he went over twenty, in 1963, he was forty-two, and he threw another seven shutouts. That season Spahn led the National League in complete games with twenty-two, two more than another lefthander, Sandy Koufax, four more than Juan Marichal, five more than Don Drysdale. It was an extraordinary confluence of pitching generations. While Spahn was leading his platoon through Nazi artillery fire, Koufax was an eight-year-old elementary-school student in Brooklyn.

Although the statistics that Spahn posted as a young man and as a veteran are similar in victories, in shutouts and even in earned run average, the youngster and the sage were different pitchers. The results were pretty much the same, but the means of accomplishing them had changed. As a youthful twenty-game winner, Spahn threw a high-rising fast ball, an overhand curve, and every so often a change of pace.

The veteran Spahn worked mostly with curves thrown at different speeds, a straight change of pace, a screwball, and a slider that he mastered after ten years in the major leagues.

He remembers pitching against Ted Williams during an exhibition game in Florida, when his slider was under development. As Spahn studied hitters, Williams studied pitchers. With the count two strikes, Spahn decided to try a slider, low and away. Williams struck out. Each man went about his business, Williams with the Red Sox, Spahn with the Braves. They next saw each other the following spring.

"What the hell pitch was that you struck me out on last year?" Williams said.

"Slider," Spahn said.

"I didn't know you threw a slider," Williams said.

"I didn't till then."

Surprise became the great weapon in the arsenal that Spahn managed in maturity. "Hitting," he said, "is timing. Pitching is upsetting timing." This is rather more complicated than Spahn makes it sound. "First of all," he says, "a pitcher has to know his own arm, his own pitches, his own stuff. All of these vary not only across the years but from day to day. You have to know your own stuff and what works this afternoon, this inning, this at bat. You're out to surprise the hitter, not yourself."

When Spahn rejoined the Braves after World War II, he roomed with Johnny Sain, a 6-foot-2-inch righthander from Arkansas who threw a curve ball that Jackie Robinson said "was just about the sharpest curve I ever saw." In 1947, Spahn and Sain each won twenty-one games. No other Boston pitcher won more than eleven. The sports-writers celebrated the Braves' pitching rotation in doggerel:

Spahn and Sain
And two days of rain.

In 1948 Spahn and Sain started almost half of the Braves games—74 out of 154—and Boston won its final National League pennant. The two men roomed together and talked hitting and pitching, curve balls and hopping blazers. Current pitching coaches talk about fast balls as "two-seamers" and "four-seamers." The reference is to how many times the seams on the baseball hit the air with each rotation. Hold the baseball across the seams as you deliver it, and four rows of seam hit the air each spin. Hold it along the seams, and two rows hit the air. The seams act like an airfoil. All other things being equal, a four-seam fast ball, traveling fast enough, rises. A two-seamer tends to sink. (In addition either pitch may sail inside or out.)

"Warren Spahn and I were as different as daylight and dark," Johnny Sain remembers. "He was left-handed. I was right-handed. I was a curve-ball, a breaking-ball pitcher, with a lot of sidearm. He was straight over the top, a little faster, a little more orthodox. Our methods were completely different. Our basics were the same. I learned by watching him. I think he learned by watching me.

"I saw hitter after hitter swing underneath Warren's overhand fast ball. It seemed to rise. I thought maybe he was getting more backspin on the ball than I was. One spring, I decided to get more backspin on

A FOUR-SEAMER

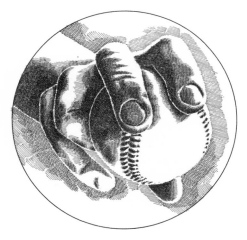

A TWO-SEAMER

my own fast ball. Throw a four-seamer. Lot of backspin. The pitch would rise and turn into a strike, or anyway a pop fly. I worked on that high backspin fast ball and I threw one to Enos Slaughter. No strike. No pop up. Slaughter hit a home run. The next time Warren mentioned the backspin fast ball to me, I told him, 'I think I'm going to put the backspin high hard one in my back pocket and leave it there.' Spahn laughed. The lesson is this," Sain says. "Every pitching arm is different."

Spahn says that his pitching was a matter of knowing his own arm and knowing the hitters and even "listening to what the hitters told me. For example, along about 1952, the hitters began to tell me that my fast ball was losing zip. I had just passed thirty. How did they tell me my fast ball was losing zip? They began hitting it." Some pitchers fight against the rough message line drives deliver. Hard-throwing Robin Roberts, a Hall of Fame righthander, was a twenty-game winner for the Phillies across six consecutive seasons. As he turned thirty, Roberts denied that his fast ball was slowing. He never had another twenty-victory season.

"I knew my arm and I knew my hitters," Spahn said, "and as I lost sheer speed, I went for variety. I'd concentrate on the kind of pitch a batter hit last time and the time before and how he hit it and what the speed of the pitch was and what the location of the pitch was. Sometimes I'd work a hitter one way in his first two times up and work him differently the third. I didn't want to pitch in set patterns or give the batter a chance to wait for a particular pitch to a particular spot. I played with the hitter's comfort zone. As I say, hitting is timing, and pitching is throwing off that timing. Now, imagine an area of comfort for a hitter. That's not just a specific area of the strike zone. It's also the miles per hour of a pitch. You stay away from the hitter's comfort zone by varying the location and the speed and the trajectory of the pitch. A curve ball has a different trajectory from a fast ball. That's obvious. My own particular special favorite for staying out of a hitter's comfort zone was the change of pace. You make him miss by getting him to swing in the wrong plane. A neat trick is to get him to swing at the wrong time.

"Some of the standard stuff you hear from managers is simplistic. *Don't give this hitter anything good to hit. But don't walk him.* Oh! *Give him the fast ball high and tight, and the breaking ball low and away.* Also oh! What felt really creative was to get out a big hitter with my change. I believe there wasn't any hitter in baseball that I couldn't get out with my change, if I set him up properly."

By the time he won his three-hundredth game, on August 11, 1961, Warren Spahn, high-fast-ball pitcher, was no more. "Most of the time," he told a reporter after that game—he defeated the Chicago Cubs, 2 to 1, at Milwaukee—"I ignore the upper half of the strike zone. These days I throw only below the waist. Of course if a batter has a profound weakness—say he can't hit a high inside fast ball—I'll still throw to that spot. But a batter with a profound weakness doesn't last in the major leagues."

If he had not seen a batter before, the veteran Spahn read important signs. "A man who drops the front shoulder when he cocks the bat is a high-ball hitter. If he drops the back one, he's a low-ball hitter.

After he takes one swing you know whether he has quick wrists. All this is important but pretty elementary. When you've pitched against a batter a hundred times, you know all about him, but you have to remember, he knows all about you, too. Then the fun starts. It's cat and mouse."

This never played out more vividly than in the saga of Spahn versus Stan Musial, which ran from June 17, 1946, to September 13, 1963. Just as Spahn's windup was a windup for the ages, Musial's swing was unforgettable. At bat Musial coiled—like a cobra, some pitchers asserted—and in his coiled crouch Musial seemed to be looking around a corner at the pitcher. When the pitch arrived Musial uncoiled, lashing out 3,630 hits in a twenty-two-year major league career. "He hit a double against me the first time I faced him," Spahn says, "and he hit a double against me the last time I faced him. He was one consistent SOB. Because of Musial, I always concentrated especially hard on the hitter who preceded him. The best way to pitch to Musial was with nobody on base. He was the hardest man in the league to fool."

Musial had a hitting technique that countered many of Spahn's efforts. He studied the ball in flight, picking up the speed in its first thirty feet. He knew who was pitching. He had committed to memory the speed at which every pitcher in the league threw. "I never had to guess at what they threw me," Musial says. "I knew. I had to concentrate very hard and so halfway in, I knew what the ball would do when it got to home plate, sink or rise or break." Both the memory involved and the concentration necessary to this accomplishment are comparable to what Spahn brought to pitching. Then, of course, there is the element of reaction time. Once Musial determined what the pitch was, he had a fifth of a second to swing. Concentrate. Remember. Decide. Uncoil and swing in a fifth of a second. When you watched Spahn against Musial, you saw gods at play.

"Musial was just the hardest man to fool," Spahn says. "I'm a left-handed pitcher and he's a left-handed batter, so I'm supposed to have an advantage. He had an overall average of .314 against me [as contrasted to a lifetime average of .331]. But I never brooded when Stan got a hit off me. The time to worry was when some two-fifty hitter knocked off my cap with a line drive. I tried to upset Stan's timing with breaking stuff and change-ups. Once Musial started timing fast balls your infielders' lives were in jeopardy. He had the most unorthodox stance I ever saw, and he must have come up against me four hundred times. But I can't recall one instance when he hit the ball without getting the fat part of the bat on it. I never gave him the same pitch twice in succession. I didn't dare. He was the only batter I ever walked intentionally with bases full. We were ahead, two to nothing, and Musial came up with bases loaded. I worked him carefully and the count went to three-and-two. That was enough excitement for that moment. I deliberately threw the next pitch way wide, forcing in a run. Then I got the next batter. If I'd given Musial a good pitch, three and two, we'd have lost."

Musial calls Spahn "the best pitcher and one of the great athletes of my era. Spahnie knew everything about his profession, and he was smart enough to change before he had to. In the early years he had the good high fast ball, a nice change, terrific control inside the strike zone, but only a fair curve. A lot of pitchers would have stayed where they were. Not Spahn. He began tinkering with a screwball, and as the fast ball began to go, he'd come at you with the screwjie. He'd thrown it low and away from righthanders, but down and in to left-hand hitters, an unusual pitch. Lots of left-hand batters like 'em low and inside. Spahnie got away with it. Then came the slider. In my whole career, there was only one time when a pitcher walked someone to get at me. That was in 1957, when the Cardinals got a threat going in the ninth inning. First base was open. Spahn came in from the bullpen and deliberately walked Del Ennis, who was hitting ahead of me, to set up a double play that would end the game. I obliged."

Spahn threw his first no-hitter in 1960, when he was thirty-nine, and his second in 1961. While he was winning twenty-three games in 1963, *Time* magazine summed him up as "the Grand Old Arm." But the next season, age laid a jeweled hand on him; he won only six games and the Braves sold him to the New York Mets, a ball club that would lose 112 games. Spahn was to pitch and coach under the manager who had been blind to his gifts twenty-three years before. Casey Stengel, seventy-four, was running the Mets, and after Spahn lost a few, Stengel told New York sportswriters, with inappropriate verve, "The hitters jump him so fast I can't do a goddamn thing." The Mets dismissed Spahn as a coach and sold him to the Giants, for whom Spahn won his final three major league ball games.

Spahn remembers Stengel calling him gutless in Boston, and he remembers Stengel dumping him in New York. He also remembers that, in between those incidents, Stengel managed Yankee teams that won ten pennants. "I knew Casey," Spahn says mildly, "both before and after he was a genius."

Spahn's own work as a pitching coach, over fifteen years, was less distinguished than his pitching. Often the finest performing artists, from Ted Williams to Jascha Heifetz, can't teach as successfully as those with smaller talents. Spahn has ideas. "I don't think pitchers throw enough today. They go once a week. They pitch five innings. They don't throw batting practice between starts. We're in an era preoccupied with jogging, getting your heart rate up, weight lifting. I think a lot of players lift and run instead of doing what's necessary to stay in pitching shape. Throw and throw. I'd pitch a game and the following day pitch batting practice, fifteen minutes for stamina. The next day I'd run some in the outfield. Day after that I was ready for another start. Kids today seem bigger, with longer fingers, and they like the split-fingered fast ball, a sinking pitch. I'm afraid the curve ball is being neglected. A pitcher with a fine curve, Carl Erskine, would have wonderful success right now.

"Something else. Attitude. How I loved to pitch. Whenever they gave me the ball and it was my turn, I always had the same thought. This is my day in the sun." The big-jawed, broad-nosed face lights in a smile. It always comes up sunshine when I get to talk pitching with Warren Spahn.

9.

THE PROFESSOR

Johnny Sain didn't try to make you pitch like he did.
He put himself in your shoes. He had allegiance to you.
He made you think. He was the best pitching coach in baseball.

JIM BOUTON

asey Stengel, so passionately and uncharacteristically wrong about Warren Spahn, developed a keen—some might say compensatory—appreciation for Spahn's Boston roommate, Johnny Sain, a tall and soft-voiced pitching scholar out of Pine Bluff, Arkansas. Stengel managed Sain briefly in 1942 at Boston when, by Sain's own account, "I was just a big strong thrower." In 1951, after Sain had matured into a big strong pitcher, the Yankees obtained him from the Braves in exchange for fifty thousand dollars and a remarkable prospect, Lew Burdette.

"Sain wins important games," Stengel told me in 1954, "as you have no doubt noticed, and he gets important outs, and I think you should write about him more, along with my very excellent players Mr. Ford, Mr. Berra, and Mr. Martin."

"Sain is quiet, Case," I said.

"Now, I know that," Stengel said, "and I can see where you would like the feller to say more because it would help you in your line of work. But the way he is, which you know, shouldn't bother you. He don't say much, but it don't matter, because when he's out there on the mound, there ain't nobody he can talk to."

In time Sain grew more voluble, although he never did chatter like Billy Martin, or even remotely like Stengel himself. "Looking backward," he remarked not long ago at the Downtown Athletic Club, in New York City, where as a senior citizen he had come to sign autographs for paying customers, "I hold a few records you won't find in the books. I threw the first pitch in organized baseball to Jackie Robinson and I threw the last pitch to Babe Ruth. In 1943 I was in navy preflight school at Chapel Hill, North Carolina, and we were playing baseball weekends. They took us up to Yankee Stadium one day in May to play an exhibition. The Yankees played the Indians first, and after that they put together a team of Yankee and Indian subs to play against us, North Carolina Pre-Flight. Ruth managed the subs. I was pitching, and we were a few runs ahead in the fourth when Ruth decided to put himself in as a pinch hitter. He was forty-eight and his legs were gone. The manager came over and said to me, 'John, this is just an exhibition to help war relief. Just an exhibition. Don't throw the Babe curves.'

JOHNNY SAIN

"That was part of it. Then it turned out that if Babe didn't swing, the umpire would call the pitch a ball. No matter where it was. No swing. A ball. Ruth hit a long foul and then I walked him, or they said I walked him. So the last pitch ever to Babe Ruth was ball four.

"Jackie Robinson made his major league debut on April 15, 1947, opening day at Ebbets Field. That broke the color line. Some writers have asked, wasn't I concerned that a pitch might get away and bean Robinson and, what with me being a Southerner from Arkansas, cause a race riot in Brooklyn. No thought like that crossed my mind. Robinson was a rookie and a kind of rule of thumb is that you show rookies break-ing stuff. This wasn't like Ruth. I was allowed to throw curves. So I con-centrated on giving him breaking stuff. I had trouble that day with Pete Reiser and Pee Wee Reese, but Robinson didn't get a hit off me. He was outstanding, a great player, and he got his hits off me in time. But not on that historic first day."

Someone came up and said he remembered Sain with the Braves and with the Yankees and with three other teams and could he ask a question. What, in Sain's opinion, was the best pitch in baseball? "Well, I know Whit Wyatt said the best pitch in baseball is a strike," Sain began, "but let's think about that a bit. You get strike one. Fine. But now you have to throw another pitch and probably make it differ-ent from the one before. Strike two. Fine. But you still have a job to do. So this is what I say: The best pitch in the game, even if it's just a lollipop, is the one-pitch out."

Johnny Sain's journey toward pitching scholarship began in small-town Arkansas, in villages called Pine Bluff and Havana and Belleville. His mother was born in Havana, Arkansas—"about five hundred sixty people, between Little Rock and Fort Smith, not exactly the Havana of the Caribbean"—and his father ran a garage in Pine Bluff. "Dad was a small-town auto mechanic. I helped him when I could. I kind of grew up in Dad's garage. There was a vacant lot across the street and when the kids came in out of the country, came into town, I would play catch with them and throw with them on the vacant lot. Dad had been a left-handed pitcher. I never saw him pitch but he was always very encouraging about my playing ball. Something I want to bring out is on that vacant lot in Pine Bluff there was always somebody who could run faster. There was always somebody that could run faster than I could and throw the ball harder than I could and hit the ball further than I could. I never considered myself as having extraordinary natural talent. I want to bring that out because a lot of youngsters look at themselves and say, 'I can't do this. I can't do that,' and get discouraged. I plugged along.

"I was always mechanically inclined, probably related to my father's work. If I watched how he did something on a car, I could teach myself to do it. That's how I learned pitching. I'd see other pitchers do things, and I'd question them and watch them and try to figure out just how they did what they did."

After graduating from Havana High School, Sain signed to pitch for Osceola in the Northeast Arkansas League. He spent six seasons in the minors and four in the profound obscurity of the Northeast Arkansas League. "I wasn't overpowering," he says. "I had real problems. Four different times in the minors, I got released. I was studying how to pitch, how to win, and it came slowly. In Nashville, 1941, my sixth minor league season, my record was only six-and-twelve. Next season, it was wartime. Fellers were going into service and the Boston Braves gave me a look. As I said, I was still a thrower. They used me as a reliever mostly and I finished four-and-seven. I was twenty-five years old and I hadn't set the country on its ear, but I would not let myself get discouraged. I was determined.

"I joined the navy about the same time Ted Williams joined the marines. We both wanted to be pilots. Flying airplanes came easily to us. We took preflight training at Amherst and North Carolina. My eyesight was twenty-fifteen. Ted's was twenty-ten. And I guess we had good coordination. But we'd both been out of school awhile and we were in preflight classes with very bright college kids. We only had high school educations. What, with the navigation and the Morse Code and the academics that you had to learn to be a navy pilot, there was some struggle. Some staying up late studying. We applied ourselves.

"People would come up to Ted—he hit .406 in 1941—and say, 'That can't be very difficult for you. You've got great vision.' That annoyed him. Lots of people with good vision can't hit major league pitching at all, let alone hit at a .400 clip. Ted became a great hitter because he *applied* himself to the craft of hitting. He became a fine pilot because, on top of the physical skills, he applied himself to the craft of flying. We talked about that, applying ourselves to flying and applying ourselves to baseball, and we became close. Every spare moment I had in service, I threw a ball, or thought about throwing a ball. I was in my late twenties and I was simply not going to give in to doubts, or negative thoughts. I wanted to succeed in the major leagues and I had no time to waste.

"When I went to Corpus Christi, Texas, where I won my wings, I played ball every chance I could. Other flyers used their spare time to go into town or play cards or loaf and there's nothing wrong with that, but I spent my spare time throwing. If I found a catcher, I'd throw to him. If I couldn't find anyone, I'd throw at a target on the back of a building. I left dents in buildings at every naval air station where I was sent. In four years in the Northeast Arkansas League, class D, the lowest classification of professional ball, there wasn't one manager who thought I would succeed in a big way. When I moved up to Nashville in the Southern Association, Double A, still two rungs below the majors, the manager Larry Gilbert told me to switch to first base. Larry said I didn't have enough on the ball to pitch in the majors. When I got to Boston, it was wartime; Casey Stengel said I could go only five innings. Relief pitcher. He said I'd never be a big-league starting pitcher." Sain's voice was soft and even. His intensity is well contained.

"In the navy, I learned aeronautical physics and I did a stint as a test pilot. No big deal, but I didn't fight my part of World War II with a fungo bat. If you are going to survive as a test pilot, you learn aerodynamics. Aerodynamics is the interaction of moving bodies with the atmosphere. A plane in flight is a moving body. So is a pitched baseball. In navy flying my work was dives and loops and rolls. In my spare time I worked on grips and spins and point of release. One fellow who was impressed with my pitching more than Stengel or Larry Gilbert was Ted Williams.

"My getting out of service was not a big event in Boston baseball history. I was a pitcher near thirty who'd won only four major league games. Ted's discharge was something else. New England was thrilled that he was coming back." (In 1946 returning veteran Williams led the Red Sox to a pennant with an average of .342. He was voted the most valuable player in the league.) "Ted was in contact with all the important New England baseball people. I was a nobody. He was a supergreat. He talked me up as a feller who knew how to pitch, and when I got to spring training, 1946, Billy Southworth, who was managing the Braves, said that on the basis of what he had heard, I could be a twenty-game winner. The Braves hadn't had one for about ten years.

"Understand, Southworth didn't mean I *would* win twenty. He meant simply that he would give me an opportunity. I made the most of that. I did win twenty right on the nose, and I pitched twenty-four complete games. The next year, I won twenty-one and so did Warren Spahn. That's when they started that poetry, Spahn and Sain.

"The year after that, 1948, I won twenty-four and the Braves won the pennant for the first time in a generation or maybe two. I know it was a very long dry spell."

"Since 1914," I said. "Thirty-four years. The 1914 team was last on July fourth, but came on and won the pennant. People called them 'the miracle Braves.'"

"We weren't a miracle team in forty-eight," Sain said, "but we had a lot of hard workers. My fast ball was no more than average, eighty-five, eighty-seven miles an hour. I call that a 'short' fast ball, not an outstanding pitch all by itself. My bread-and-butter pitches were breaking balls. I had different spins and I could throw overhand or three-quarters or sidearm, and I could change my speeds. I didn't overthrow, and I didn't let the count dictate my stuff. That is, if I fell behind, I didn't simply throw my fast ball. I continued to mix speeds, deliveries, spins."

Across one stretch in 1948, Sain completed nine games in twenty-nine days, one completion every three days. All this without the fast ball of a Feller, Spahn, or Koufax; all this from someone who seemed destined to finish in an obscure minor league; all this from someone who taught himself to pitch and followed his dream with intelligence and fortitude, even when the dream seemed, at least to others, less tangible than a rainbow, less real than mist.

Sain opened the 1948 World Series by beating Cleveland and Bob Feller, 1 to 0. He lost the fourth game, 2 to 1. Then Billy Southworth elected to save him to start the seventh game. Cleveland won the 1948 Series in game six. Sain was a break-even World Series pitcher, but his earned run average for the series was the lowest of any Boston starter, an economical 1.06. After twelve years of professional pitching, John Sain at last had become an overnight success.

"As far back as I can remember, the National League has been a league of curve-ball pitchers," said Tris Speaker, the great center fielder who batted .344 across twenty-two seasons. Speaker was a top Cleveland scout in 1948. "I go back aways to 1907 in the majors. Sain comes out of that curve-ball tradition, and as I watched him in the Series, I got to thinking about Christy Mathewson. Matty had some of the best breaking stuff I ever saw, and the fadeaway. When he wanted to, he could throw a fast ball with plenty of swift. But Matty seldom used the fast ball to retire a batter. He threw it high or wide, to show you the speed and upset your timing. Then he'd get you with the curve or the fadeaway. Sain doesn't throw a fadeaway, but with his deliveries and spins, he has a dozen different curves. He's a great pressure pitcher, not because he has a blazing fast ball or one startling curve or something freaky like a knuckleball. He's great because he knows how to adapt his pitching to the situation."

One renowned former Ohio farmer traveled to Boston for the Series. "When I come up in the 1890s," said Cy Young, then eighty-one, "I had a good overhand fast ball and a good overhand curve. But that wasn't enough to keep getting out 'Cap' Anson and Ed Delehanty and the young feller who come up later with Detroit, Ty Cobb. So I started throwing sidearm some, like Sain. That turned out to be just what I needed. I threw some sidearm and I kept the ball low and that's this young man Johnny Sain all over."

Including the Series, Sain had now pitched seventy-six complete games in three years. His arm ached after the 1948 season, "but I didn't say anything to anybody. Remember this was in the 1940s. Sports medicine was uncertain stuff. Up to that time, I don't believe I ever saw any pitcher whose sore arm was helped by a doctor." He dropped off to ten victories in 1949, catching, he says, "a lot of static." He won twenty again in 1950, making it four out of five twenty-victory seasons.

"As a pitcher, you should use everything, even adversity and pain," Sain says. "With my arm bothering me, I concentrated on more speed changes and more kinds of deliveries." But in 1951, he fell into a wretched midseason slump. The team drifted. The Braves fired Billy Southworth and replaced him with Tommy Holmes. Sain was pounded in six out of seven starts, and Holmes wondered if he would ever win another game.

The Boston sporting press was numerous and contentious. "Are you thinking of quitting?" Roger Birtwell of the *Boston Globe* asked Sain.

"A lot of people have given up on me," Sain said. His voice was low. He looked out across Braves Field. Then he said, strongly, "But I haven't given up on myself. I don't rely on the opinion of others. Only one manager, Billy Southworth, really believed that I was a big-league pitcher."

Birtwell's story, with its implied criticism of Tommy Holmes, ran in the *Globe* on August 1. At the end of the month, the Braves sold Sain's contract to the Yankees for fifty thousand dollars and the rights to Lew Burdette, a lanky young righthander from Nitro, West Virginia, who was coming along nicely in the Pacific Coast League.*

That Yankee ball club, under garrulous Casey Stengel and the dour general manager, George Weiss, was the most consistently winning team in baseball history. From 1949 through 1960 the Yankees won the pennant ten times, ten out of a possible twelve. In their ten World Series, the Yankees won seven. But the teams varied with the season. Joe DiMaggio went and Mickey Mantle arrived. Tommy Henrich left and Roger Maris came. The only starter on the 1949 champions still playing regularly in 1960 was Yogi Berra. We are talking about one franchise here, the Yankees, and we are also talking about many different teams.

One knack the Stengel-Weiss brain trust displayed was locating a veteran with just enough legs or bat or arm remaining to help out

---

*The Braves, playing out of Milwaukee in 1957, upset the favored Yankees in the World Series, 4 games to 3. Burdette won the second game for the Braves, 4 to 2. He then pitched shutouts winning games five and seven. His Series earned run average against a slugging Yankee team was 0.67.

through the pressures of a pennant race. They brought the slugger Johnny Mize to the Yankees in 1949 when Mize was thirty-six; he became the best pinch hitter extant across four seasons. They acquired Enos "Country" Slaughter, "The Spirit of St. Louis," from the 1954 Cardinals, and got fine work during his twilight years. Slaughter batted .304 for the Yankees in 1958, when he was forty-two years old. Braced by the mountain air and swift-running spring water of the south Bronx, Long John Sain was one more veteran who became a winner again in Stengel's triumphant baseball machine. He started in spots, relieved in others, and won fourteen games for the 1953 champions. A year later, working entirely in relief, Sain led the American League with twenty-two saves. With that accomplishment, he became the only pitcher in the annals to have led one major league in victories for a season and to have led the other major league in saves.

This dogged and inspiring major league career—rooted equally in forgotten rural ball parks and in the disciplines of a navy test pilot—finally wound down in 1955. Sain's arm was gone. He had started and relieved and been a workhorse, always ready, never one to complain, even when he had to pitch nine complete games in a month, always ready in Osceola, Arkansas, and Boston and New York. It ended in Kansas City in 1955, when he was thirty-eight and his arm was about a hundred and he couldn't get out any more major league hitters. "If that had finished my baseball days," Johnny Sain says, "I wouldn't have had a complaint in the world. Seventeen years as a professional pitcher. Four big-league pennants. Pitching in four World Series. If that had been the end, I still would have borrowed that remark from

Lou Gehrig. I would have considered myself the luckiest man on the face of the earth."

But that wasn't the end at all. The Yankees hired Sain in 1961 as pitching coach. He showed up with a briefcase full of inspirational books and tapes and a machine he was patenting as the "Baseball Pitching Educational Device," which everyone soon called "the Baseball Spinner." Baseballs were mounted on rotating axes—one axis per ball—and you could snap one in a variety of fast-ball spins and the other in rotations for sliders and curves. The baseballs were anchored. Except for rotating, they didn't move. Using John Sain's Baseball Pitching Educational Device, you could practice spinning your delivery at home or in a taxi or in a hotel room without endangering lamps, mirrors, or companions.

Across fifteen years Sain brought knowledge and technique and teaching tools to the staffs of four American League teams. Everywhere he went he created twenty-game winners, more twenty-game winners than any pitching coach before or since. The assembly is as varied as it is impressive.

Sain stayed with the Yankees from 1961 through 1963. Whitey Ford won twenty-five in '61, Ralph Terry won twenty-three in '62, Ford won twenty-four in '63, and Jim Bouton won twenty-one. None had won twenty before Sain took charge. None won twenty games after Sain left the Yankees. Bouton had to go to work and write books for a living. Terry enjoyed success as a professional golfer. Ford evolved into a pitching coach, although not one in the class of Johnny Sain.

When Sain moved on to coach the pitchers at Minnesota, Jim

"Mudcat" Grant, who'd never amassed fifteen victories, won twenty-one games in 1965. A year later Jim Kaat cracked twenty for the first time. Grant never again won twenty. Kaat did, nine years later when his path crossed with Sain in another town.

Sain next went to work for the Detroit Tigers. In 1967 Earl Wilson won twenty-two. Denny McLain won thirty-one in '69 and twenty-four the next season. Without Sain, McLain became, in just two seasons, a twenty-two-game *loser*.

Sain moved on to the Chicago White Sox in 1971. He stayed there for five seasons. Wilbur Wood won twenty-four games twice, Jim Kaat won twenty twice, and Stan Bahnsen won twenty-one in 1972. In sum, we find a total of sixteen twenty-victory seasons produced by nine different men, only one of whom ever had a single twenty-victory year for any pitching coach but Johnny Sain. That record is incredible and matchless.

The large question is a consideration of how Sain worked his magic. A smaller one, but interesting, is this: Why, if he was that good, did Sain move around so much?

Sain is a conservative man, retired now in northern Illinois, who puts on a jacket and tie to go downtown and who just might show up at a village board meeting in Oak Brook to make sure that young developer with the sixteen-cylinder green Jag isn't going to change the character of the town. But as a pitching coach, Sain, conservative citizen, was a revolutionist. This tall, quiet gentleman from the American heartland became a Robespierre of pitching coaches. Here are some of his revolutionary dicta:

Pitchers don't have to run, or not nearly as much as the conventional wisdom demands. "I've always felt," he says, "that a lot of pitching coaches made a living out of running pitchers so they wouldn't have to spend that same time teaching them how to pitch."

There is no one way to teach. "You have to vary your methods with the individual. If you have a ten-man pitching staff, you may have to use ten different methods of teaching."

Pitchers, even big strong pitchers who can throw fast balls through the Washington monument, are at their core delicate flowers. They need to be nurtured, encouraged, supported, admired.

A coach owes his primary loyalty to his pitchers. To perform a completely honest job, that loyalty takes precedence even over other important loyalties: to the boss, the field manager, and to the employers, the people who own the team.

It is better for a pitching coach to be unemployed than to be dishonest. "I loved being in baseball," Sain says, "but rather than be a baseball wheeler dealer, a clubhouse politician, I'd have sold cars. I've flown fighter planes. I can take people for test drives. I know how to change a spark plug. I can even make some sense with bankers if I have to."

Baseball people who are not pitchers are not nearly as interesting as those who are. "You can play without three outfielders," Sain says. "You learn that when you're a kid. But without a pitcher? No game today. To me pitchers are the most special people around."

The Yankees fired Casey Stengel in 1960 after he had won his tenth pennant in the Bronx. Officially, Yankee management felt annoyed that the team lost the World Series to Pittsburgh. "The truth," Stengel insisted, "is that I'm being fired because I'm seventy. I won't make that mistake again next year."

Ralph Houk replaced Stengel, and the Yankees won pennants for three straight seasons. Jim Bouton, who wrote *Ball Four* with the late Leonard Schecter, is intelligent, committed, and resolute in speaking out. He didn't think much of Jim Turner, "Ol Milkman Jim," Stengel's pitching coach, Bouton says. (Having known both, I attribute that at least partly to a clash of personalities. Under Stengel, Turner got excellent results. But he was a company man. His loyalty flowed from his paycheck.)

"Ralph Houk," Bouton says, "hired Sain because he was feeling shaky having to follow Stengel. Then after Houk won those three pennants, he wanted to get rid of Sain. By then Houk was confident. What general—Houk started thinking of himself as a general—wants a lieutenant on his staff who's smarter than he is?"

In Minnesota, Sain's pitching staff won a pennant in 1965. At Detroit Sain's pitchers won the World Series in 1968. He is as proud, he says, of the five Series he reached as pitching coach as the four Series in which he worked as J. Sain, Arkansas bulldog righthander.

"I wouldn't want you to make it seem in your book as though I thought I knew everything about pitching," Sain began, when we talked not long ago. "In any complicated field, there are as many ideas as there are different people. Broadly, pitchers use two distinct methods. The first comes from real estate. You know that saying, the three biggest factors when you buy a house—location, location, location.

Apply that to pitching. It sounds easy, to throw the fast ball at the letters on the inside corner, throw the slider kneecap high on the outside edge. It isn't easy to have pinpoint location with a ball traveling eighty-five or ninety miles an hour. Very few people can actually pitch to spots.* The other approach emphasizes quick movement, late movement on the ball. I'm a great advocate of that. I think the natural tendency of pitchers is to start out throwing hard and keep trying to throw harder. You look at the hitter and you want to say, 'Here comes my fast ball. It's going by you.' Some were simply overpowering and that's the staff every coach would like to have, a bunch of pitchers who just walk out, say here it comes, and overpower everybody."

Sain paused and you could pause with him and begin to imagine a staff of overpowering pitchers. We open our rotation with Walter Johnson. Next day we start a lefthander, Sandy Koufax. Then Bob Feller works. Finally toss a coin, Lefty Grove or Nolan Ryan. That covers four days. On the fifth day you have no ball game. All the hitters have sold their bats and taken up golf.

"With normal arms, in the real world, things are different," Sain said. "Let's say you're a hitter and somebody overpowers you and overpowers you. If you're smart, and a lot of hitters are smart, you're going

---

*Bill Veeck told me that before he brought Leroy "Satchel" Paige from the Negro American League to the Cleveland Indians in 1948, he asked the venerable righthander to warm up, just throwing fast balls over the plate. That was too easy, Paige said. No challenge. He placed a book of matches on top of the plate. He then threw ten straight pitches over the matchbook. At forty-two, Paige's blazer was history. But practicing location, location, location, he went 6-and-1 in just part of the 1948 American League season, winning games at a .857 clip.

to find a way to combat that. Shorten your swing. Slap the ball to the opposite field. There's a saying some hitters could turn a thirty-thirty around, could time a thirty-thirty bullet. Exaggeration is one way to make a point, but seriously I don't know anybody who was very successful trying to overpower Ted Williams and Stan Musial. Say, I walk out to the mound, and I can throw hard. Extremely hard. I throw the first pitch by the hitter. I do that a few times, a few at bats. But later on, I'm going to need a different approach. A good hitter adjusts. That's one reason he is a good hitter. He's learned that if I'm throwing as hard as I can and he's swinging as hard as he can, I'm going to beat him. He's going to make out. So he gives in. That's not surrender. Not at all. That's adjustment. He isn't trying to hit the ball out of the park. He's trying to make contact. Even the greatest power hitter won't homer even once in ten at bats, on the average. Contact hits, singles, can kill a pitcher as dead as the long ball. All right. Our intelligent hitter has observed my extremely fast pitches and has cut down on his swing. I pick that up. He's watching me. I'm also watching him.

"Here's what I do. I throw with the same motion, the exact same arm speed, but up to now I've been putting extry on the ball. Extry." Some rural Arkansas remains in Long John Sain. "This time I don't put extry on it. What does that do?"

"The pitch is slower," I said.

"Right, and this is important: *Not much slower*. Extry is a subtle thing. The pitch is only about a foot slower—in the same length of time out of my hand the pitch travels one foot less toward the hitter than the hard fast one, the pitch with extry. One foot is enough. The hitter is geared to extry but there isn't any extry. The hitter is a foot out front. He's shortened his swing but all he gets is a little foul ball. I've fooled him, thrown him off. Somebody watching thinks, *What happened to the hitter on that one? That last pitch didn't look that fast.* It wasn't supposed to be that fast.

"A casual fan doesn't pick that up. But the hitter, particularly the smart hitter, does. Watch his lips. He'll begin talking to himself using a lot of the words I wouldn't want my family to read in your book."

Upsetting a batter's timing, varying velocity, is one weapon with which Sain armed his charges. The moving, lurching fast ball was another. "It helps to get a visual picture of someone throwing a fast ball," he said. "As you release, you put backspin on the baseball. If you throw enough and put enough backspin on the pitch, you get a fast ball that goes against gravity. Hops? I think it does. An airplane lifts off. If a physicist wants to argue, let's just say backspin levels off the baseball. Now, throw exactly the same, but turn your fingers as you release the ball. Just slightly. That's enough to change the direction of the spin. Now the ball goes with gravity, moves down a little bit. What do you have coming out of the same motion? A hopping fast ball in the first case. A sinking fast ball in the second."

Simply to call any pitch a fast ball is to settle for an incomplete description. Simply to call any pitch a curve is probably even looser. "There are a lot of curves," Sain said. "Throwing right-handed, I liked to throw mine just about at the shoulder of a right-hand hitter. I thought in terms of that curve sweeping across the plate. For a left-handed hitter, I liked a curve that broke down, more than wide. Keep on top of the ball as you release it, snapping your wrist down. That should give some idea. Pitches with or without extry. Fast balls working against gravity or going with it. Curve balls sweeping wide or breaking down. That's a bit of the mechanics of pitching. Then comes the matter of psychology. The psychology of the game and the psychology of the different people you work with."

"Let's talk in terms of extremes, John," I said.

He nodded.

You could not find two more extremely different individuals than Jim Kaat and Dennis McLain. Kaat is to solid citizenry what Gibraltar is to rocks. A large and significant model. McLain, to put this as tactfully as possible, is a risk taker. After his pitching years were done, he served hard jail time for a felony conviction.

McLain won twenty games for Detroit in 1966, while Sain was coaching at Minnesota, but slipped back to an energetic but ordinary seventeen victories and sixteen losses the following season. A lot of his problem traced to attitude. McLain had a swaggering manner, which some felt was wrapped around a core of insecurity. He liked to fly. After Sain became the Tigers' pitching coach, he helped McLain prepare for licensing exams and shared a test-pilot tale, or two or three.

McLain had passed a checkout in a Lear jet and he was qualified to fly cargo, but he could not fly passengers in jets without being accompanied by a copilot. Somehow McLain wangled a commission from General Motors to fly a load of parts from Detroit to St. Louis. He flew by himself at thirty thousand feet, his first long solo flight, and tried, as I've heard ball players say, "to give it the old nonchalant."

"How was it?" the pitching coach and old test pilot asked his macho charge.

"John," McLain said, "when I set down back here in Detroit, I'll tell you the truth: I didn't have a single dry thread on me."

Sain took that in, then said, "Why, you son of a gun! From now on you're gonna be all right out there on the mound, even with bases loaded and nobody out." In turn, McLain took *that* in. He was not much interested in listening to a coach, but a navy test pilot, one who didn't wet his threads even in power dives... well, damn, even difficult Denny respected that. Sain tutored. McLain responded. Over two seasons under Sain in Detroit, he won fifty-five games. Summing up years later, McLain said, "I don't think Johnny Sain taught me very much about throwing the baseball. I knew about throwing the baseball. He didn't teach me throwing, but I grant you this: He sure taught me a lot about *pitching*."

During the 1970s in Chicago, almost by accident, Sain helped Jim Kaat acquire a rapid delivery that unnerved batters. Kaat had won twenty-five for Minnesota under Sain in 1966, but he never approached that number again in Minnesota. The Twins gave up on him during 1973 when his record slipped below .500. He went to the Chicago White Sox, where he was reunited with Sain, and at the old Comiskey Park the coach asked him to wind up at half speed, "just for a little review, Jim." After several half-speed windups, Kaat suddenly and impulsively went from a stop position and threw the ball.

"Kaat's delivery was terrifically fast," Sain said, "and the baseball flew out of his hand. We worked on that. He would be standing there with his hands in front of him and then all of a sudden, just go *wham!* He started doing that in games, standing there and just going *wham!*

That quick fast ball became an outstanding pitch. The hitters got to where they'd put up a hand to the umpire as they stepped into the box when Kaat was pitching. That was proof how he was disrupting their timing. He had the hitter on the defensive before he threw the baseball. Jim Kaat [now a splendid play-by-play announcer with the Yankees], was a very sharp person. With that new quick delivery in Chicago, he had two more twenty-game years."

Talking flying with McLain, quick-pitching with Kaat, hard sliders with Whitey Ford, Sain's forte was communication and bonding. "What did you tell them about knocking down hitters?" I asked him.

"I never said to knock anybody down, and I never said don't knock anybody down. That's a matter of individual style. I always adjusted to the individual style of the feller I was trying to help. I meant to respect their attitudes and their thinking, and of course they have to think. If you can't think, you can't pitch. You can't play baseball. Knowhow is the name of the game. You have to have courage. If you're afraid and you can't fight that down, you aren't going to win."

Sain made a modest little summation. "Give me a pitcher who has some courage and can think, and I believe I can help him a bit."

Did the greatest of retired pitching coaches believe that he, like his friend Warren Spahn, deserved a bust in the Hall of Fame? (He has not been chosen yet.) Sain looked thoughtful. The Arkansas sandlots came back strong. "Unlike some others, I had to plod my way to success. I'll answer your question with a question of my own. Do you send a mule up there with the thoroughbreds?"

10.

THE COLLIE THAT

WORKED LIKE

A DOBERMAN

The hell with all the hitters. The hell with all of them.

SAL MAGLIE

cross fourteen seasons in Brooklyn and Los Angeles, Dodger teammates called Don Drysdale "the Big Collie," a nickname that has no more bite than "Lassie." Drysdale was large and open and convivial, and that, mostly, was what the baseball people remembered at his funeral, in 1993. He died, suddenly and alone, in a Montreal hotel room when he was fifty-six, and his widow, Ann Meyers Drysdale,* wanted a suggestion of the Big Collie's joy to lighten a sad

---

*Ann Meyers was an Olympic basketball star. She is a member of the Basketball Hall of Fame in Springfield, Massachusetts.

DON DRYSDALE

summer day. Nine hundred people crowded into a funeral chapel at the Forest Lawn Cemetery in Glendale, and at the altar Orel Hershiser read an open letter he had composed to Drysdale's three young children. "Your father used to say that if you hurry in and out of the clubhouse," Hershiser began, "you'll hurry in and out of the game. You have a responsibility to your *teammates* and to the fans.

"'To some of us, he hurried in and out of life too soon. He didn't give us enough time to tell him we loved him." Hershiser wept. The youngest of Drysdale's children, four-month-old Drew, stirred in her mother's arms. Bob Uecker, catcher, broadcaster, and raconteur, moved to the microphone. "I'm the one who introduced Annie to Don. He wanted to go out with her right away. Annie wasn't so sure. She said all right, she'd go to dinner with the big feller all right, but only if her mother came along. Don said to me—he was pleading—'You've got to be her mother's date.' Didn't faze me. Not at all. I just said to Don, 'Hey. What's the mother look like?'" Laughter sounded in the chapel, even as some were still dabbing away tears. "I'll never forget the first time Don touched me," Uecker said. "I was very strongly touched. It was right here." He pointed to a spot on his neck, where one of Drysdale's ninety-mile-an-hour brush backs nailed him. "Annie says the baby, Drew, is just like Donny, even looks like him. Sheesh. What's it going to be like eight years from now in Little League when some cute little girl in a skirt starts throwing knockdown pitches?"

Across his major league career the Big Collie hit no fewer than 154 batters. Lassie, go away. This isn't Lassie. When one considers Drysdale at work on the mound, a Doberman comes to mind.

....

Pitching terrorism is often overstated, possibly because a great knockdown pitch is as dramatic to behold as a home run. The surprised batter falls backward, defining hot haste, his head going down, his feet skidding forward, his bat sailing over a shoulder as he dives toward safety and the earth. "He really undressed the guy with that one," the ball players say. I remember watching from a vantage point close to field level in the old Polo Grounds, Joe Black of the Brooklyn Dodgers knock down a Giants' pinch hitter named George Washington Wilson. The year was 1952 and the Giants were not yet wearing batting helmets. Black threw ninety-five miles an hour, and Wilson went down so hard that he ducked out from under his baseball cap. The knockdown pitch sailed through a small space, the distance between George Wilson's fast-descending head and his baseball cap, which floated down more slowly. Talk about an unholy trinity. Cap, skull, and the baseball rocketing in between them. I felt suddenly and deeply grateful that I did not to have to face major league pitchers for a living.* But anticlimactic though it is, the truth of such situations is that the dramatics are greater than the actual peril. With good eyesight and coordination, each a given among major leaguers, the batter almost always gets his head out of the way of a knockdown pitch. I have no good statistics here, but my impression today is that the average major leaguer is more in danger of signing with the wrong agent than he is of stopping a fast ball with his brow.

The ball is hard, but that is something you first learn—or at least I learned—not at bat but in the infield. Good coaching teaches an infielder to keep his glove low; it is easier to come up for a high hop than it is to grope for a ball that stays down. As I learned on sandlots outside a small New York State town called Lake Mohegan, ground balls bounce irregularly off pebbles or divots and veer into one's wrists. The

---

*I sometimes caught Black winter days in the gym at the old Carlton YMCA in Brooklyn. Keeping his arm loose, he threw a rubber ball. Ninety-five miles an hour being what it is, I had to use a glove.

sensation is like being struck by a rock. But that's part of playing ball. If the pain proves to be greater than the enjoyment you get from playing, you are ready for tennis, where the ball is softer, or synchronized swimming or chess.

In extreme—and rare—cases, a baseball can do fatal harm. Research by the writer Robert McGarrigle brought to light an accident that shook the village of Indiana, Pennsylvania, in 1904. The Babcock Baseball Club of Johnstown traveled to play the Indiana Normal School on June 21, and in the bottom of the seventh a foul tip struck Grove Thomas, Babcock's catcher, over the heart. Thomas, who was wearing a chest protector, rose. The *Indiana Evening Gazette* reported, "He rubbed his chest as he walked away from the plate area. Then he turned and started back to his position, but suddenly groaned. He fell unconscious atop home plate and died within seconds. Two physicians responded to no avail. The grandstand was well filled with fans, many of whom were girls of the Normal School. The awful suspense, which was darkened and dampened by a light rain, was very trying and many of the girls burst into tears." (No description of Thomas' chest protector survives. It was probably a leather strip, backed by felt padding.)

The one fatality in major league ball took the life of Raymond Johnson Chapman, Cleveland's trim and speedy shortstop, on August 17, 1920, after he had lost sight of a high inside fast ball at the Polo Grounds. (The Yankees played home games at the Polo Grounds from 1913 to 1923, when the Stadium was completed.) Chapman, who crowded the plate, led off the fifth inning against the formidable

Yankee righthander Carl Mays, nicknamed "Sub" for his underhand, or submarine, fast ball. The count on Chapman went to 1-and-1. Mays now intended to throw a low sinking fast ball. "But just as my arm reached the farthest point of my back swing," Mays said long afterward, "I saw Chapman shift his back foot into the position he took for a push bunt. At the last split second, I changed to a high and tight pitch." That is to say, as Mays told the story, Chapman was turning in the batter's box, to shove a bunt between the mound and Wally Pipp, the Yankee first baseman. Mays' response was to throw a pitch that would be hard to bunt.

Shortly before his death, in 1971 at El Cajon, California, Mays recounted what happened next. "Usually a batter would fall away from the high, tight pitch. This time there was a sharp crack. The ball bounded like a bunt between me and the third-base line. I ran over, fielded it and winged it to Pipp." Only when Pipp didn't start the usual ball toss around the infield did Mays realize that Chapman had not bunted, much less run to first base. He was lying beside home plate, semiconscious. After five minutes Chapman rose and walked toward the dugout. Near the bench he staggered. He had to be assisted to the clubhouse. There he said to a friend, "I'll be all right. Tell Carl not to worry." Chapman lay down on a rubbing table. The pitch had fractured his skull in two places. Trainers applied ice packs to his head. He lapsed into unconsciousness and died in a hospital at 5:00 A.M. the next day.

Baseball people were shaken but not for long. Cleveland went on to win the 1920 World Series, defeating the Brooklyn Dodgers. Sub

Mays won twenty-six for the Yankees the year of Chapman's death and twenty-seven more in 1921.

"Chapman draped himself over the plate," Mays said. "I always dreaded pitching to him. I think he was draped so far over the plate that the pitch that hit him was a strike. I don't like the idea of pitchers throwing at batters to hit them. But I don't like the idea of batters digging in, defying the pitcher to throw to the inside corner." Batters and pitchers both are responsible for safety, Mays said. A batter puts himself in peril when he crowds the plate, or these days overestimates the security of a batting helmet, or simply, in Carl Mays' words, "when he digs in and swings from the heels and all he's thinking about is hitting the ball out of the park." Mays' final point sounds clearly through major league baseball today. Pitchers say, "I threw at him not to hurt him but just to make him think. It wasn't a beanball. It was a thought pitch."

My father, the college third baseman, had stopped off with teammates to see the game in which Ray Chapman was hit. He remembered that Chapman made no effort to get out of the way of the pitch and that once struck he remained erect for several seconds, then fell very slowly. Either Chapman lost sight of the ball or, upon seeing it, he froze. The pitch was not a strike, but neither was it an unusual knockdown; just one more high, tight big-league fast ball, but the only one that ever killed a man. Mays was known as a brush-back pitcher. Other old-timers famous for knockdowns were Burleigh Grimes, "Ol Stubblebeard," who knocked down hitters by way of setting them up for low outside spitballs; Bullet Joe Bush; Walter Mails, nicknamed

"Duster"; and none other than Babe Ruth, who hit eleven batters one season when he was a hard-throwing young left-handed pitcher.

As baseball evolved, knockdown pitches were worked into the fabric of the game. Harry "Cookie" Lavagetto, who became a solid .270 hitter, recalls trying to win a job with the Pittsburgh Pirates in 1935. "Where I came from," Lavagetto said, "the San Francisco Bay area, the Depression hit hard. If I could make the major leagues, about ten people named Lavagetto in Oakland were going to come off home relief. I was hanging on in an intersquad game. I came up against a tough old righthander named Guy Bush. Not Bullet Joe Bush. This was Guy Bush, a big feller that they called 'the Mississippi Mudcat.' I got around on a fast ball and cracked a single. When I got to first base I was so happy, I started to giggle. I couldn't help myself. My whole family was going to be eating. Bush looked over and said, 'Who are you laughing at, you little dago bastard?' Then he stayed in the intersquad game to pitch to me again. Next time I came up he threw the first pitch at my head. I go down. Second pitch same thing. Guy Bush walked me on four pitches. Every one was at my head. When I got to first this time, Bush looked over and said, 'I don't hear you laughing now, dago.'"

Lavagetto smiled his mild smile. "That's how baseball was played during the old days, during the Depression. But there were controls, a kind of balance. If they threw at you, then your pitcher threw at them. Once or twice some tough umpire would try to stop it, but usually the players worked it out among themselves. Take the 1941 Series, when I was with the Dodgers. Red Ruffing and Spud Chandler, a couple of big righthanders with the Yankees, threw at Pee Wee Reese and me. So Whit Wyatt threw at DiMaggio. Knocked him on his ass into the dirt. DiMaggio made a terrible fuss. Wyatt shouted, 'You think you're too good to go down?' They started toward each other but the umpires moved fast."

One classic response to particularly vicious beanball was exemplified by a play Jackie Robinson made in the summer of 1953. Sal Maglie of the New York Giants was "Sal the Barber," mostly because his high inside fast balls "shaved" hitters' chins. Maglie was candid and friendly when he wasn't pitching. "You have to make the batter afraid of the ball or, anyway, aware that he can get hurt," Maglie told me matter-of-factly one afternoon over drinks at his apartment in Riverdale. "A lot of pitchers think they do that by throwing at a hitter when the count is two strikes and no balls. The trouble there is that the knockdown is expected. You don't scare a guy by knocking him down when he knows he's going to be knocked down."

"Then when, Sal?" I asked.

"A good time is when the count is two and two. He's looking to swing. You knock him down then and he gets up shaking. Now curve him and you have your out. Of course, to do that you have to be able to get your curve over the plate on a three-and-two count. Not every pitcher can." Maglie could break three different curves over the plate, three and two. He had particular success against such free-swinging sluggers as Roy Campanella and Gil Hodges. But it is simplistic to say Maglie intimidated Campanella and Hodges. Rather, his unpredictable patterns disrupted their timing and concentration. He had less success with Pee Wee Reese and Jackie Robinson, and one day in Ebbets Field, by throwing a shoulder-high fast ball behind Robinson, Maglie brought matters to detonation.

The knockdowns thrown at Lavagetto, the fatal pitch thrown at Ray Chapman, roared toward the temple. A batter gets away from that pitch by ducking backward. (Chapman's freeze reaction, though not unknown, is rare.) Angered or frustrated by Robinson that afternoon in Brooklyn, Maglie threw his best fast ball behind the hitter, shoulder high. That was and is dangerous and inexcusable. As a batter strides forward, he loses height. Reflex makes him duck backward. A batter's head moves directly into the path of the fast ball thrown behind him shoulder high.

Robinson started to duck into Maglie's pitch and then his phenomenal reflexes enabled him to stop, as it were, in mid-duck. The ball sailed just behind the back of Robinson's neck. Robinson glared but did not lose his poise. Maglie threw an outside curve, and Robinson bunted toward Whitey Lockman, the Giants' first baseman. By making Lockman field the bunt, Robinson was forcing Maglie to leave the pitcher's mound and cover first. There he would be in Robinson's path, and Jack, going at full and full-muscled tilt, intended to run over Maglie, signing his name in spikes on the pitcher's spine. Saturnine, Faustian, brooding Sal Maglie refused to leave the mound. At a critical moment, the Barber lost his nerve. Davey Williams, the Giants' second baseman, rushed over, and as he was reaching for Lockman's throw, Robinson crashed into him, a knee catching Williams in the lower back. Robinson's knee was so swollen a day later that he could not play. Williams never really recovered. He dropped out of the major leagues two seasons later, at twenty-eight.

The next day Alvin Dark, the Giants' shortstop, said to me, "Robinson did a terrible thing. He hurt an innocent person. He's no hero. He's a Hitler."

"And Maglie?" I said.

Dark shook his head. Rage was consuming him. "Your friend Robinson," he said, "is just like Hitler."

"Actually," Robinson himself said a few days later, "I'm sorry that Williams got hurt. But when Maglie threw behind me, he was starting a really dangerous business, and I was going to put a stop to it before he hit Gil or Campy or Pee Wee in the head." He puffed air through his cheeks. "Don't ever throw that fucking baseball behind me." Dark, a stubborn man, never withdrew his characterization of Robinson as a Nazi.

After that I saw Maglie start eight games against the Dodgers, but I never saw him throw another fast ball behind a hitter. The grim, intimidating beanballer had been intimidated himself, and by a bunt.

Attempts to eliminate beanballs by fiat trace at least to 1879 when *The Reach Guide*, a dominant sports publication, reported that the National League "would henceforth fine" pitchers who tried to bean batters as much as twenty dollars, a week's pay. In 1932 the American League authorized umpires to eject pitchers for throwing beanballs. In 1950 both leagues formally prohibited pitches aimed at the head. The codes have been modified at least four times since. Today's governing dictum, 8.02 (d), reads:

A pitcher shall not intentionally pitch at a batter. If in the umpire's judgement, such a violation occurs, the umpire may elect either to

1. Expel the pitcher, or the manager and the pitcher, from the game, or

2. Warn the pitcher and the manager of both teams that another such pitch will result in the immediate expulsion of that pitcher and the manager.

If in the umpire's judgement circumstances warrant, both teams may be officially "warned" prior to the game or at any time during the game. (League Presidents may take additional action.) To pitch at a batter's head is unsportsmanlike and highly dangerous. It should be and is condemned by everybody.

Umpires should act without hesitation to enforce this rule.

That seems explicit. This rule has been in the books since 1988. Yet in a typical recent season, at least fourteen batters have charged at mounds, intent on punching pitchers they believed were throwing at their heads. Four batters were suspended. Assaults continue, making one wonder why such a clearly written rule has not stilled tumult and wonder also why batters by the dozen feel free to swing at pitchers. As more than one has said, "This is not supposed to be hockey." (That sport's random and sometimes numbskull violence was deliciously ridiculed by the comedian Don Rickles, who said, "I was watching a fight last night when a hockey game broke out.")

Robinson tried to get at Sal Maglie while staying within the rules of engagement. You can bunt anywhere you want. You can run over anyone in your base path. But whatever an opposing ball player has done, you cannot start punching him and stay within the rules. Like Stan Musial and George Brett and Harmon Killebrew, Robinson played hard but legal baseball. Why, then, this recent breakdown, what some would call the hockey-ization of baseball? A number of baseball people suggest that lax schools, permissive parents, and easy access to drugs have created a climate in which rules are no longer respected. This may be true, or true to an extent, but we can still wonder why 8.02 (d) has not been enforced as rigorously as no-parking regulations on any given Tuesday in Manhattan.

Some umpires are bothered by the word *intentionally*—by being asked to decide on the spot whether a fast ball aimed at the letters inside slipped and sailed toward the batter's skull or whether the pitcher was, in the baseball and Amazon jungle term, head-hunting. Some years ago this problem was played out by the late and legendary John "Jocko" Conlan, one of eight umpires selected for the Hall of Fame. Conlan was putting a son through Harvard Law School, "on the money I made calling balls and strikes." Conlan eventually began to think of himself as a lawyer once removed or possibly a justice on the United States Supreme Court.

"How am I supposed to know what's on a pitcher's mind?" Conlan said. "How much does the league pay for mind reading?" We had met by chance at a Chicago airport, with time between planes. Jocko was always a good one for a quick beer and a snappy argument.

"It isn't always that difficult to tell intent, and don't pretend that it is," I said. "You know the count, the game, situation, the pitcher, his history, his control. Put all those things together and you can usually tell intent."

"Hah!" Conlan cried. "*Usually!* Not good enough. *Intent!* Not good enough, either. At most, I can tell *possible* intent. That's not good enough to put a man out of a game."

I recalled a summer afternoon for him when the St. Louis Cardinals were playing the Montreal Expos and Bob Bailey was batting against Bob Gibson. Bailey was a "mistake hitter"; he got most of his 1,564 major league hits on belt-high fast balls and hanging curves. Gibson threw a high, hanging curve ball, and Bailey walloped a home run into the left-field stands. Mike Jorgensen was the next Montreal batter. Gibson said hello with a ninety-five-mile-an-hour fast ball into the ribs. Jorgensen's cry at impact must have reached halfway to Toronto. "Pure rage reaction," I said. "Gibson was mad that he'd thrown a bad pitch and took it out on an innocent, Mike Jorgensen."

"Fine for an airport bar," Conlan said. "Not fine on a ball field. Suppose," Conlan said, "I'd been working the game and I walked out to the mound and warned Gibson?"

"Warned? Why not eject him?"

"The pitch was nowhere near the batter's head. I warn Gibson. 'If you throw inside like that again, you're out of here.' Now," Conlan said, warming to his brief, "the next pitch Gibson throws hits the next Montreal batter in the head and kills him. I'm a baseball expert. No doubt about that. With my warning, I've just ruled that Gibson intentionally threw at one hitter. The batter after that gets killed. The Montreal district attorney indicts Gibson for murder. I have to testify in court under oath that, yes, in my opinion Gibson was throwing at the head of the batter, trying to bean him. And he succeeded. My testimony sends Bob Gibson to the electric chair. That's where that damn knockdown rule ends up."

"The circumstances you're playing with, Jocko, are so remote, they're nonsense."

"So you insist, but you're safe enough. All you get paid for is typing. I'm out there in the front lines. I'll call anything they want me to call that I can see. But I don't want to rule on a pitcher's intent. The players themselves have to stop the head-hunting. You can't ask the umpires to be, uh, what the hell's the word? You been to college, like my son."

"Psychic."

"Right," Conlan said. "I've been a great umpire. I know that. But I've never claimed to be a psychic. Fair or foul. Safe or out. Ball or strike. All of that is plenty tough enough."

Player controls are reasonably complex. As Jackie Robinson demonstrated, the bunt is one way for batters to retaliate. But it is limited counterweapon. Only batters with high bunting skills can use it. Pitchers, like Maglie, can decline the challenge. A second check has been simply to have your pitcher knock down any opposing players: the rival pitcher in the National League, the opposing catcher in the American League. Chuck Dressen, a fierce competitor, preached endless escalation here. "If they throw one, we throw two. If they throw two, we throw four. If they throw four . . ."

"I don't have a PhD, but I can do arithmetic," says Carl Erskine, who pitched under Dressen for three seasons in Brooklyn. "Four, eight, sixteen, thirty-two, sixty-four. If you're talking about sixty-four knockdown pitches in an afternoon, you aren't talking baseball. You're talking raw violence." Dressen thought that by, using gross exaggeration, he could get Erskine to throw at the head of rival batters. Not sixty-four times a game, but once in a while. I don't believe he ever did. Erskine pitched two no-hitters and set a World Series strikeout record without knocking down anybody. He believed, as rule 8.02 (d) says, that to pitch at a batter's head is unsportsmanlike. Tommy Glavine, the splendid lefthander with the Atlanta Braves today, feels the same way. "You can play and win without hurting other people," Glavine says. As evidence, he can point to his Cy Young Awards for 1991 and 1998.

Others on that Dodger staff—Black, Clem Labine, Don Newcombe, and the new kid named Drysdale—knocked down hitters when they felt it was appropriate. Sometimes they were protecting teammates. Sometimes they were setting up an outside pitch. The same applies today in Atlanta. A hitter is unwise to lean across the plate when facing the hard right-handed stuff Roger Clemens throws. Nor is it sensible to underestimate either the fast ball or the competitive nature of Greg Maddux.

. . . .

Two figure filberts, John Thorn and John Holway, have calculated that in one season (1985) at least 690 major league batters were hit by pitches. Four hundred–plus American Leaguers. Some 280 in the National League. They wrote, "The difference is obviously accounted for by the presence of the designated hitter in the American League: AL pitchers do not have to bat and thus are safe from retaliation." The point is not entirely persuasive. I don't recall many instances of pitchers throwing at other pitchers. A sophisticated big-league counter-knockdown focuses on the other team's catcher. He is calling for the beanballs, sometimes with a little spin of the right hand indicating, "Flip him." A catcher has to know when a knockdown is coming. Otherwise, at major league speed, a knockdown becomes a wild pitch.

Elrod Hendricks caught in the American League between 1968 and 1979, mostly for the Baltimore Orioles. In recent years he has worked as the Orioles' bullpen coach. Ellie Hendricks is large, hearty, and erudite in surprising ways. He can talk knockdowns one minute and then move on to his avocation, playing flute. ("The best tone I ever heard came from the classical player Jean Pierre Rampal. He uses a gold flute. I make do with silver." So much, for the moment, for Mozart.) "As a catcher, you're in the middle when the knockdowns start," Hendricks says. "One Yankee game, some pitches came close to Thurman Munson's head. He started getting angry. I'm catching. Damn, Thurman said, but we're throwing at him. And he said worse than 'damn.'

"I'm crouching back there. I told him no, we weren't. Some pitches just drifted inside. I don't think he believed me. The next time I came to bat, the Yankees plunked me with a fast ball in my chest. Catfish Hunter. A control pitcher. He got me. Right over the heart. But you know, that's part of the game, moving the ball in and out, giving a shot, taking one. By the time you make the major leagues, you don't want to blow your composure because a pitch comes close to your head or your body. I got the most out of my ability by concentrating, not blowing up. I was never a great hitter but I wasn't a raging bull up there, or a scared hitter, either, for that matter. I put all my concentration into getting the bat on the ball."

Gene Michael, whose work as general manager created interesting Yankee teams in the mid-1990s, played major league shortstop for ten years. "Being hit by a pitch and not rubbing, not showing pain, that was important, when I was playing [1966–75]," Michael says. "They're all running out to get at the pitcher these days. I don't think they really want to fight. They want to run out to make a point, but they hope it's broken up before the fighting gets serious. To me that's not macho at all. You run out there, you let the pitcher know he's bothering you when he comes inside. And isn't that what the pitcher is trying to do?"

Tony Kubek, a retired network broadcaster, was a solid Yankee shortstop for nine seasons (1957–65). He is a tall, sandy-haired, gentle follow, best remembered as a sober citizen in the days of such free spirits as Mickey Mantle and Whitey Ford. (Trying to rein in Mantle and Ford, general manager George Weiss once hired private detectives to shadow them. The morals police became confused and followed Tony Kubek. Later the detectives reported that they had shadowed him in Detroit all the way from the ballpark to the recreation room of a YMCA. He played an hour or so of Ping-Pong. After that he connected with a teammate, Bobby Richardson. Each consumed a malted milk.)

"I'm for the law of the jungle," says gentle Tony Kubek. "That's the one control that works. You get one knockdown, you give one knockdown. Good umpires let that pass. Then after each team has had one knockdown pitch, they step in. But first, go by natural law. Once in a while things get excessive. By the time Charlie Dressen took over the Tigers [1963], he was a very angry guy. Our Yankee clubs were beating him, and one day he stood up in the Detroit dugout and flipped a coin. We know what that meant. Flip the hitter [with a fast ball at the head]. Dressen kept flipping the coin. He wanted to knock down everybody in our starting lineup, Maris, Mantle, Elston Howard, even me, although I couldn't hit with those guys. There's where you do need an umpire with the power to say, one way or another, Charlie, put that coin away. But most of the time the law of the jungle keeps everything in check."

Buck Showalter is short, intense, intelligent, a successful manager across four seasons in the Bronx and now successful again with the expansion team, the Arizona Diamondbacks. (As far as I can tell, Arizona is the only big-league club ever named after a venomous reptile.) "A brush back that straightens up a hitter leaning close is part of pitching inside," Showalter says. "Pitchers have that right. They have the right to work both the corners. But certain people go too far. I tell my pitchers, if you think there is something macho in hitting a batter in the face, then watching him lie bleeding in the batter's box, then there's something wrong with your idea of what macho is. Maybe there's also something wrong with you."

Can you win in the major leagues advocating sportsmanship, as opposed to the terrorism of Dressen and Casey Stengel? Mathewson

did it seventy-five years ago. Koufax did it thirty-five years ago.*
Showalter has been winning in a sporting way in two major leagues
with very different franchises and, indeed, across two centuries.

One curiosity about brush-back pitching is this: Some of the most
genial of men have been most fearsome. "Walter Johnson was a be-
nign person," said the late Shirley Povich, who began covering the
Senators for the *Washington Post* in 1922. "For years baseball writers
referred to Walter as 'the Big Swede.' After a long time, he mentioned
that he wasn't Swedish. His ancestry was Scotch and German. I asked
why he had been silent for so long. 'The Swedes are nice people,' Johnson said. 'I didn't want to offend them.' He was a rube from Weiser,
Idaho, when he came up, but he was also a gentleman. He wore cellu-
loid collars and high-button shoes. He went to church. He often expressed dread at hitting batters. He told me many times, 'I know I
throw hard and I don't want to hurt anybody.'

"I remember the scene in Griffith Stadium when Johnson hit
Eddie Collins [a career .333 hitter], driving a fast ball into the ribs.
Johnson was the first to reach Collins, who was writhing in the dirt of
the batter's box, and was the most solicitous of the group that gathered there. For five minutes Collins lay prone. There was a cheer

---

*In twelve seasons, Koufax hit only eighteen batters. However, even Koufax's sportsmanship had
limits. Once after Lou Brock stole two bases on successive pitches, Koufax said, "Lou, I don't
like to be embarrassed. If you want to run like that, you're going down." Koufax threw a hundred
miles an hour with great control. Brock was brave but not self-destructive. He stopped running
on Koufax.

when he rose unsteadily. He received a pat from Johnson and hobbled to first base with a gimpy stride. On Johnson's next pitch, Collins stole second."

That was the compassionate Walter Johnson. But what major leaguer actually hit the greatest number of batsmen? The competitive Johnson. Same chap. Reminding batters not to crowd the plate, Johnson plunked either 206 or 208, depending on the source. "He didn't want to hurt anyone," Povich said, "but something else was just as strong in Walter. He didn't want to get beat."

Factored on a per-inning basis, Don Drysdale hit more batters than anyone in the annals, except for Joe McGinnity of John McGraw's fearsome old Giants. Nobody called McGinnity a collie. He was a flint-heart, Iron Man Joe. Early Wynn, who hit nine batters one season, was said to have been so mean that during a family outing in Alabama he knocked down his mother. "I had to," Wynn said. "Mom was a good curve-ball hitter." This story, which Wynn spun out for Red Smith and myself one spiritous night at the Players' Club in Manhattan, recurs constantly in various versions. When we gathered, I was preparing a magazine story about Wynn, and Smith was mining for column material. "The point of the knockdown is not to injure anybody but to get someone upset," Wynn said a few years later. "If I could make you and Red Smith write that I was mean enough to bean my mother, that would only help my effectiveness. Hitters can read. Most can, anyway. Besides, my mom knew better. I'd never bean her. Brush her, maybe.

"Are you sure the waiter heard our order?

"Whenever I wanted to hit somebody I could," Wynn said, "but then I'd never go for the head. I could always drill any hitter in the ribs. Get my fast ball in the ribs and you remember. After the pain passes you cough for a week."

Clem Labine once plunked 6-foot-4-inch Joe Adcock squarely in the helmet. Adcock, a first baseman for the Milwaukee Braves, had hit four home runs against the Dodgers the day before. I went into the Braves' locker room and Adcock was sitting on a trainer's table, looking irritated but unhurt. He showed me his blue helmet. "Look at this," Adcock said. The pitch had hit the helmet so hard that red marks from the stitches showed on the blue plastic. "Mention that to your fucking friend Labine."

"But there was no intent to hit him, much less hurt him," Labine said. "Adcock was supposed to get out of the way of that pitch and then make out on an outside curve. I didn't need another base runner then. It isn't my fault he didn't have enough sense to duck. I wasn't trying to hit him. Tell that to Adcock." Somehow I never got around to doing that.

Six-foot-five-inch Stan Williams of the Dodgers once threw a fast ball into Henry Aaron's batting helmet. He apologized later. "I'm sorry I hit you on the helmet, Hank," Williams said. Aaron glared. "I meant to hit you on the neck." Aaron *hated* being thrown at. We were walking down a sidewalk in Philadelphia once when I asked him how he felt about being knocked down. He turned his back and crossed the street in what he believed was a pointed no-comment. He didn't realize— Aaron was a better hitter than thinker—that a rapid shuffle away from the question was comment enough. While Aaron detested being thrown at, on the field he possessed enough mental discipline so that he did not let knockdowns distract him for longer than a few seconds.

I don't imagine anyone likes being thrown at, but the exemplary response was expressed by the exemplary Willie Mays. "They can throw at me all they want," Willie said, "but when that knockdown pitch comes in, I ain't gonna be there. The pitch after that, the one they throw for a strike, that's the one I'll be around to meet."

Mays hit 660 home runs in twenty-two seasons. Aaron played a season longer and hit the record total, 755. But Mays had to spend a decade playing alongside San Francisco Bay, hitting into a pitcher's wind. Aaron played fifteen seasons in Atlanta, where the air is thin and the old ballpark was called the Launching Pad. Had they played under comparable conditions, Mays would have outslugged Aaron. Or so I believe. Had the Giants stayed in the Polo Grounds, the major league ballpark with the shortest fences on the planet, Mays' power numbers would have crashed computers.

Pitchers could not rattle Mays with knockdowns. In fact, many believed that a knockdown served only to fuel his competitive fire. "You make Willie mad and then he just hits you better," conceded the redoubtable Early Wynn.

I remember Don Drysdale, the preeminent modern knockdown pitcher, as a tall, skinny boy of twenty who came tiptoeing into the clubhouse at Ebbets Field one summer day in 1956, open-mouthed with awe. He was joining the most illustrious Dodgers team, the one I called "the Boys of Summer," a roster bright with brilliant players: Jackie Robinson, Pee Wee Reese, Duke Snider, Roy Campanella, Carl Furillo, Gil Hodges. Drysdale was a smart youngster from a baseball family. He knew who everybody was. That's why he entered as quietly as he did. If this Dodgers team could be said to have had a weakness, it was pitching. Although four old Dodgers starters were twenty-game winners, none was capable of taking over a World Series as Hoss Radbourn and Mathewson had and as Allie Reynolds of the Yankees did to a lesser extent. In 1956 Don Newcombe, the mighty Big Newk, won twenty-seven games for Brooklyn. That October against the Yankees, he started twice and never made it past the fourth inning. He lost both games and finished the Series with an earned run average of 21.21. He did not recover his confidence and was never a big winner again.

The old Brooklyn Dodgers were a remarkable organization, and their search for young pitchers produced three unusual characters in a hurry. One was Roger Craig, never a big winner—indeed, Craig twice was a twenty-game loser for the Mets—but an innovative coach and manager during the 1980s. Another was Sandy Koufax, who, for a variety of reasons, did not become a twenty-game winner until his ninth season. The third was Drysdale, the Big D, the Collie who worked like a Doberman.

Some years ago, as this book began to assume a shape, Drysdale and I spoke for a long time at the Dodgers' training base in Vero Beach, Florida, called, reasonably enough, Dodgertown. The place was a Naval Air Station during World War II, which Branch Rickey purchased for the Dodgers two years after the Japanese surrender. Rickey wanted a Florida enclave where his black players could train free of racist threats and eat in a clean, well-lighted place. Rickey built four diamonds, installed platoons of pitching machines and sliding pits, creating an innovative baseball center with, among other things, a pitching area where the strike zone was outlined by strings. Generations of Dodgers pitchers sweated in the springtime, getting their best stuff through stringed quadrangles. Most of the players lived in what had been navy barracks; a few stars were allotted the cottages, once inhabited by flight officers. Dodgertown was a self-contained community, with dining rooms, card tables, and a bar—off-limits to the players—a huge, flat expanse rimmed on three sides by orange groves. On the fourth side, to the west, the village of Vero Beach dumped garbage.

Over the years, the wildly energetic Walter O'Malley and his less-gifted heirs remodeled Dodgertown past recognition. The barracks and cottages were replaced by a living quarters that looked like an endless motel. The late Jim Murray of the *Los Angeles Times* called the architectural style "Bakersfield Modern." Roadways were named for former Dodgers stars. Conference rooms sprouted on the sandy soil. The old rustic, integrated baseball camp evolved into the Dodgertown Spring Training Base and Conference Center, suitable for corporate meetings, rates furnished on request, group discounts available, call collect.

Drysdale looked vigorous and assured as we sat at a table beside the modern dark-wood corporate bar that the Dodgers use as the focal point for their dogged hospitality. Through windows in the lounge, you could see hard-surface tennis courts and a pool, where the players' wives and children idled in spring. (Children were barred from the earlier Dodgertown. Walter O'Malley said, "Some damned kid might come down with measles and infect my entire team.")

Drysdale was fifty-six, still youthful in manner, ebullient and proud of the athletic beauty of his second wife, Annie, who just four days before in Los Angeles had given birth to Drew. "When she gets better," he said, "we'll go back to playing tennis. She can beat me. Annie isn't just a good athlete for a woman. She's a good athlete." He smiled and took a drink and drank it quickly. "You still remember me from Brooklyn?"

I was a few years older than Drysdale, and I had covered the Brooklyn Dodgers for four seasons before he arrived. Four seasons constitutes an epoch in baseball time. "You were tall," I said, "and skinny, and you looked scared."

"Was I ever," Drysdale said. The voice was intense and mellifluous. He had been broadcasting games for twenty years, and he spoke in the even, measured tone you hear on radio. "I was afraid of New York and afraid of the manager and afraid of the veterans and afraid of not making it and afraid of what everyone would write. Buzzy Bavasi told me he'd seen lots of pitchers come and go, people like Ralph Branca and Rex Barney and Jack Banta.* They had a world of promise, but then they fizzled out. Buzzy said it was hard to make the major leagues, sure, but the harder thing was this. Stay there. I never forgot those words. Stay there. Stay a big leaguer. Stay a winner. I was fortu-

---

*Ralph Branca, who won twenty-one games for the Brooklyn Dodgers at the age of twenty-one, was washed up at twenty-eight. Rex Barney, the Dodgers' hardest thrower and ace at twenty-four, was through at twenty-six. Jack Banta, another overpowering righthander, started and relieved in forty-eight games for the Dodgers at twenty-four. He disappeared into the minors two seasons later. Both Bavasi and Rickey believed that all three had at least the potential to become Hall of Famers. None came close.

nate in ways I didn't understand at the time. Pee Wee Reese, the captain, made me feel welcome. He said I could be a big winner and that's what the team needed, a big, strong winner. No one would be rooting for me harder than he was. Jackie Robinson made me feel that I belonged. On some clubs in those days there was a war between the veterans and the 'rooks.' Every rookie was threatening to the veterans. But with the old Brooklyn Dodgers, hey, suddenly I had a bunch of brand-new uncles."

Drysdale's father, Scott, had played minor league ball, but back problems retired him and he had to go to work for a western telephone company as a repairman. Scott Drysdale earned extra money and stayed close to baseball as a "bird-dog" scout in California, a free-lance operator, loosely linked to the Dodgers. Scott drew no salary, but if the Dodgers signed a prospect he recommended, he earned a fee. "Bird-dogging" is the baseball term for scouting as piece work. Scott did not have to travel far to spot his most imposing prospect. The kid was sleeping in an upstairs bedroom. Scott recommended his son to Harold "Lefty" Phillips, the Dodgers' crack West Coast scout, who signed Don as soon as he finished high school.

Drysdale was raised a valley boy, in Van Nuys. He played infield at first, but in time at Van Nuys High "my body kind of came together and all of a sudden I could throw like hell." He became a star pitcher in his senior year. Drysdale pitched one season at Bakersfield, another season in Triple A, and then materialized in the Brooklyn Dodgers' dressing room. "I could throw ninety-five miles an hour, right up there with Koufax," Drysdale said, "but at nineteen I had some things to learn." That season, 1956, the Dodgers bought the contract of Sal

Maglie, who had been struggling in Cleveland. Maglie won a number of important games and lost a classic. He was the Dodgers' starter whom Don Larsen of the Yankees defeated on October 8, pitching the first and only perfect World Series game.

Although Maglie had limited later success as a pitching coach, he was, Drysdale says, "an important influence. I learned more from Sal than from any single individual." Drysdale became the Dodgers' best pitcher as a twenty-one-year-old in 1957, the team's last summer in Brooklyn. He won seventeen, and pitched four shutouts. Five years later he won a Cy Young Award. He pitched in eight all-star games, and during the spring of 1968, he worked fifty-eight consecutive scoreless innings. Shoulder trouble forced him to quit in August 1969. "I deeply regret having to retire," he told reporters at Dodger Stadium. "But as they say, some things are inevitable—death, taxes, and retirement from professional sports. The elasticity is gone from my arm. I haven't been able to throw a good fast ball all year." Drysdale told himself proudly that he had followed Bavasi's precept. He had become a star and *stayed* a star. He won more games (209) and struck out more batters (2,486) than anyone in Dodger history up to that time. (Both marks have since been eclipsed by Don Sutton.)

In Drysdale's pitching prime, a *Sports Illustrated* reporter wrote about "his creamy good looks and his hair-tonic hairdo" and his appearance as "a made-in-Hollywood boy next door." Lowell Reidenbaugh of *The Sporting News* provided a more compelling description. Working hyperbole with care, Reidenbaugh described Drysdale as "having the face of a choirboy, the physique of Goliath, and the competitive instincts of a tarantula."

Drysdale's life rang with excitement and victory and controversy. He married a lively, strong-minded California beauty named Ginger Dubberly. When they appeared on the Groucho Marx quiz show, *You Bet Your Life,* a year later, they struck viewers as an American dream couple. Drysdale bought race horses and a restaurant, sang with Milton Berle in Las Vegas, won acting spots in television series. When baseball negotiations still ran under feudal rules, he banded with Sandy Koufax to take on the Archduke of Feudalism, Walter O'Malley. "We want together a million dollars for the next three years," Drysdale said. The reaction in O'Malley's personal tectonic plates is said to have registered significantly on a Cal Tech seismograph. Eventually, Drysdale settled for $115,000 per season. His knockdowns prompted Aaron to call him "mean." Others said he threw a spitter. When Herman Franks managed the San Francisco Giants, he told reporters that Drysdale was applying Vaseline to the baseball. The effect, as with a spitter, Franks explained, would be to make a fast pitch drop. Drysdale's only on-the-record response came in a television commercial. A rival manager accuses him of loading the ball with "greasy kid stuff." Drysdale marches off the mound, tramps into the clubhouse, and emerges holding a jar of the hair tonic he uses, the popular, nongreasy Vitalis.

At the bar in the corporate Dodgertown of 1993, Drysdale spoke with easy candor and open optimism, someone still in the middle of the journey. "I don't know what Ginger wanted exactly," he said, "but it wasn't exactly me. She said I was too wrapped up in myself. I suppose I was, but when the marriage went, after about a dozen years, that was my first major defeat. A bad time," he said. "After the divorce, I drank too much. That's done now. I like to drink socially and I'm one of those people who can do that. Annie's been great for me and now I feel like a kid. I mean, I'm a new father, past fifty-five years old, and right now I'm also one hell of a happy camper."

We had another drink. "Did you throw the Vaseline ball, the way Herman Franks said?"

"Never. Never had to. I threw a good spitball. Gene Mauch, when he was managing the Phillies [1960–68], said I threw the best spitter in the league. You have to go back with me here. I was playing for Montreal. When was that, 1955, before the Cuban Revolution. We were playing the Havana Sugar Kings and their pitcher was giving us fits with spitters. I took a crash course. Put saliva on the ball. Keep your fingers off the seams. I didn't know the aerodynamics and I don't know them today. But when I wet the ball and kept my fingers on the smooth part, the bottom would drop out of the pitch when it reached the plate. A pretty good fast ball that falls off the table. In Brooklyn they'd had the master. Preacher Roe. Anyway, I had a fast ball and a spitter. A lot of fast balls, really. High and in. Low and away. High and away. I regard these as different pitches because there are different release points. And then I had a hard breaking ball, but none of that, nothing, means a damn thing in the big leagues, unless you have mental toughness."

I mentioned that some Dodgers prospects whose careers came up short were fine sensitive fellows, perhaps a bit too sensitive.

"I'm a fine sensitive fellow," Drysdale said. "Ask Annie. But that's not what applies on the mound. The greatest thing Sal Maglie taught me was this: The hell with all the hitters. The hell with *all* of them. (Except the hitters on your own ball club. They're the ones who put up the runs that you need.) I'll tell you the truth. I threw spitters and I threw at batters' heads. I'd knock a guy down. He'd get up. His uniform is dirty. He's mad. I knock him down again. He looks at me. Am I crazy? Am I a killer? No. I'm just a competitor about to strike him out with a ninety-five-mile-an-hour fast ball on the outside at the knees, which he doesn't take the time to figure will be coming because he is too damn busy wondering, *Am I a killer? Am I nuts?* and worrying about his head. I threw at Henry Aaron and I threw at lousy hitters. I bothered Henry in the early years. But he adjusted. After a while, he started getting up from the knockdowns and walloping shots. He hit seventeen homers off me. I'd give him the knockdown. I'd give him the spitter. He wasn't afraid of me, that's for sure, but that isn't my point right here. I never was afraid of him, or any other hitter, and I got Henry out a lot. Willie McCovey hit the hell out of me for a couple of years, big strong left-hand batter. He hit me for power. Not many did that.

"After my rookie year, I pitched forty-nine shutouts, forty-eight in twelve seasons. That's an average of four a year. Not many hit me for power at all. I talk about the mental game and they look at me and there I was six foot five, and two hundred ten pounds, and throwing ninety-five and they're thinking, *Oh, sure, what the hell is mental about that, and when did you ever graduate from Harvard, Drysdale?* I got good marks at Van Nuys High and sure I'm big and strong, but believe me, without mental toughness, not another damn thing matters. I'm an action guy. I'm not what you'd call an intellectual. I don't sit home reading Shakespeare or Keats or that Italian poet from the middle ages."

"Dante," I said. "The feller could write. Dante Alighieri."

"Yeah. I knew it wasn't Carl Furillo. So I'm not intellectual, but I can think and everything begins with that. I thought a lot, as I was getting established, that somebody was looking over my shoulder. Somebody else wanted my job. There was no room to ease up. When I first came here to Dodgertown, there were sixteen, eighteen farm clubs, six or seven hundred players, a lot of them pitchers, and a lot of those ready to pitch in the big leagues, or close. When I got my chance, a hundred other pitchers were breathing down my neck. You could fold in the spring with all that pressure. You could fold later on. Maybe that's what happened to the guys Bavasi mentioned, Branca and Barney. I always was competitive and I had good support from Reese and Campanella. I came up with good mechanics, that is arm and leg and body in synch. I learned mechanics in the backyard, from my father. Sometimes in high school I'd let my arm get low and then, instead of the fast ball sinking, it would stay on the same plane, running into a right-hand hitter, moving flat. Easier to hit. Whenever that happened my dad whistled in the stands. Even when the Dodgers came out from Brooklyn to California, I'd drop my arm sometimes. My dad, up in the stands, he'd let loose a whistle. I heard that whistle so many times as a kid that even in a crowded big-league ball park, fifty-five thousand people, I could pick it out. Pick out Dad's whistle and what it meant. Get my arm up, dammit it. Get it up.

"Some say that Maglie taught me how to knock down big league hitters, but that's too simple. He'd say, 'Kid, you've got to watch the hitter. What is he trying to do? Look at his feet when he swings, or even sets to swing, and you can tell whether he's trying to pull the ball or go the other way. What's he been doing to you lately? What pitches has he hit hard? What has he missed?' This takes a strong baseball mind. Not academic. Not analytical. Just a specific kind of baseball thinking. Who's the hitter? Where are your fielders? Who's on a roll?

"All right. You know who you're dealing with. Now, upset him; get him really upset! In later years I often did that with change-ups. I threw the fast ball and a spitter and a *slurve,* a cross between a slider and a curve. With right-hand hitters, I used the fast ball and slurve. With the left-hand hitters, it was more fast ball, change, and straight slider. To me the knockdown pitch upsets a hitter's timing, like a change-up. It's not a weapon. It's a tactic."

I stared. He laughed and said, "I guess you don't agree."

"If you were going at my head," I suggested, "I'd rather have you do it with a change-up than a fast ball."

"Well, sure," he said, "the knockdown rattled some, but sharp shots through the box must have hit me fifty times. Those figure fellers got a record of the guys I hit, but no record of the guys that hit me. I never backed off. I never let fear enter my baseball mind. The truth is, no good hitter does, either."

It was getting close to dinnertime. "Let's watch a game together late in the season," Drysdale said. "We'll look for knockdowns together. You can upset a good hitter's timing but you can't really frighten him, any more than a football lineman frightens a good quarterback. Knock him down. Call him a chicken. Then he throws for the TD next play. Fear on the field? Exaggerated. Way out of line. A pitcher's arm isn't a loaded rifle. Now let's go eat. I want you to hear about my new family."

In a popular 1967 study, *A Thinking Man's Guide to Baseball,* Leonard Koppett advances the interesting and lurid proposition that pitching is akin to terrorism. Koppett writes: "Fear is the fundamental factor in hitting, and hitting the ball with the bat is the fundamental act of baseball. The fear is simple and instinctive. If a baseball, thrown hard, hits any part of your body, it hurts. If it hits certain vulnerable areas, like elbows, wrist or face, it can cause broken bones and other serious injuries. If it hits a particular area of an unprotected head, it can kill. A thrown baseball is, in short, a missile."

Koppett, who covered baseball for both the *Herald Tribune* and the *New York Times,* is always a thoughtful commentator. Which is not to say that he is always correct. Mathewson did not think that fear was particularly important in the confrontation between major league pitcher and major league batter. Branch Rickey, probably baseball's greatest theoretician and a rookie catcher for the St. Louis Browns in 1905, believed that a hitter knew a variety of fears. "First and foremost," Rickey said, "he's afraid of failing, of making out. Second, he's afraid of being made to look ridiculous, before his teammates, before the crowd, before the sharpies of the press. Third, but only a distant third on a major league level, he may have some fear of getting injured." Koppett's description of a major league turn at bat as a confrontation with a missile is dramatic but, I believe, off the mark, a Scud falling, as it were, on an empty patch of sand.

But the fear of which Koppett writes applies properly to lower levels of the game. Fast balls have caused numberless youngsters across the generations to quail and lurch away from the path of the baseball as they swing. They focus not on *getting a hit* but rather on *not getting* *hit.* * Since it is difficult to swing effectively while trembling, these children are never effective players. Body language gives away the terror in a frightened hitter, and sandlot kids, like any other kids, can be merciless. "Watcha fraida? The ball doesn't bite."

Baseball is a constant process of selection and refinement, whether in the Little League, among pickup teams, or in the majors; but on all levels, the people who can't hit—except for pitchers—are picked last, if they are picked at all. The baseball experience of children frightened by fast balls becomes a horror. First there is the terror the ball creates. Then comes the caustic needling. On top of that, there are episodes of rejection, being picked last or not being picked at all. Faced with these circumstances, youngsters look for other forms of recreation. Fear of the baseball weeds out weak players early.

Successful major league hitters, Barry Bonds, Sammy Sosa, Chipper Jones, and the rest, go about their business aware of stress—you don't want to strand the tying run at second base—but for them fear is history. "I've been hitting major league pitching since 1978," that splendid batsman Paul Molitor told me late in the 1990s. "That's what I do for a living. Some people look at computer screens every day. I look at ninety-mile-an-hour fast balls. If I was afraid, by now I'd have to be shell shocked, which according to my wife and friends, I'm not."

Ty Cobb, who played from 1905 through 1928, remains the most successful batsman in the annals. From 1907 through 1919 Cobb was

---

*There is no single completely satisfying explanation of the nature of fear in sport. I knew one youngster, terrorized by baseball, who skied joyfully down icy slopes that would have given pause to tough Swiss Alpine troopers. Skiing is a much more dangerous sport than baseball.

the leading hitter in the American League twelve times, and his lifetime batting average, .366, is the least approachable of baseball records. The fastest American League pitcher in Cobb's era was Walter Perry Johnson of the Washington Senators, called "the Big Train." Johnson won 417 games across twenty-one major league seasons. He was a long-armed righthander—about Mathewson's size—and he threw a little above sidearm, snapping his thick wrist at the moment of release. The Johnson fast ball, which moved at perhaps a hundred miles an hour, rode up and in to a right-handed batter. Some suggest that Johnson's blazer was the single hardest pitch that anyone ever has thrown. Although Johnson hit more than two hundred batters, he was profoundly concerned lest he seriously injure someone. "And that," Ty Cobb told Shirley Povich, "was what I used to get my edge. I'd crowd the plate against Johnson, putting my toes right up against it. Johnson didn't want to hit me, so he'd work the outside corner. When he missed a couple of times and fell behind, he'd let up, take something off his fast ball to be sure to get a strike. I'd step back and that would be the ball I'd hit." The greatest fast ball of all time stirred no fear, none whatsoever, within the dauntless competitor Ty Cobb.

Mathewson in his later years recounted a knockdown incident from the first game of the 1911 World Series, which he won for the Giants, defeating the Philadelphia Athletics 2 to 1. Charles Albert "Chief" Bender started for the Athletics, and Bender was throwing harder that day than Mathewson had ever seen him throw. Twice Bender drilled Fred Snodgrass, the Giants' young center fielder. When Snodgrass came to bat for the third time—in a "pinch"—Bender smiled at him. "Look out, Freddie," he said, "you don't get hit this time." Then he threw a fast ball at

Snodgrass' head. Snodgrass ducked. Ball one. "If you can't throw better than that," Snodgrass shouted, "I won't need to get a hit."

Bender continued to smile. ("He had perfect teeth," Mathewson remembered.) Then he threw a fast-ball strike that overpowered Snodgrass. "You missed that a mile," Bender said, grinning again. Snodgrass set his jaw in anger and began overswinging. "Grinning chronically," in Mathewson's phrase, Bender struck out Snodgrass with a curve that broke down into the dirt. Snodgrass was not afraid of Chief Bender's pitches. He was a solid hitter who finished with a lifetime average of .275. What happened, Mathewson said, was that a combination, the knockdown pitches, the sarcastic banter, the condescending grin, distracted Snodgrass. Then, having struck out his man, Bender pushed the needle deeper and twisted. "You ain't a batter, Freddie. You're a backstop. You can never get anywhere without being hit!"

Although beaten that day, Chief Bender won two other games. The Athletics won the World Series, 4 games to 2. Across six games, the rattled Fred Snodgrass, a .294 hitter all season, batted .105. But as Mathewson interpreted the episode, he was a victim of gamesmanship, obviously and distinctly quite different from being terrorized. "Chief took Fred's mind right out of the game," Mathewson said.

Mathewson himself never talked to hitters. "Talking on the mound disconcerts me," he said, "as much as it does them. Repartee is really not my line."

I once asked Branch Rickey if Mathewson threw at hitters. We were seated on a leather couch in a Pittsburgh hotel lobby and Rickey was lighting a cigar. The question produced strenuous puffing and cumulonimbus clouds of smoke. "Never," Rickey said, firmly. "Absolutely not. Mathewson *deceived* hitters. He didn't intimidate them. Besides, he never wanted to hurt another soul. He was the greatest pitching competitor I ever saw, but he only beat your brains out in the most figurative sense."

Mathewson took his Bible studies seriously. He pitched in 647 major league games, but never, not even in the World Series, would he consent to pitch on Sunday. This statement by a rugged Christian gentleman found an echo in the 1960s, when Sandy Koufax, the Dodgers' great Jewish lefthander, declined a World Series' start because the game fell on Yom Kippur. There is an odd and stirring link between Mathewson and Koufax in Branch Rickey's words. From the mound they both beat your brains out but in the most figurative sense.

I did plan to visit Drysdale again, as he suggested, later in 1993. Games get more competitive as pennant races build, and we were going to look further into intimidation, fear, timing, the knockdown. The Big Collie would talk about the Doberman side of pitching, with examples spreading out in front of us. His "Italian poet," Dante, wrote seven hundred years before, "In the middle of the journey of our life, I came to myself in a dark wood where the straight path was lost." But for Drysdale that spring it was not the middle of the journey; it was already very late in the season. The hardest thing, Pee Wee Reese told me, was seeing Don's father, Scott Drysdale, silent and bereft in terrible grief at the funeral for his big handsome son on a clear and sunny day in Southern California.

11.

A BULLPEN

NAMED BRUCE

If it wasn't for the splitter, I'd still be a printer's
assistant back in Mount Joy, Pennsylvania.

BRUCE SUTTER

Early in the 1980s, Dorel Norman Elvert Herzog, a country slicker who answers to "Whitey," set about reviving a St. Louis Cardinal team that had fallen into indolent mediocrity. Whitey Herzog is one of the soundest baseball men of his generation, but trusting him runs against rules I had to learn two score and several summers ago. My instructor at the time was the horse-racing columnist for the *New York Herald Tribune*, Joe H. Palmer, a man of startling erudition, who formerly taught freshman composition at the

University of Kentucky and who could write entire paragraphs in pre-Norman English. If I was (a) going to survive as a writer and (b) make sense as a person, I had better remember basic guidelines, Professor Palmer remarked.

1. Never eat at a restaurant called "Mom's."

2. Never carry a bundle by a string.

3. Never trust a man named "Whitey" or "Doc."

When I wondered about the third rule, Palmer turned irritable. If I'd grown up in a respectable place like Kentucky, he said, I would have long since met a lot of people named "Whitey" and "Doc," been fleeced a few times, and consequently not have bothered him with such a foolish question.

Whitey Herzog grew up in New Athens, Illinois, and after an eight-season career as a journeyman outfielder, managed with great success in Kansas City, where his teams won three pennants in a row. Then he marched east, across Missouri, and took over the Cardinals. He was certainly shrewd, confirming a bit of Joe Palmer's Theory of the Whiteys. But where to this day I shun restaurants called "Mom's," I would certainly hire Whitey Herzog to run my big-league ball club, if I possessed a spare $300 million and could buy one. August A. Busch, the late Baron of Budweiser, handed Herzog the Cardinals—he hired

Whitey as field manager and general manager during the 1980s—and said, in effect: *Fix this team*. "They had power hitters but you don't get much out of power hitters in Busch Stadium," Herzog said sometime after taking charge. The park stands a few hundred yards west of the Mississippi River, and the summer air is hot and humid, which seemed to have the effect of taking distance off high drives before Mark McGwire was invented. "This is a turf stadium," Herzog said. [It was at the time.] "You want speed here, that's what I've been angling for. You want a fast team that pounds hits through the infield. You'll die hitting long fly balls."

"And the pitching?" I asked.

"I'm not going to tell you we have a great starting rotation. But I've got some bullpen, some amazing damn bullpen. I don't think you've seen anything like my bullpen before. Stick around. My bullpen is named Bruce Sutter."

Later that afternoon, the Cardinals guarded a narrow edge over a good Montreal Expo team that had Tim Wallach, Gary Carter, André Dawson, and Al Oliver, a team that led its division in batting and home runs. St. Louis took a one-run lead in the ninth inning when Herzog brought Sutter into the game. Sutter was bearded, like an Amish farmer, and he worked in a great hurry, *pitch-pitch-pitch-pitch-pitch*, and suddenly, the fine Expo batters disappeared. One grounded out to the mound. Two others struck out on pitches that dropped into the dirt. Not big glorious overhand curve balls, in the Sandy Koufax manner, pitches breaking down in a rainbow arc from chest to ankle.

Sutter threw what looked like an ordinary fast ball. It came toward home plate thigh high. Then the baseball fell into a black hole. I don't believe I had ever seen so many good hitters take so many terrible swings at pitches out of the strike zone, and in such haste. *Pitch-pitch-pitch. Swing-swing-swing. Ball game.*

Bearded Bruce Sutter hurried off the mound and shook hands quickly with Darrell Porter, a square-jawed catcher with eyeglasses who had drawn the nickname of a comic-strip character. "What a battery," I said to Herzog. "Superman pitching to Clark Kent."

He grinned. "I thought we'd get your attention."

"What was that pitch?" I said.

"We call it the split-fingered fast ball."

"Like a fork ball."

"No," Herzog said. "A fork ball is a fork ball. This is a faster pitch. To batters, it's the sinker from hell."

"Why do they swing?"

"Because it comes up there looking like a strike. The speed doesn't give away anything. It's pretty fast. You can't pick up the rotation, so you don't know what the hell it is. Now, if I used Sutter to start ball games, maybe the third time the hitters came up, they'd do a little better than what you just saw. But I don't use him to start. Into the game. Pitch quick. Cardinals win."

Herzog worked Sutter in seventy regular season games that year, 1982, almost half the schedule. Sutter won nine and saved thirty-six; he walked off the mound, having posted the final out, no fewer than forty-five times. Sutter got the final out in just about half of all the games the Cardinals won. "I'll tell you what my attitude was," Sutter remembered recently. "The manager's bringing me in? We've got a lead? Gentlemen, this ball game is over."

The 1982 Cardinals defeated Atlanta, 7 to 0, in the first game of the league championship series, without needing relief pitching. The second game was close. Sutter came in to start the eighth inning with the Cardinals down, 3 to 2. Atlanta's lineup bulged with muscular batters: Dale Murphy, who led the league in runs batted in; Bob Horner, who hit thirty-two home runs; strong, solid Chris Chambliss. Sutter retired six in a row. The Cardinals won the ball game, 4 to 3, in the ninth. Next day, Herzog brought Sutter in with two men on base in the seventh inning. Sutter retired seven Braves in a row. The Cardinals, with a bullpen named Bruce, had won their first pennant in fourteen years. Sutter's earned run average for the championship series was easy to remember: 0.00. He did give up two runs to the Milwaukee Brewers in game five of the World Series. But he won game two and saved games three and seven. The Cards and the bullpen named Bruce were champions of the baseball cosmos.

Sutter was twenty-nine years old and at a pinnacle, and modern baseball had come to one of its defining moments, as ancient baseball did when little Candy Cummings threw his dazzling curve ball for the Hartford Dark Blues, or as art-deco baseball did when Whitlow Wyatt threw his new hard slider and brought the Brooklyn Dodgers their first pennant in twenty-one seasons. In essence, a pitch took center stage.

Sutter suffered early from a tender elbow. Later what he called "nerve pain in my arm" sidelined him. He was always in a hurry, and as he says, "trying to come back too quick, I tore my rotator cuff." Despite modern surgery and rehabilitation, that shoulder injury is often ruinous. It forced Sutter to retire in 1988, when he was thirty-five. Under the category of games started, he tied an all-time major league three-century record. Bruce Sutter, the greatest split-finger pitcher in the annals, never started a game. Not one. His bottom line reads: Starts: 0.00. Victories: 68. Earned run average: 2.84. Saves: 300.

As an almost contemporary pitcher, Sutter benefited from the explosion in ball-player salaries. For several seasons he earned $1.66 million a year—more than Mathewson or Sain or Spahn or Drysdale earned across a career. Financially comfortable in retirement, he drifted away from organized baseball and concentrated on family matters. "Right now," he said when we last talked, "I'm raising money for a new high school field and working with some charities and helping out my children. [He has three.] Being retired like this, I'm too busy to take a job."

In 1986 *Sports Illustrated* declared in a prominent article that the split-fingered fast ball was "The Pitch of the '80s." That sort of *diktat* has been booming out of the publication since its founder, Henry Luce, a devotee of diktats, discovered sport in 1954. In this instance the writer, Ron Fimrite, focused on Roger Craig, Drysdale's old Brooklyn teammate, who with equal portions of grit, intelligence, and personal promotion got himself anointed as "the guru of the split-fingered fast ball." Craig was an effective manager, particularly in San Francisco, but in retrospect something less than a guru. *Apostle* might be a better term. Sutter's name was mentioned in only four paragraphs.

Fimrite did add solid research of his own. After the spitter was outlawed, he suggested, "the search for an equivalent pitch has taken pitchers along paths once explored only by the alchemists." Medieval alchemists sought to transmit base metals into gold or to find the panacea that would cure all diseases or to create eternal life. But given the wonders of the splitter, we can forgive Fimrite excess enthusiasm. He postulated that knuckleballs and fork balls developed to replace the spit ball. "The split-finger is but the newest of the substitute spitters," he wrote, "but with its breathtaking drop it may yet be the closest to the real thing."

Journalism marches on, and in October 1988 *Playboy* ran an extended interview with Craig, then managing the San Francisco Giants.

> CRAIG: Ask me another baseball question. A real one.
>
> PLAYBOY: Why do players tug on their crotch so much?
>
> CRAIG: The crotch cup hurts if it's not right.
>
> PLAYBOY: You never finished saying what unique thing you've given to baseball.
>
> CRAIG: Unique? The split-fingered fast ball.

Aside from the inherent *Playboy* vulgarity, the interview is uninformed journalism. As best I could put the story together, the true history of the split-finger begins with a right-handed pitcher named Fred Turner Martin, out of Williams, Oklahoma, who all but destroyed his own career. Freddie Martin surfaced briefly with the championship 1946 Cardinals as a thirty-year-old rookie. "He was a well-seasoned rookie righthander," Stan Musial remembers. "He knew how to pitch. Not the greatest fast ball, but he was smart."

Late in May, Martin, lefthander Max Lanier, and second baseman Lou Klein quit the Cardinals—a franchise noted for excellent baseball and severe parsimony—and went to play for a so-called outlaw league in Mexico. (Musial, offered a $50,000 bonus to move south, declined. The Cardinals then raised his salary to $18,500, for which he won his second batting championship, hitting .365.)

At the time Major League Baseball—Baseball Inc.—denied ball players the right of free negotiation. Albert B. "Happy" Chandler, the commissioner, immediately suspended the three Cardinals "for life." When the Mexican venture collapsed, "life" turned out to be two seasons. Back with St. Louis in 1949, Martin worked well as a reliever, but the following year his arm went bad and the Cardinals released him. Martin drifted into the minor leagues and a variety of coaching jobs. He had long fingers and like Johnny Sain (and Sandy Koufax and Christy Mathewson and Ol Hoss Radbourn) he experimented with a variety of grips. By the time Martin devised the splitter, it was too late to rescue his own pitching life. But his career crossed the career of Bruce Sutter during 1973 at Quincy, Illinois, in a felicitous meeting of two baseball men who didn't seem to be going anywhere at all.

"When I graduated from high school," Sutter says, "I was seventeen. Everybody around me said that I should try college instead of pro ball. I guess that says something about my stuff. There was no split-finger fast ball then, but I was a good pitcher at Donegal High School in Mount Joy, and the Washington Senators drafted me. I listened to the people around me and decided not to sign. Instead I enrolled at Old Dominion University in Virginia. I played fall baseball with them. After a while I realized that I was doing things backward. It would be sensible for a young athlete to use a baseball scholarship to get educated. But that wasn't what I was doing in Virginia. I was young and pretty much bored by education, or anyway, classes. I just wanted to play ball. So I dropped out and went to work in a printing place in Mount Joy. That spring I started pitching for a semipro team in Lancaster, young fellers, high school and college kids, eighteen to twenty-one. The team was called—I'm not kidding —the Hippies Raiders. I won for the Hippies Raiders and a Chicago Cub scout saw me. He liked me, but he didn't exactly go nuts. He offered a five hundred dollar bonus to sign. Not five thousand dollars—five hundred dollars. I was ready to report right there, right then. The scout said there wasn't any rush. I could go on pitching for the Hippies Raiders in the small towns and the farming country where I grew up. The Cubs would wait for me to come to their minor league camp the following spring."

Sutter began at the bottom of the minors, pitching for a "co-op" team in Bradenton, Florida. Most minor league teams work with a single major league organization that supplies players, manager, coaches, and even the trainer. A few, very few, minor league teams operate independently, seeking out and paying their own talent. That tends to be costly.* Somewhere between the farm team and the independent falls the co-op. A co-op club is staffed by players from a variety of major league organizations. These tend to be marginal minor

---

*I purchased a controlling interest in the Utica Blue Sox of the New York Penn League in 1983 and ran a reasonably tight ship. The Blue Sox won the pennant on the last day of the season and then won the league championship play-off, all there was to win. My triumphs stopped at the ledger book. Putting together a championship team, I lost 90 percent of what I invested.

leaguers, rather than top prospects. Bruce Sutter was a marginal minor leaguer. He could throw "average hard," about eighty-six miles an hour, but so can legions of young men. Then something popped in Sutter's elbow and he spent the rest of that summer trying to get well.

That winter Bruce Sutter, working as printer's assistant, paid for elbow surgery on his own. He felt that if he let the Cubs know he was undergoing surgery, they would release him. His baseball career would then be over, just about the time he reached his twentieth birthday, on January 8, 1973. "I went to spring training," he told me, "and, of course, I didn't tell anybody about the operation, and, of course, they kept asking me how my elbow felt. Then it happened. A pitching coach saw me with my shirt off and said, 'What is that scar on your elbow?' I had to tell him, but I think it worked out, because they stayed with me, even with my scar, a little longer, waiting to see if my elbow came around. They sent me to play for Quincy in the Midwest League. A month into that season, I clicked with Martin."

On a country ball field in downstate Illinois, Martin said, "Kid, why don't you try holding the ball like this and see what happens?" Martin demonstrated the split-finger grip.

"I threw it," Sutter says, "and the first time I did it, the ball broke down. Right away it broke down. I don't know why it came so quickly. I have big hands and long fingers, but maybe, aside from that, it was something in my natural motion. Anyway, it broke great that first time and then it was just a matter of . . . well; now that I think about it, a lot of things. Learning to throw it for a strike. Learning to bounce it in the dirt. Getting the hitters to chase the one that bounces. Fooling them. Keeping them fooled." Howard Bruce Sutter, late of the Lancaster Hippies Raiders, had the arm, the hand, the fingers. He had the pitch. Now he had to learn to play the head game.

Radar guns were clocking Sutter's fast ball at 86–87 miles an hour. His split-finger traveled 78–82. The similarity in speeds is significant, because it was just about impossible for a batter to determine early— early enough—whether Sutter was throwing an 86-mile-an-hour fast ball or an 82-mile-an-hour splitter. A fast ball coming in thigh high is a good pitch for most batters to hit. A splitter coming in thigh high drops under the batter's swing, often all the way down into the dirt around home plate. That is the swinging strike that makes so many in the grandstands wonder, *Why is a big leaguer swinging at a terrible pitch?* For starters, it is not a terrible pitch. It is not a terrible pitch at all. It is, in fact, a wonderful pitch. We lack decades of analysis of splitters. No physicists have published studies, and, as a happy concomitant, no magazine has yet published a story denying that the splitter drops. Considering the pitch, we are left on our own, naked as it were, which is how it is for batters on the field.

"All right," Bruce Sutter begins an unpretentious but profoundly knowledgeable lecture, "a baseball has two seams, which run in lines. Take the point where those seams are closest together. Put your index finger on one seam and your middle finger on the other. Now spread your fingers about a quarter inch so they rest on either side of the seams. If your fingers are long enough, you'll be sort of reaching around the ball and your fingertips will come to rest on the front seams. [If your fingers aren't that long, the splitter isn't your pitch.] The ball is touching the meaty area on the inside of your fingers but actually you grip it—apply pressure—only with the fingertips on the seams at the front of the ball. Very different from the grip for any other pitch.

THE SPLIT-FINGER FASTBALL

"Okay. The second thing is positioning your thumb underneath. When you set your grip so that there are those two parallel seams on top, inside your fingers, you find two seams on the bottom of the ball. Nothing complicated. Just the nature of how a baseball is stitched. Your thumb underneath goes on the back seam, not the front one. That makes the ball move out in your hand a little bit, away from the palm.

"Now something else. Pressure the ball more with your index finger than with your middle finger. That's hard for some to do; they're used to applying most pressure with the middle finger. It just so happened that I always threw off my index finger, even when I was a little kid, even when coaches didn't want that. There it is. Fingers spread, wrapped around the ball. Thumb on the back seam on the underside. Most pressure from the index finger. Let 'er rip."

"You just threw that?" I asked. "Right after Martin showed you all of this, Bruce, you just threw the pitch?"

Sutter grinned through his formidable burghermeister beard. "It just come natural."

"And the first one you ever threw actually made that crash-dive drop?"

"Yes. That's what happened. But it was some time before I could control the splitter the way I had to. After a while, I found out that I did best throwing for the top of the catcher's mask. That became my target. If I used a wide finger-split, the ball would end up in the dirt. If I split the fingers a little less it would be a strike at the knees. Once in a while, maybe one pitch in ten, to cross 'em up, I'd play real dirty. I'd throw a straight fast ball that didn't drop at all.

"Before I learned the splitter, the Cubs were ready to release me from a bottom-level minor league team. Back to the print shop, kid. That's what it would have been. Two years after I learned the splitter, I was pitching in the major leagues."

The Chicago Cubs last won the World Series in 1908, the season Mordecai "Three Finger" Brown defeated Christy Mathewson in a play-off for the pennant. Theodore Roosevelt was president. In the long reach since Roosevelt's regime, the Cubs have achieved comic or tragic stature, depending on one's point of view. They try, they compete, they blunder. The Cubs have enjoyed generous support from fans on the north side of Chicago. For decades the owner was the leader of the Wrigley family, czars of an empire of chewing-gum. The ownership has lately passed on to the Tribune Corporation, the mega newspaper company. The ball park, Wrigley Field, is pleasant and comfortable. Money has never been a problem. The Cub problem has been something else: winning.

The Cubs have been unique in an unusual category: inability to recognize Hall of Fame talent. In 1941 the Cubs dealt Billy Herman to the Dodgers for two faded infielders and a handful of silver (sixty-five thousand dollars). Herman, the best second baseman in the league, helped the Dodgers win their first pennant in twenty-one years. He was voted into Cooperstown in 1975. In 1964 the Cubs traded Lou Brock to the Cardinals for Ernie Broglio, a right-handed pitcher in decline. Across three years as a Cub, Broglio won seven games. Brock played sixteen seasons in St. Louis, batting as high as .313. In 1974 he stole 118 bases, a mark that still stands as the National League record. Eleven years later Brock joined Billy Herman as a spurned Cub in Cooperstown. Ferguson Jenkins was the best starting pitcher in modern Cub history. The Cubs traded him to the Texas Rangers after the 1973 season, and Jenkins at once became a twenty-five-game winner. Jenkins entered the Hall of Fame in 1990.

The Chicago team with which Bruce Sutter entered the major
leagues was run in uncertain ways. Four different people managed the
Cubs across five seasons. Herman Franks replaced Jim Marshall in
1977; Marshall had replaced Whitey Lockman in 1974; Lockman had
replaced Leo Durocher in 1972. By the time Sutter left the Cubs after
the 1980 season, Joe Amalfitano had replaced Franks and Preston
Gomez had replaced Amalfitano. Philip K. Wrigley was forever looking for a miracle manager. Instead he found chaos.

"How can you manage properly," Jim Marshall asked me once,
"when the boss makes you feel you're living in a revolving door? Just
about when you get to know the personnel, you're gone." We were
having a drink at Dodger Stadium. "Under those conditions," Marshall said, "every little loss feels like Waterloo. You're always on the
edge of a disaster. Sutter came up when I was managing. I knew right
away that he was something and that the split-finger fast ball was
something else. Before I really got to work with him, I was gone."

Mostly on his own, Sutter emerged as a wonder on a losing ball
club. As a rookie in 1976 he won six, saved ten, and recorded the lowest earned run average on the staff. The next season, he relieved sixty-
two times, won seven, saved thirty-one, and posted an ERA of 1.35,
lowest in the majors. In 1979—six victories, thirty-seven saves—Sutter won the Cy Young Award. He was established as the most valuable
pitcher in the league and probably in the game. But on December 9,
1980—you may suspect what is coming—the Cubs traded Sutter to
St. Louis. In the great Cub tradition, they swapped the best relief
pitcher on earth for three journeymen. Later I suggested to Whitey
Herzog at Busch Stadium that what he had done to the Cubs at the

trading table approached larceny. "Naw," he said, "I give 'em good players. They just didn't all work out."*

Herzog used Sutter at St. Louis in sixty to seventy games a year. At the end of the 1984 season, Sutter moved on to the Atlanta Braves, at $1.66 million a season. Herzog elected not to match that offer. Sutter had won five and saved forty-five in 1984, but I suspect Herzog had spotted certain signs of wear in Sutter's arm late that season. Or he may have felt that Sutter's agent was asking for too much money in the climate of mid-1980s. Or a little of each. That December, Sutter signed with Atlanta, bagging the best contract in the annals for a relief pitcher. "What are you going to do for relief pitching without Sutter?" someone asked Herzog in the spring.

"We're gonna have bullpen by committee."

With three men doing the work of Sutter, the Cardinals won the 1985 pennant. Sutter struggled with increasing arm miseries in Atlanta. He had been pitching three or four times a week for ten years. He saved twenty-three in 1985, but his earned run average jumped. In 1988, at the age of thirty-five, his arm was worn out and Sutter had to retire.

By that time his pitch had swept baseball. Orel Hershiser was throwing it, and Jack Morris and Ron Darling and Mike Scott. Roger Craig was peddling a videotape on the secrets of the splitter and soliciting offers for a split-finger book. "I don't remember the date," Sutter

---

*The best of the three, Leon "Bull" Durham, gave Chicago seven competent seasons, marred by his disastrous play in the league championship series of 1984. Infielder Ken Reitz played a single season for the Cubs. He batted .215. Utility man Tye. Waller appeared in only forty-seven games.

says, "but I was the guy who showed Roger Craig how to throw a splitter. I was with the Cubs. Craig was pitching coach for San Diego. Fred Martin [who died in 1979] was there with me on the major league club that day, and on the sideline there I showed Roger how to throw it. Then Fred spent some time talking to him about it. I'm sure Roger came up with modifications. But it was Fred Martin and I showed him the pitch. I was the first one on the scene who made an impact with the splitter. Then the curiosity of other pitchers came out. 'How do you throw that?' Guys asked me that a lot. I'm not stingy. When they asked me how, I told them."

To keep a pitching arm healthy, Sutter suggests a regimen of work. "If you want to build up your legs, you work your legs, right? Bike. Run. Use your legs to build up your legs. I think it's the same with your arm. Some guys may start, then say, I gotta rest for four days now, so I can pitch the fifth. That way you never build up strength. I believe in working your arm. Pitch batting practice between starts. Keep using it. I would relieve eight days in a row, nine days in a row. Twice Herzog came to me and said I want you to watch this one from the stands. I don't want to be tempted to use you again.

"I used to play long catch in the outfield before games. I liked to throw long distance. I think that helped my arm. That and certain stretching exercises. Whoever first said pitching is not a natural motion is right. It strains the arm, the elbow, the shoulder. What pitch strains an arm the most? That depends on your physique. Some guys throw sliders for years. Some kill their elbows with a slider. The splitter was easy for me, but it isn't a pitch for everybody, not even everybody with the hands and fingers to throw the thing. The biggest question is how do you get the batters out. That's different for different people, too, as you know. Take intimidation. How could a pitcher intimidate Dave Parker, who ran around six foot six and two hundred forty pounds? You couldn't hit him in the head. He was too quick. You couldn't hurt him with inside pitches. He was too big. You can't physically intimidate him. No way. But big and strong as these hitters are, I never met one who wasn't embarrassed by being struck out in a clutch. I mean, like this: Ninth inning. Tying run on base. I strike the hitter out. His team gets beat. Some reporter says, hey, how come you swung at a pitch in the dirt? The man, whoever he might be, is going to be embarrassed. Now, next game I'm working on the hitter's psyche. Pretty soon, all of them start to go, 'Dammit. *That* guy's warming up again. He's gonna make me look terrible.' Then they go, 'Shit, we gotta get a lead before the eighth inning. If we don't *that* guy is going to come in and show us up and end the game.' I haven't met too many who enjoy looking ridiculous in public.

"I was *that* guy. I was an intimidator. Not because I was knocking everybody down. Because I'd get everybody out." The split-finger intimidator paused behind his full dark beard, to let the point rattle around his listener's brain. Like Spahn and Sain and Mathewson and Drysdale, Bruce Sutter was a master of the head game. It is my thought that Sutter was not simply a great innovator, not merely the perfector of the pitch that changed the game, not merely a man who recorded the remarkable total of three hundred saves. Sutter is the greatest and most significant of all pitchers across the generations who has not been elected to the Hall of Fame.

12.

I love the competition. Me with the ball. The hitter with the bat. And all the rest is horseshit. Except I like the money.

BOB GIBSON, 1971

In a heavily promoted television production that appeared during the millennium mania of 1999, ESPN offered a portrait of Sandy Koufax, the great left-handed pitcher who courts obscurity and grows ever more private. As his sixty-fourth birthday approached, thirty-three years after his last Dodgers' season, Koufax agreed to a brief interview, for which ESPN people lustily congratulated themselves. I was reminded of what happened shortly after sound came to motion pictures. That long-ago publicity campaign announced:

GARBO SPEAKS!

SANDY KOUFAX

I don't remember what words spilled forth from the Norn goddess. (With her face, words were superfluous.) On ESPN Koufax looked splendid—gray-haired and splendid—and was predictably courteous and bland. He appeared amid a sea of talking heads—mine included—assembled, cropped, and edited to support the network's shrill contention that Koufax was the greatest pitcher of all time. How did ESPN know who was the greatest pitcher of all time? The network had compiled a list of "the fifty greatest athletes of the twentieth century." Koufax was the only pitcher on the roster. Good-bye, Cy Young.

Take a hike, Christy Mathewson. Walter Johnson, Bob Feller, Nolan Ryan, Bob Gibson, you fellers have missed the bus. One might ask how the earnest, ambitious young people who work at ESPN knew the fifty greatest athletes of the century. The answer is, of course, that they did not. Their ratings were an electronic parlor game, not to be taken very seriously.

I once asked Pete Rose to name the greatest pitcher he faced in a playing career that ran across three decades. This is what Rose said. "That would be three. Hardest thrower—Koufax. Toughest competitor—Bob Gibson. Most complete pitcher—Juan Marichal. In a jam Marichal could throw any one of five pitches for a strike." According to Rose the greatest modern pitcher is three people. That idea, too complicated for an arbitrary list, cuts to a core, to a truth. There is no one greatest pitcher. The head game does not lend itself to simplisms.

In 1905, as we've noted, Christy Mathewson of the New York Giants started thirty-seven games, finished thirty-two, and posted a winning record of 31 and 8. He led the National League in strikeouts and finished with an earned run average of 1.28. Then, as the Giants won the World Series, Mathewson shut out the Philadelphia Athletics three times in six days. Was Koufax better than that? Nobody was better than that. Baseball's mahatma, Wesley Branch Rickey, saw both men work (and was unhappy that he failed to sign Koufax in 1954; he was then running the Pittsburgh Pirates). "If I had to pick one or the other for my staff," Rickey told me, "why, that would be sheer pleasure. Taking nothing away from the younger fellow, I regard Mathewson as the finest pitcher who ever lived. If I had to use one word to describe Matty, that word would be *adaptable*. He could learn a new pitch quicker than any man in history, any new pitch at all, and with that wonderful mind he had, Matty knew how to work the new pitch into his repertoire for absolutely maximum effect." Imagine Mathewson today with a knuckler, a splitter, a slider, in addition to the stuff he already had.

"Didn't Koufax throw harder?" I asked.

"I believe, sir," Rickey said, suddenly formal, "that I have spoken my piece."

So did Al Campanis, one of Rickey's leading acolytes, during a pitching conversation we had in the 1970s. "Only two times in my life has the hair literally stood up on the back of my neck," Campanis told me. "Once was when I saw Michelangelo's work in the Sistine Chapel. The other time was when I first saw Sandy Koufax throw a fast ball."

No one has more admiration than myself for the work of Koufax, across his prime years, 1963 through 1966. During that time he was *one* of the three or four best starting pitchers ever. But to call him *the* greatest pitcher is silly, and to call him without reservation a great athlete is iron-headed. Across twelve major league seasons, Koufax batted .097. The ESPN show was visually attractive, easy viewing, slick and superficial. Koufax is visually attractive, but *slick* and *superficial* are among the last words I would choose to describe him. He is complex, sensitive, inward, and aware not only that he was a great pitcher but that he was a great Jewish pitcher in a game where ethnic needling is as much a tradition as second base.

Koufax appeared—*materialized* may be more appropriate—as a subdued nineteen-year-old in spring training, 1955, on a veteran Brooklyn Dodgers team, peopled by such Hall of Famers as Jackie Robinson, Pee Wee Reese, and Duke Snider. He had been studying architecture at the University of Cincinnati. He was wild, but all left-handers start out wild, everybody said. Still, Koufax had a particularly bad time with his control, even in batting practice. One day when a series of batting-practice pitches sailed wild into the backstop or bounced, Pee Wee Reese, who was hitting, said through clenched teeth, "Throw the fucking ball over the plate." Reese, the team captain, seldom spoke harshly. This must have been a terrible moment for Koufax. He was an awed Brooklyn kid, suddenly working on the same ball field as Brooklyn legends, and he was messing up badly.

In those days I used to play half-court two-man basketball in Vero Beach, teaming with Joe Black, the fine relief pitcher. Koufax joined our games, choosing as his partner a bespectacled publicity man who seemed to be playing hoops for the first time. Black and I moved way ahead, trying not to giggle. Then Koufax took over. He drove to a corner and sank a gorgeous left-handed hook shot. He faked the same drive and tanked a jumper. He could drive, leap, and maneuver, but most of all Sandy could shoot. In this game, if you scored you kept the ball. Black and I didn't get the ball back that day.

"Joe," I said later, "help me figure this out. The kid can sink a hook shot from the corner. He's got the most delicate touch. Then he goes out in batting practice and can't throw a fast ball over the plate. How can you have so much control on the court and none on the mound?"

"Up here," Black said, pointing to his head. "The problem has got to be up here."

The Dodgers moved on to Miami for exhibition games, where the fierce tabloid reporter Dick Young and I wrote our first-edition stories in the cabana of a hotel called the Sea Gull (which I confess we renamed the Siegal). Baseball's ethnic needling infected everyone. Koufax's mother, an attractive dark-haired woman, was staying there, and one afternoon as I shoved paper into my portable typewriter, Mrs. Koufax asked, "Did you put Sandy's name in the paper this morning?"

"I wanted to, Mrs. Koufax, but he didn't pitch."

She dropped her voice. "You're a Jewish boy. Sandy's a Jewish boy. Put his name in the paper today, please."

Unhappily I said, "It doesn't work that way, Mrs. Koufax." After she left Young leered and said, "I guess she thinks you work for the *Tel Aviv Herald Tribune*."

Well before Koufax, Dodgers' pitching had been spinning in a sea of troubles. Wonderful youthful arms appeared in camp. Rickey and his successors would suggest, "Another Matty." Or, "This kid brings it harder than Lefty Grove." Then the big careers never developed. Ralph Branca came out of NYU and won twenty-one games for the Dodgers in 1947, when he was twenty-one years old. After that Branca never won fifteen. A rangy righthander named Rex Barney arrived with an overpowering fast ball and forecasts of a phenomenal future. He never learned control, leading Bob Cooke to write in the *Herald Tribune*, "Barney pitched as though the plate were high and outside." The year before Koufax appeared, a very fast lefthander named Karl

Spooner broke in with the Dodgers by pitching successive shutouts. He struck out twenty-seven batters in his first two major league games. Here he was at last, the kid who couldn't miss. Next spring Spooner developed "a slight shoulder twinge." Two years later, out of baseball, he was installing linoleum on kitchen floors.

As a rookie Koufax did not enter a relaxed pitching environment, and the Dodgers did not seem to have any idea what to do with him. During the 1955 season he worked only forty-one innings. The season after that, he pitched fifty-eight. The Dodgers won the pennant both years and used a total of thirteen pitchers in fourteen World Series games. Koufax never got into any, and a grave problem was being joined. To ignore a young pitcher, notably one with the Sistine Chapel in his arm, is no way to develop talent. Spot his starts. Throw him into long relief. Keep him working. Remember the great commandment, "An arm will rust out before it wears out." Besides, sitting on the sidelines, about as important as a bat rack, shrivels confidence. Talk to the youngster. Make him feel that he's part of the team, an important part. Tell him you care for him. Tell him he's going to be great. One reason Willie Mays became so good so quickly was that his manager, Leo Durocher, kept telling him he was the finest ball player on earth. With that support, Willie came to believe that he was. In his second full major league season, Mays, at twenty-four, won the most valuable player award.

Dour Walter Alston, the Dodgers' manager, was small if any help to Koufax, and Koufax spent his first six seasons as a losing pitcher, condemned to Dodger Siberia. Drysdale told me that Koufax wondered if his six years in the gulag were dictated by latent anti-Semitism in Alston. It is a fair question. Alston had more of his share of trouble with Jackie Robinson, and the man was no stranger to prejudice. But at this date one cannot be sure.

In one of Koufax's early seasons—neither he nor I can pin down the year—a tabloid came barreling into his complicated life. Milton Gross, a columnist for the *New York Post,* ran down a tip that there had been a divorce in Koufax's family. Gross found Koufax's biological father, a man named Brown, or Braun, selling phonograph records in downtown Brooklyn. Irving Koufax, CPA, the man who had been presented as Koufax's father, actually was his stepfather. The *Post* splashed this story in great headlines across its front page. Koufax would not comment. Whatever divorce may be today, in the sedate Jewish community where Koufax grew up, divorce was a scandal. Koufax had been staying inside a shell. Now he built a shell around the shell.

He pitched a splendid World Series game in 1959, losing a 1–0 decision to the Chicago White Sox, but his period of greatness dates best from June 30, 1962, when he pitched a no-hitter against the Mets. That season he led the National League with a 2.54 ERA Then came the years of thunder. In 1963 (25-and-5 with eleven shutouts) he started the World Series in Yankee Stadium by striking out the side. A key was Bobby Richardson, the Yankees' number two batter, who got most of his hits off high fast balls. Koufax knew that. He threw Richardson three high fast balls and struck him out. Then Koufax gave the Yankee dugout a hard look. I saw that look. I know what it said. "I can pitch it to your power and I'll still strike you out." The uncertain youngster who had fled the mound for an asphalt basketball court was history. Mr. Sanford Koufax now embodied absolute command and with it an appropriate arrogance. He won the game 5–2 and wrapped up a Dodgers sweep by beating the Yankees in game four, 2 to 1. In his eighteen innings he struck out twenty-three.

He went on to win the Cy Young Award three times and to dominate baseball as few have. He possessed a great hopping fast ball, an enormous overhand curve, superb control, and tremendous pitching intelligence. From 1963 through 1966 he posted an earned run average of fewer than two runs a game three times. The other year, 1965, his ERA reached 2.04, but that was also the season in which, pitching 335 innings, he struck out 382. He had finesse, he could outthink most hitters, but the overwhelming impression was power. "Sandy," someone said, lifting a term from the minors, "is just too good for the league."

Soon a Koufax start was drawing ten to twenty thousand extra fans, depending on where the game was played. "You know," Walter O'Malley told me over lunch, "in all the years I had the Dodgers in Brooklyn I would have given my eyeteeth for a big Jewish star. How that would have worked at Ebbets Field. I come out here [to Los Angeles]. I can fill the ballpark with nine Chinamen, and what do I get? Koufax." The ethnic element was never far away.

The ESPN special suggested that a tip from the Jewish Dodgers catcher Norm Sherry—"don't grip the ball so tightly"—transformed Koufax from lost soul to Hall of Famer. That's neat, and ridiculous. After six years in the majors, Koufax's record stood at thirty-six victories and forty losses. Pitchers, including Mathewson, including Koufax, forever fiddle with grips and spins. To attribute Koufax's sunburst to the sudden discovery of a looser grip after six years of living and breathing pitching is unconvincing. The difference between the journeyman Koufax and the triumphant Koufax lay not in the finger, hand, or arm. The difference lay inside his head. Slowly and painfully he taught himself to make a mighty fortress of the mound. He defended that fortress in the manner of the Spartans at Thermopylae (but more successfully).

In one of his great years, *Time* magazine published a long feature saying that you could find Koufax between starts plugging in his portable phonograph and listening to the Mendelssohn Violin Concerto. Ah, those preppy Yalies who used to run *Time*. What would a Jewish pitcher listen to except the plaintive work of a Jewish composer? Koufax expressed disgust. "I listen to Sinatra a helluva lot more than I listen to Mendelssohn," he said.

Some other ball players gave him a nickname. If they thought it would flatter him, they were delusional. They called him "Superjew."

Koufax threw up complex defenses. The late Ed Linn, a gifted collaborator who had worked with Bill Veeck and Durocher, signed on for the obligatory autobiography of a superstar. Any anti-Semitism along the way? he asked. None, Koufax said. Linn dug deep and found Koufax's old sandlot catcher, a fellow with an Irish background who was working as a Brooklyn police detective. The detective told Linn that he and Koufax played for a mixed Jewish–Irish team near Coney Island and that their big rival was a squad of Italian Americans. The Italians disliked Koufax not out of innate bigotry, but because they thought he threw too hard for the league. This led them to call him names. After a while Koufax silenced the Italians by throwing fast balls into their ribs. Linn liked the story and wrote it. Koufax excised it from the book. He built up the most complex defenses you are likely ever to find in a ball player.

In 1966 Otto Friedrich of the *Saturday Evening Post* asked me to write a long piece about Jewish life in America, as part of a series he was publishing on the Jewish experience around the world after the Holocaust. I wanted to touch on Jews in sports and thought of two athletes, Al Rosen, who hit thirty-seven homers as a Cleveland rookie and batted in at least a hundred runs in each of his first five full seasons, and Koufax. Since I was in Los Angeles first, I talked to Sandy in the Dodgers' clubhouse. He was polite, even cordial, but said he wished I wouldn't do a story like that. "Too much is made of me as a Jewish pitcher," he said, "and not enough just as a pitcher."

I respected that and remarked on an irony. Sandy's mother had pleaded with me, on ethnic grounds, to put his name in the paper. Now he was avoiding publicity, particularly that which stressed his Jewish background. I thought that twist might amuse my old hook-shooting half-court basketball buddy.

It did not. Koufax fixed me with a glacial smile and announced that what I said could not be true because his mother had never been to Florida. But a one-time Dodger publicist remembered Mrs. Koufax well. "When she was in Florida for spring training," Irving Rudd said, "she always wanted a lot of tickets." I had run into a case of intense denial. When Koufax retired, after the 1966 season (27–9), stories blamed circulatory problems in his left arm, or arthritis. I think it is fair to say also that the glare of public life had worn him out. He was fed up with people asking about his mother, his parents' divorce, his Jewishness. He was burned out as a public figure.

Koufax's revisionist history contrasted vividly with Al Rosen's thrilling account of his own life as a Jewish big-league star and, staying closer to the mound, just as vividly with Bob Gibson's story of his life as a black athlete. Decades ago bigotry was more patterned than it is today, by which I mean that anti-Semitism and prejudice against blacks went hand in hand. Generally the same people—in baseball or outside it—who thought that Jews were devious, avaricious, and "too smart," argued that African Americans were dumb, inarticulate, shiftless, and obsessed above all by lust for white women. For many years an unofficial alliance existed among Negroes, as they were then called, and Jews. Such blacks as Paul Robeson and Jackie Robinson spoke eloquently against anti-Semitism. The large Jewish community in Brooklyn constituted the core of Robinson's early support at Ebbets Field. Liberal Jews made up a major part of Robeson's adoring audiences even to the infamous day in 1949 when hoodlums in American Legion hats stormed a planned concert in Peekskill, New York, and with the connivance of New York State Troopers, stoned innocents and stopped the event before Robeson sang a note. It is simplistic to present all bigotry as the same, but in at least one significant way slavery and the Holocaust are linked. In each instance, people treated others as less than human.

BOB GIBSON

"How did my family happen to get to Omaha, Nebraska?" Bob Gibson said, repeating a question. "I have no idea. When you're black you probably can't trace your family history back very far. They tell me my father died three months before I was born. We were poor people. Not only didn't I know my father, I've never even seen his picture. There were no cameras in the four-room shack where I grew up." Gibson's mother worked in a laundry and raised six children. He remembers the little house without affection, for it was there, when he was a small boy sleeping soundly, that a rat bit one of his ears.

"I liked sports from as far back as I can remember, but when I started high school I didn't have the body of an athlete. I was only four feet ten inches tall. But something happened at Omaha Tech. Growth happened. By my senior year, I stood six feet." Gibson could now high jump six feet one, good for the techniques of the 1950s when the Olympic record stood at six feet eight. He could broadjump twenty-two feet and run or hurdle with any schoolboy in Nebraska, except he didn't like jumping or footraces. Baseball and basketball were his sports, and he set his dreams on a career as a scholar-athlete at the University of Indiana. He still remembers a final word from a university official in Bloomington. "Your request for an athletic scholarship has been denied," an associate dean wrote, "because we have already filled our quota of Negroes."

He settled for Creighton in his hometown, and the picture of Creighton's 1954 varsity basketball team is surprising. Thirteen players stand against a gymnasium wall. Gibson is the only black. After graduation he signed two contracts. One was with the Cardinals farm team in Omaha. The other was with the Harlem Globetrotters. Playing two professional sports across twelve months in 1958, he grossed eight thousand dollars, "which seemed a fortune." Presently the Cardinals realized what they had and talked him away from basketball. In the mid-1960s, as the strains of pitching were driving Koufax into retirement at the age of thirty-one, Gibson emerged as the greatest pitcher on earth. We came to know each other by reputation. He'd heard of my first book, *The Passionate People,* in which prejudice was an important theme, and I knew him as a lustrous twenty-game winner who twice threw three complete games in a single World Series. He invited me to spend time with him around opening day in 1971 so I could get some sense of what he did and hopefully write what I found. "Accurately," Gibson said. "That seldom happens."

We began at breakfast in the coffee shop of a hotel in Chicago, where that afternoon at Wrigley Field Gibson would open the Cardinal season against a worthy adversary, Ferguson Jenkins of the Cubs. (Strapping Fergy Jenkins, also black, is the first native of Canada elected to the Hall of Fame.) Gibson that morning was somewhat troubled by the press. "I have a reputation for being difficult to interview," he said, "but all I object to are asinine questions. *How do I feel about being thirty-five*. That's this year's favorite. You want to give me an answer for that?"

"Ten years worse than you felt about being twenty-five."

He is a handsome, even-featured fellow, and now he broke into a small smile. "And it's always *what pitch did the guy hit*? Can't they see?"

"A lot of times you can't be certain from a press box, and anyway, the writer may be looking for confirmation. Asking a question is less asinine than getting it wrong."

"I guess," Gibson said. "I object to how information is used. The papers always have the big hit coming off the high curve or the belt-high fast ball. Read the papers and you never find out that a hell of a lot of hits come off good pitches." He looked at me and said slowly, quietly, forcefully, "This the major leagues. Up here a lot of good pitches get hit."

"We've both seen very bad pitches get popped up."

"Pitching is inexact," Gibson said. "It begins as a craft, working with your hands. But the longer you go, if you know how to think, the more it becomes an art. You hear about knockdowns, and to protect the Cardinal hitters, I've thrown my share. But with the years, I throw at batters less and less. As the art, the thinking, takes over, I've come to realize that not everyone is bothered by knockdowns and some of them are afraid of my fast ball, whether I throw at them or not."

At coffee a well-dressed stranger extended a hand and said, "I want to shake with a great pitcher." Gibson stared unsmiling but did as he was asked. "That's all," the man said. "I just wanted to shake your hand." Gibson thanked him and the man moved on. "You get suspicious," Gibson said. "People come over for 'one question' and then it turns out they don't want to listen, but talk at you and there goes breakfast. But this was very straight, very nice."

That afternoon, the wind slanted off Lake Michigan through the high-rises on Marine Drive and the squat homes near Clark Street. It lashed across Wrigley Field, and despite clear skies, the day seemed colder than its thirty-five degrees. Behind glass in the heated press box, Stan Musial, then a Cardinal vice president, dropped into the seat next to mine. "You don't have to worry about Gibby and the weather," Musial said. "He can pace himself just fine." Gibson was fast and commanding and so was Fergy Jenkins, and you could tell very quickly that runs would come hard.

In the fourth inning two Cubs reached base and Gibson concentrated on John Callison, a left-handed batter with a smooth compact swing. Gibson threw a fast ball up and in, where he wanted it, and Callison hit it with the handle of his bat. The ball fluttered toward short right field, a sick pigeon that landed beyond everybody's reach. Chicago, 1 to 0. In the sixth Joe Torre, who would bat .363 for the season, drove a home run to left. The 1-to-1 tie held through nine innings. Barney Schultz, the Cardinals' pitching coach, suggested some relief, but Gibson said he thought he'd "pitch one more inning." Shadows falling across the park put home plate in darkness. Still the mound was bright. "Change speeds now," Musial said. "Batters can't pick up the ball."

With one out in the tenth, Gibson threw a fast strike past Billy Williams, a lithe left-handed batter out of Whistler, Alabama. A slow breaking ball stayed wide. Gibson returned to the fast ball and threw it low, an excellent pitch in uneven light, and Williams slammed a tremendous home run into the wind. Chicago, 2; St. Louis, 1. A cold day's labor had come to nothing. Standing on the mound Gibson twice quietly repeated the same phrase, "Oh, fuck." Then he squared his shoulders and walked off the field. In the dressing room a reporter asked if he was feeling tired. "No," Gibson said. "I never get tired pitching ten innings in thirty-five-degree weather."

We drank a nice red Pomerol at dinner. "How did you like the afternoon?" Gibson said. "Good pitches got hit. I got asinine questions. Just what I told you."

"Why did you go out and make yourself pitch the tenth?"

"I had a chance to win. I don't ever want to come out when I have a chance to win." He looked distant, then directly at my eyes with sudden, surprising intimacy. "I love the competition. Me with the ball. The hitter with the bat. And all the rest is horseshit. Except I like the money."

We talked about varieties of bigotry then, and Gibson said, "Where I come from, what I put up with, where I am. It's kind of hard to explain, but what I feel is hope. A lot of hope." Can one say that these two superb competitors, Koufax and Gibson, were steeled by the bigotry they encountered, that prejudice helped make each man as tough as he was? That is not a question Koufax will touch. Gibson remarks that many blacks were not steeled by bigotry but broken by it. "But still I feel this hope, and hope is something that's difficult to define." Emily Dickinson did as well as anyone:

Hope is the thing with feathers
That perches in the soul,
And sings the tune without the words
And never stops at all.

13.

THE POPE

OF PITCHING

Why turn something as simple
as throwing into a science project?

LEO MAZZONE

I f you lived among the corn and soybean farms rolling up from the
Sangamon River in central Illinois and followed minor league
baseball during the summer of 1969, you saw Leo Mazzone pitching in his prime. Mazzone won fifteen games that season for the De-
catur Commodores in the Single A Midwest League. Strong and
stocky, he possessed a good fast ball and a fine pitching head. He was
a battler. But the Commodores finished well under .500, twenty-eight
games out of first place, and Mazzone never again won as many as ten
games in a season.

LEO MAZZONE

Single A lies three notches distant from the major leagues, and people whose playing careers peak there, amid creaky wooden bleachers and flaking fence signs, usually move on only to obscurity. What happens to most pitchers who peak in Single A; what becomes of them? Nothing happens to most of them. They don't become.*

---

*During the year I owned the Utica Blue Sox, a couple of pitchers on our roster peaked. When last I heard, one of them, Johnny Seitz, was driving an eighteen-wheeler in western Pennsylvania. The other, Roy Moretti, was working for the sanitation department in Victoria, British Columbia. "Not pretty work," Moretti said, "but the pay is steady and the pension program is fine."

"Maybe with a break or two," Mazzone says, "I could have made the majors, but that makes me sound like a thousand other guys, doesn't it?" Only for an instant. For after Mazzone retired from pitching, in 1975, he set forth on a bench career unsurpassed in recent baseball history. He managed successfully in the minors for a few years and then put most of a decade of study and teaching into the head game. Working mostly against the conventional grain, he passed a succession of small miracles. Numbers alone make that clear. From June 22, 1990, when Mazzone joined the Braves as pitching coach, through 1999, Atlanta pitchers won the Cy Young Award six times. After Mazzone's appearance in the old Atlanta ballpark, starting in 1991, the Braves staff posted either the lowest or second-lowest earned run average in the major leagues every season for the balance of the century. I don't believe any pitching staff has ever dominated for as many years. Fine throwing arms? Indeed. Greg Maddux, Tom Glavine, and John Smoltz brought high skills to Atlanta. "They're very gifted young men," pronounces Henry Aaron, now a graying, portly vice president with the Braves. "But the guys in our rotation have been able to pitch, with just a few exceptions, injury free and at their best level for all the time they've been here. That's a tribute to Leo's program. It enables our pitchers to get the most out of their gifts."

Aaron broke Babe Ruth's home-run record in 1974 at the old Atlanta ballpark, Fulton County Stadium, which was subsequently nicknamed the Launching Pad. Atlanta is a bit more than a thousand feet above sea level, and baseballs seemed to leap off bats in air thinner than the air in, say, New York or San Francisco. That old arena was demolished in 1997 to make way for Turner Field. Sometime earlier Mazzone and his crew, with three or four of those Cy Youngs, had demolished the nickname. "The Launching Pad," he said during a pleasant evening of conversation, prime steak, and red wine, "was a myth. We demonstrated that. But we've had to work against a lot of things that weren't myths, that are real." Mazzone is a stocky, cheerful character, originally out of the railroad town of Keyser, West Virginia, "two or three hours" distant from Washington, D.C. His manner is open and pleasantly rough-hewn. It might take a stranger some time to recognize that he was listening to a scholar.

"Look at today's hitters," the coach said. "Bigger, stronger. Plus they're armored, with all that new protective gear like the huge elbow pads some of them wear. Look at today's ballparks. They're smaller than the ones they replaced. You know what's happened there." I certainly do. To cite a single case, consider the shrinking playing field at Yankee Stadium. The old Stadium ran 461 feet to the wall in dead center field and 457 in the so-called left-center power alley. The field in the Stadium, A.D. 2000, runs 410 to center and 411 at its deepest point. Hank Greenberg never forgot a high 460-foot drive that he walloped in the Bronx during the summer of 1938. Joe DiMaggio fled backward, caught it, and—contrary to the image of DiMaggio as ever cool—became so excited that he ran toward the infield holding up the baseball and neglected to double a runner off first base. That mighty drive could not be caught today. Instead it would be a very long two-run homer. So are many long fly balls that were caught in earlier days when

Vince Scully described Willie Mays' glove as "the place where triples go to die."

"Mounds are lower," Mazzone said. "You don't have to go around with a ruler. You know when you sit in the dugout, a high mound sort of blocks your view. The view from the dugout gets better all the time. And the strike zone keeps becoming smaller. I watch reruns of a lot of World Series games on a cable network. Those old Yankee pitchers like Allie Reynolds were always getting strikes on high hard stuff that's called a ball today. The strike zone then was wider, too. North to south, east to west, today's strike zone is shrinking all the time." ("Like a cheap shirt in a Chinese laundry," the politically incorrect Early Wynn once suggested in his later years.)

"Then there's the actual baseball," Mazzone said. "I know it's juiced. You know it's juiced. So does everyone who pays attention, and I don't care who denies it. One day Greg Maddux comes to the plate for us and he swings a little late [Maddux bats right-handed] and hits a home run into the right-field stands. That's a lot of power the other way. Maddux rounds the bases and comes into the dugout and sits down next to me. He says, 'Leo. I can't do that. I can't do what I just did.'"

Armored batters, smaller playing fields, lower mounds, a shrinking strike zone, and livelier baseballs. That works out to five blows against every man who goes out to pitch a big-league game today. These changes, which obviously tilt the balance against pitchers, are not accidental. The home run is box office. The long fly ball is less so.

Baseball today, intertwined with television, approaches show business and makes crowd-pleasing, show-business adjustments.* What is to be done? In the name of Radbourn, Mathewson, Gibson, Sutter, and Sain, how can good work from the mound survive? "Command your fast ball," preaches Leo Mazzone, the pope of pitching. "Put the radar guns in the garbage. [He means sheer speed doesn't amount to that much in the majors, where all the hitters' eye-to-hand-to-bat speed is phenomenal.] Learn to throw a fast ball with touch, with movement. Use your fast ball, a fast ball that moves, that sinks, that rides. Then pitch off the fast ball and change speeds."

Hoss Radbourn would recognize Leo Mazzone and, I suspect, approve. The big Atlanta pitchers of the new millennium, Maddux, Glavine, Smoltz, throw almost as often in modern summers as Radbourn did in 1884. But then differences enter. Supervised throwing, *frequent* supervised throwing all summer long for the Braves, is part of Mazzone's sophisticated program that proceeds from, among other things, consultations with an exercise physiologist. The Braves' pitchers work hard but every one, at least while I was with the club, could

---

*An abiding difference remains. Watching a video of *Singing in the Rain* we know that Gene Kelly is going to dance his grand umbrella dance on that soaking Hollywood set and do it perfectly every time. Attending *Hamlet* we have the foreknowledge that the hero will die and that Horatio then will say, "Good night, sweet prince." Six nights a week and at the Wednesday matinée. Movies and plays are scripted. This isn't so with baseball. We don't know in advance who will win, much less what will happen, or indeed, whether slim Greg Maddux will drive out an opposite-field home run. That is one of the wonders of the game. Adding a script, as World Series fixers were able to do in 1919, is catastrophic.

comb his own hair and put on a sports jacket without assistance. Mazzone tips his hat—revealing a thoughtful brow and a bald dome—to Johnny Sain's dictum than an arm will rust out before it wears out. "I worked with Sain. I know how to listen. Johnny Sain is the best curveball coach who ever lived."

Mazzone goes into each season with two interrelated goals: Keep the pitchers healthy and keep them winning. His methods include weight lifting, stretching exercises, jaunts to nowhere on a treadmill, and—Leo's trademarks—large helpings of hard work and practical good sense. The program includes aspects of physiology and psychology and defies the venerable belief expressed in dugouts across decades, usually about like this: "Pitchers ain't athletes. Pitchers are pitchers."

Leo Mazzone is at once self-confident and unpretentious. Recently the Braves employed a rangy right-handed closing relief pitcher named Mark Wohlers, who possessed a lively one-hundred-mile-an-hour fast ball and a lively slider. From 1995 through 1997 Wohlers saved ninety-seven games. He struck out 282 batters in 211 innings. That is premier, but not unprecedented, relieving. Working in short bursts, closers can be overpowering; they have no need to worry about pacing themselves. Nor do hitters get to adjust to their stuff on a second or third go-round. Still, anyone striking out more than one batter an inning in the major leagues is earning his pay.

In 1998, when Wohlers was twenty-eight, he strained his left oblique, a muscle that slants across the lower chest and abdomen. The oblique is critical in body pivots but the injury seemed minor.

Wohlers retreated to the disabled list for three weeks. On his return he was unable to throw strikes. Mazzone worked with him. After a while Wohlers reported that he was losing feeling in his pitching hand. Sometimes the loss was so acute that he couldn't tell whether or not he was holding a baseball. Doctors—the Braves employ no fewer than five—probed and examined Wohlers with a full range of high-tech medical machinery. Nerve damage? A circulatory problem? Nothing showed up. The team psychologist, Jack Llewellyn, met with Wohlers. Still the big pitcher could not throw strikes. Wohlers sank into the minor leagues and late that season pitched twelve innings for Richmond. He walked thirty-eight and gave up twenty-eight runs. Subsequently, the Braves released him. "People come up to me all the time," Mazzone said, "and ask what went wrong with Mark Wohlers." The coach shook his head, then lapsed into baseball English. "If I knew what the fuck went wrong, I would have fixed it."

The forceful argot of the game is not classroom language, but I believe that Leo Mazzone, like Mathewson and Rickey, is essentially what Thomas Jefferson called "an academical" man. Leo's thoughtful program in Atlanta has, at the simplest level, killed at least one slogan: The saying "Pitchers ain't athletes" is dead. If you are not an athlete, you have no chance of making the Braves staff. Pitching continues to be mysterious—What, in fact, did happen to Mark Wohlers?—but Mazzone has brought it a long way out of the swamps of myth, superstition, bad medicine, ignorance, and cant. Today we look at Radbourn's nineteenth-century regimen as primitive. But looking back to the days when I began covering major league baseball in the middle of the twentieth century, the general approaches to pitching retained the reek of the medievalism.

Starters usually worked every four days. The good ones finished what they started, more often than not. Typically in 1950 Robin Roberts of the Phillies finished twenty-one of thirty-nine starts. Bob Lemon of the Indians finished twenty-two of thirty-seven. A pitcher who had trouble finishing—Allie Reynolds did for a time—was suspect. To say of a pitcher, "He can't go nine" was an indictment. Relief was unsophisticated and spotty. Jim Konstanty of the Phillies, the best closer in the 1950 National League, saved twenty-two. Second best was Bill Werle of the Pirates, and he saved only eight. The bullpen was pretty much an afterthought. Many teams warmed up relievers one man at a time. The idea of warming up a righthander to come in against a righthander batter, and a lefthander to face a batter who swung left, was still aborning. It is a simple percentage move. When you think about it, what's so complicated about warming up a lefty reliever and a righty reliever simultaneously? Nothing, but few managers of the fifties thought to do it. One who did was Casey Stengel. Mantle and Berra hit very well, but Yankees pitching was the real key to the team's dominance of baseball, to the team's winning five consecutive World Series. Stengel's handling of his pitching was a generation ahead of the work of the rival managers he faced in those series, Eddie Sawyer of the Phillies, Leo Durocher of the New York Giants, and Charlie Dressen.

Conditioning was haphazard. After starts, pitchers generally shagged flies during batting practice. Or stood in the outfield chatting while others shagged flies. Some theories were, to put this gently, bizarre. Charlie Dressen, who managed the Dodgers to two pennants early in the 1950s, offered me pitching ideas on more than one occasion. Oral sex, Dressen believed, was a killer. He said, "You see, kid, if you get blowed, it makes you sweat in hot weather. I got guys on my staff can't beat the Cardinals in St. Louis because they get blowed. It starts 'em sweating and after a while they can't stand up to the heat that comes up from the river." That led him to his next pronouncement, the one about premature infants: "Incubator babies can't never go nine." These assertions may sound comical nowadays, but they were not funny to pitchers who were subjected to unsettling personal quizzes by their manager. Once you conclude, as several pitchers did, that your manager is a nutcake, problems follow as the night the day.

Dressen was an extreme—Sherwood Anderson would have called him a grotesque—but he was not unique. All sorts of crackpot theories resounded through dugouts and clubhouses and even medical offices well into the second half of the twentieth century. Rotator-cuff surgery was unknown in the 1950s. To restore Karl Spooner's sore shoulder, the Dodgers' medical staff ordered the extraction of several teeth. That helped neither his pitching nor his ability to chew. A renowned orthopedist routinely advised athletes with shoulder agonies, "Pitch to the point of pain and then keep going. That will break up the adhesions." The prescription often broke up shoulders. In practice, Joe Black, who peaked in 1952, remembers, "Elbows got better. Shoulders never did." Black, a college graduate, was one of the few big-league pitchers in those days who threw year round. To keep his arm strong, he worked out with a rubber ball during the winter, sometimes enlisting me as a January catcher. Rubber ball or not, Joe threw so hard I had to use a glove; a fielder's mitt, but still a glove. Any object moving ninety-five miles an hour commands respect.

Many pitchers developed a side occupation good in both winter and summer. That was drinking whiskey. Even during the season, most worked only one day in every four or five; they always had time on their large hands. For decades major league baseball games began at 3:00 P.M. and lasted until about 5:00. Fine pitchers worked a four-hour week. Leisure and the transient nature of the business were doorways to a boozy life. John Lardner, Ring Lardner's eldest son, wrote a definitive article on drinking ball players in SPORT magazine during 1950, called "They Walked by Night." Most of Lardner's night walkers were pitchers. He cited Rube Waddell, who chased after fire wagons when the twentieth century was young. "He never did that," Lardner told me, "when sober." In 1930 a Cardinal starter named Flint Rhem disappeared for forty-eight hours during an important series in Brooklyn. Lardner wrote, "On reappearing, Rhem said that he had been kidnaped by gunmen, held incommunicado in a hotel room, and forced at the point of a gun to drink 'large quantities of liquor.' The story was accepted by Branch Rickey, Cardinals general manager, who said you couldn't disprove it by the way Rhem smelled." Rhem won twenty only once, but others with longer and more successful careers heard the chimes at midnight and sometimes 3:00 A.M. The great Cleveland Indians staff of 1954, with Early Wynn, Bob Lemon, and Mike Garcia collectively winning sixty-three games, enjoyed martinis before dinner and martinis plus stingers afterward. Mornings, you could tell where the Cleveland pitchers had been the night before. They left a trail of olives.

Why did the ball clubs countenance such frivolity? Occasionally front-office sobersides did engage private detectives to collect evidence of uncertain training, but as long as a pitcher stayed out of jail and showed up for work, the general view was that drinking didn't hurt. Richly nurtured by evening martinis and midmorning Bloody Marys, Early Wynn won twenty-two games (and the Cy Young Award) in 1959, at the age of thirty-nine. He then started three World Series games in a week. "With fellers like Wynn and Lemon," said Al Lopez, a calm and practical sort who managed both Cleveland and the Chicago White Sox to pennants, "the best thing was leave them alone. Whatever they did at night, they came to the ballpark on time the next day, and when it was their turn, they pitched like hell." Wynn retired with 300 victories. Lemon won 207. Across fourteen seasons, Garcia finished 142–97, for a winning percentage of almost .600. These were highly intelligent men who could not pronounce, much less spell, the word *teetotaler*.

In those old laissez-faire days, what did starting pitchers do when not sipping or starting or chatting in the outfield? On some teams, they threw a bit "to stay loose." A few clubs asked a few pitchers to throw batting practice or even to jog. But overall, conditioning was haphazard. Having been raised, so to speak, in that loose (and highly enjoyable) atmosphere, I was at once startled by Leo Mazzone's Atlanta program.

Tom Glavine would pitch against the San Diego Padres on a pleasant August night at Turner Field, the only big-league ballpark that was not built but retrofitted. The stadium, originally constructed for the 1996 Olympics, was reworked into a handsome baseball facility, with a Bermuda-grass playing surface and a huge Coca-Cola bottle rising above the left-field seats, lest one forget that this is the land of Scarlett, Coke, and Cobb. In the summer of 1997 the old ball field, Atlanta Fulton County Stadium, was imploded. The ground it occupied was paved over and became the parking lot for Turner Field. (One does not associate such words as *implosion* and *retrofit* with the old-time ballparks, Ebbets Field and Sportsman's Park.)

The Braves were playing good baseball during the last August of the twentieth century, but on this evening trailed the first-place New York Mets by two percentage points. (They would win the pennant after defeating the Mets in an exciting play-off series.) Glavine is a trim, serious six-foot lefthander, a New Englander who relocated amid the Cokes and Cobbs of the new South and who in 1991 became the first Braves pitcher to win a Cy Young Award since Warren Spahn did it in 1957, when Richard Nixon was vice president. Glavine won another Cy Young in 1998, but this is no fire-snorting, overpowering latter-day Lefty Grove. Glavine's fast ball is respectable, eighty-seven to ninety miles an hour or so. By varying grips, he throws several fast balls, pitches that move in different ways, including a notably effective sinker. His change-up, which also moves, rides in at about seventy-nine—slow enough to throw the hitter off stride, but not so slow as to give him a chance to recover. The essence of a major league change of pace is slower, but not *much* slower. As Mazzone puts it, too slow and you have a nothing ball, and probably a home run.

THE CIRCLE CHANGE

Casually, Mazzone was making a significant point: The major league change is not what we as children called the slow ball. We even made up contests: The urchin who threw the slowest pitch won. That was and is quite literally kid stuff. A working major league change is likely to be a faster pitch than a good high school fast ball. "In fooling the hitter by a few miles an hour," Mazzone said, "it's important you use the same arm motion that you use with the blazer."

Branch Rickey advocated the "pull-down-the-window-shade" change. The pitcher throws out of a fast-ball motion, and as he releases the ball, he pulls down hard, as with a stubborn shade. That takes speed off the pitch but makes the baseball spin rapidly. The batter, seeing the furious spinning, thinks he is looking at a fast ball. That's it. His timing is shot. As Leo Durocher put it, "Stick a fork into him, Gertrude. He's done!" During the Dodgers' years in Brooklyn—or was it Camelot?—Carl Erskine and Johnny Podres threw outstanding pull-down changes. Even today Brooklyn patriarchs' eyes mist as they recall how Podres' change rattled the New York Yankees in the autumn of 1955 and brought the borough its only World Series victory. But the historic pull-down change, while relatively easy to describe, is damnably difficult to throw. ("I suspect," Erskine says, "it went out of fashion because aside from Podres and myself, practically nobody else could master it.")

Favored today is the "circle change." The pitcher holds the ball deep in his palm, so that as he grips it, his thumb and index finger form a circle. He then throws exactly as he would when delivering a fast ball, but since the ball is held near the palm, not with the fingertips, it moves with diminished velocity. By adjusting grips, the circle change can be made to fade. This off-speed, fading delivery looks, Joe Garagiola says, "like a big fat salami. I meant it's right there. Until you try and get your bat on it, that is."

"I don't really like the terms *slider* or *curve* all that much," Mazzone told me. "Give me a hundred experts, show them a good sharp breaking pitch. Half will say it was a curve and the other half will say it was a slider. What we want at Atlanta is a quality breaking ball [one that breaks late and breaks sharply and, as a rule, finds a low corner of the plate]. To us, that isn't a nasty curve or a nasty slider. We call it an Atlanta Braves–quality breaking ball. The opposition can call it whatever the hell they like."

Glavine throws a "four-seam" breaking ball. That is, he grips it across the horseshoe pattern of the seams, so that all four spin across the air with each rotation. His arm speed, his touch, and his wrist snap combine to give the ball a quick down-breaking movement that fools hitters. Some recent breaking balls have been huge and dramatic, notably pitches thrown by Dwight Gooden and Aaron Sele. Glavine's style and stuff are all subtlety. He has never struck out two hundred batters in a season, but he's been a twenty-game winner four times. His hallmark is a four-hop ground out to shortstop.

If you watch Glavine from the stands, you may have a hard time understanding his artistry. As the saying is: "He lives on the outside corner." He is not a brush-back pitcher, but he will come inside with fast balls riding into a batter's thumbs. What you do notice from a decent seat is that Glavine shuns the heart of the plate. Out. Down. Away. Sometimes in. Riding fast ball. Sinking change. Breaking ball that snakes backward, crossing the outside corner at the knees, a sidewinder with a bite fatal to hitters. Always a little more speed. Or a little less. Tom Glavine on the mound is not a thrower but a pitcher. Ol Hoss and Matty would applaud.

This night Glavine moved easily into the third inning, when suddenly he made a cluster of mistakes. He walked his opposing pitcher, Matt Clement, on four pitches. At the time Clement was batting .079. Two infield outs moved Clement to third. Glavine walked Reggie Sanders. Then with the count 2-and-2 on Phil Nevin, a pretty fair power hitter out of Cal State Fullerton, Glavine found the middle of the plate with fast ball. Nevin walloped the pitch into the left-field seats. Glavine kept his head—he is very good at that—and made no more mistakes of consequence. He went eight innings and threw 131 pitches. San Diego did not score again, and the Braves pulled out victory in a sloppy eleventh inning, 4 to 3.

This was a competent start but not a great start. (Glavine delivered a great one when he shut out the Mets during the divisional play-off as a sellout crowd in Queens drank beer, belched, and reviled the visiting athletes.) Tom was a shade wilder than usual and he had to combat that. There were more mistake pitches than is his norm, but this game and the afternoon that followed provided ideal examples of the Mazzone system. Greg Maddux says a pitcher doesn't learn anything when everything goes exactly right. Similarly, an observer can do best studying a trip when pits and bumps mark the pitcher's road.

Mazzone and Glavine met in early afternoon and talked easily about the flawed start. Reporters had focused on "the bad pitch," the one Nevin hit for a home run. "There were really five bad pitches in that inning," Mazzone said gently. "The four that walked Clement before the home run." Glavine nodded. Mazzone's tone was in no way critical. He was a kindly uncle. ("Somehow after Leo talks to me," Maddux says, "I always feel more comfortable. He just has this way of increasing my zone of comfort.")

We tramped to the outfield and Glavine began to throw to a catcher. He had thrown 131 pitches the night before, and here he was throwing again. "Long tossing," Mazzone said. "He'll throw at seventy-five to eighty percent." That is a major league seventy-five to eighty percent. The catcher was wearing both mask and shin guards. I took a batter's position in order to get a feel for Glavine's stuff. *Whoosh, whoosh.* The August Georgia sun was hot. *Whoosh. Whoosh.* How this lefthander could throw. *Whoosh*. He backed up. He was throwing not from 60 feet but from 70, then 80, then 90. Still the baseball came in, pitch after pitch, hard and low, hard enough to make a catcher don a mask.

"Don't brush me, Tom," I called.

"I wouldn't do that," Glavine shouted.

"He's a gentleman," Mazzone said.

Glavine backed up to a point 120 feet away. I remembered Hoss Radbourn practiced long tossing to get loose. Still the baseball came riding in hard and low and nasty. *Whoosh*.

"What an arm," I said to Leo. "I knew pitchers who used their arm for only one thing the day after they worked. To lift a glass."

"Tom isn't anywhere near through just yet," Mazzone said.

When the long tossing was done, Mazzone led us to the bullpen, where Glavine walked to a mound. I had seen enough from ground zero and this time I positioned myself behind him with Mazzone. Glavine stands on the third-base side of the rubber. His favorite fast ball sinks and fades away from a right-hand hitter. His favorite change-up fades away. By standing on the third-base side of the mound, he has more of the plate to work or, put simply, a better angle. Not only physics but geometry plays into pitching.

Glavine threw for twenty minutes in the heat, with just a little light chatter from Mazzone. "Nice one, Tom. He broke his back swinging at that." Supportive stuff, but all the while Mazzone was checking technical things: the point at which Glavine released the ball, and the angle of his arm to the ground as he did. When the throwing was done—it seemed to me Glavine threw about five innings' worth of baseball after a 131-pitch start—the pitcher dropped onto a bench. "Stiff and sore?" I said.

"A little stiff," Glavine said, "but not sore."

The rest of his day? Twenty minutes on a treadmill in the Braves' weight-and-exercise room, running a steady seven miles an hour. Then leg extensions, leg curls, triceps pushdowns, about eight different exercises on weight machines. Next a set of arm-stretching and -strengthening procedures using a weighted (2.5 pounds) baseball. After that, Glavine could shag fly balls and watch the next night's big-league game from a free seat on the bench. The bad news for the cabaret set, and it is very bad news indeed, is that Atlanta's great pitchers, Glavine, Maddux, Smoltz, do not get to lead a cabaret life during the season. They have the wherewithal. Each earns millions of dollars a year. But to make that money they work very, very hard. This may be a new story for major league pitchers, an exalted class, but it is not new for mankind. "Before virtue," the Greek farmer-poet Hesiod wrote twenty-eight hundred years ago, "the immortal gods have put the sweat of man's brow."

A gracious lady from Atlanta sounded social. When she telephoned she said that one of the Braves executives had given her my number and she believed we had both attended Froebel Academy so very, very long ago and she hoped she wasn't disturbing me but she heard that I was writing a book about Atlanta. We had indeed attended the same prep. I explained a bit, not knowing whether she followed baseball. No, ma'am. Not a book about Atlanta. A book about pitching with a section on the coach who works in Atlanta, Leo Mazzone. The lady's social tone vanished without a trace. "'Rockin' Leo,'" she cried. "He's a great man."

Mazzone is best known to the public for a particular mannerism that delights television directors. When a game grows edgy and the pitching focus intensifies, Mazzone folds his arms. He then begins slowly, persistently to rock. Like the cradle, Leo will rock, and rock and rock. In games of high suspense, Casey Stengel walked to the water cooler, time after time. When taut, others chew gum or tobacco, jaws moving at high speed. I've seen sound, tough baseball men actually squirm in dugouts while crises raged. Leo rocks and rocks and rocks. To see something else like it, you do best to look at films of Orthodox Jews praying at the Western Wall in Jerusalem. To go with their rocking, they have incantations and beards. Leo, who sports a trim mustache, rocks silently in his dugout seat beside the manager, Bobby Cox.

"I don't even know I'm doing it," Mazzone told me. We had gathered again at a prime steakhouse to consider the head game, as baseball and the world at large marched toward a fresh century with all their hopes and terrors keeping stride. "I'm thinking, figuring. Count. Score. Base runners. Who's my pitcher? At any second Bobby can tell me, 'Get out there and talk to him, Leo.' As I say, I'm not aware I'm rocking. I'm too busy concentrating on the game. When you do go out there, you can't be sure of what you'll find."

Mazzone remembered a game against the Colorado Rockies when Steve Avery, a power lefthander, drifted into late-inning trouble. As Mazzone arrived at the mound, Avery was walking in tight circles, head down. He looked up. He saw Mazzone. "What the fuck are you doing here?" he said.

Leo did not falter. In strong, clear tones he said, "I just come out to tell you to go fuck yourself." Then he turned and walked back to the dugout. Shocked, Avery settled down. After the game the late Larry Bearnarth, Colorado's pitching coach, visited the Atlanta dressing room. "The pitching coach's union is going to give you a medal," Bearnarth said, "for standing up to Avery that way." There is, of course, no pitching coach's union, but Mazzone savored the collegial compliment. Presently, Avery apologized.

"You're on their side. You're working with them, not against them. 'Mad-dog' [Maddux] is very sharp. His father is a blackjack dealer in Vegas." Leo grinned across a glass of ruby Barolo and a stellar steak. "Next time you're in Atlanta, I'm really going to look after you."

"How so?"

"I'm not going to let you play cards for money with Greg Maddux." Then, cholesterol be damned, we returned to beef and pitching and some ideas about the craft. Maddux, the great cardplayer, has an analytical mind. Traditionally, when a pitcher gets ahead, two strikes no balls, he wastes a pitch, throwing a breaking ball into the dirt or a chin-high fast ball. With two strikes a hitter is wound taut. He may swing at the bad pitch and strike out. Maddux disagrees with the traditional approach. He believes that a hitter is vulnerable at 0-and-2. He may be swinging defensively, trying not to strike out. Fewer home runs are hit at 0-and-2 than at any other count, and batting averages are lowest at 0-and-2. "I go right after him, 0-and-two," Maddux says. "I want to take him out immediately." He can hold forth and even show wisdom. "Whether you just threw a great pitch or the worst pitch in history, the only thing that matters is your next pitch. You're only as good as your next pitch, right?"

"That kind of thinking," Mazzone said, "is one reason, I can tell you, that Mad-dog is his own coach." But even Maddux sometimes needs support and reinforcement. In a clutch, when he falls behind in the count, Mazzone will walk to the mound and say, "Don't sacrifice your stuff. Stay stubborn." That is shorthand for, "Keep throwing tough pitches, Greg. Keep going for the corners. Don't throw the ball down the middle just to get a strike. Don't throw a hitter's pitch. Throw a pitcher's pitch." Pope Leo and Mad-dog have been working together since 1993. They understand each other. Staying stubborn during the 1990s, Maddux won four consecutive Cy Young Awards. No one had done that before.

John Smoltz, who won the 1996 Cy Young, was young, powerful, and adrift in the Detroit organization when the Braves acquired him. The Tigers staff did not like the mechanics of his delivery, but efforts to change his motion met with unhappy results. When Smoltz pitched for Glens Falls, New York, during 1986, the weekly *Baseball America* rated his arm "best in the [Double A Eastern] league." But Smoltz won only four and lost ten and allowed 131 hits in 130 innings. As Branch Rickey so often preached, pitchers whose records show more hits than innings (and more walks than strikeouts) are in trouble. The Braves acquired Smoltz during 1987. Two years later, at twenty-two, he pitched for the National League in the all-star game.

"When we got him," Mazzone said, "he had about zero confidence. We let him go back to his natural mechanics, and I concentrated on trying to get him to relax. We use a system of checkpoints, and there's just one I follow with Smoltz. When he's in his motion and he comes out of the glove, I don't want him to drop his hands too low."

"Make him wild?"

"Not primarily. Coming up from too low puts a strain on his arm."

Large as Smoltz is (6 foot 3 and 220 pounds), he needed arthroscopic surgery in 1994 to hack a spur from the back of his right elbow and to remove a calcium-rich field of bone chips. He recovered smartly, and in 1995 he was throwing hard enough to strike out one batter an inning. The season after that he won twenty-four. "But he always has to be careful of that elbow," Mazzone said, "and the program we have for him takes that into consideration. There are a lot of ways to throw a lot of pitches and you always need to make allowances for individuality. If you don't, you get the situation the Tigers created with Smoltz. Great arm, but a losing pitcher." Maddux teaches and Smoltz follows a so-called throw-and-turn breaking ball. Smoltz throws without turning his wrist until his right hand has passed his head. Then he snaps the wrist, spinning the baseball out of a four-seam (across-the-horseshoe) grip. After releasing he draws his elbow in toward his body and that protects it from overextension. Unlike Glavine, he doesn't throw the day after he works. If Smoltz starts on a Tuesday, his program goes like this: Wednesday off. Pitch from the mound Thursday and Friday. Saturday off, start Sunday. Smoltz is approaching his middle thirties, and he still fired until spring training, 2000. Then he tore a ligament in the elbow, and an operation sidelined him for the season. One surgeon told me, "Throwing a baseball a hundred times at ninety miles an hour is simply not a natural thing to do.

Whatever the conditioning, a certain number of arms are going to break down. The program in Atlanta kept Smoltz going for five full seasons after he first needed elbow surgery. Believe me, from a medical standpoint, that's an achievement."

When knowledge of pitching physiology was more primitive, Carl Erskine threw great overhand breaking stuff in Brooklyn for ten years. As Erskine approached his middle thirties, his arm was a bitter pinch of pain and the Dodgers dispatched him to Johns Hopkins, where an eminent orthopedist said, "Throw sidearm." Erskine remembers thinking, "I've been throwing overhand all my life. Now you want me to change my motion completely? And keep pitching, with a motion I've never even tried, and *stay in the major leagues*?" They don't play Sunday slow-pitch softball up there, and they didn't then. Erskine retired. Today, with modern physiology and Leo Mazzone, he would have gone on for another five years. Or so I believe.

Mazzone talked a bit about technical matters. Pitching posture. Varieties of windups. Fielding from the mound. Dealing with base runners. Grips. Tactic and strategies.* He said there had been some opposition to his program of almost constant throwing, when he first suggested it, but support from Hank Aaron and Bobby Cox helped him carry the day. "I'm sure their support helped, Leo," I said. "The results you got helped more."

---

*In 1999, working with a writer named Jim Rosenthal, Mazzone published a slim text called *Pitch Like a Pro: A Guide for Young Pitchers and Their Coaches, Little League Through High School*. I know no work on pitching technique, as understood today, that is its equal.

He smiled a warm smile. The Barolo had been very good. He was relaxed. He wasn't rocking. "You know," he said, "if you write that I know everything about pitching, you can make the two of us look foolish."

"How so?"

"Because," this unassuming scholar said, "when Maddux, Glavine, and Smoltz graduate, I may get stupid very, very fast."

A LISTING OF

ARMED MEN

L ists have been popular for a long time, surely since W. S. Gilbert's Lord High Executioner sang in 1885 that he had a little list ("of society offenders who never would be missed"). The millennium frenzy produced joblots of lists, the most intensely publicized being the ESPN list of the greatest athletes of the century. Number one turned out to be Michael Jordan. Think about that, not for a hundred years but for a moment. The greatest athlete of the century couldn't hit .250 in the minor leagues. Myself, I would suggest that the greatest athletes of the century were two: Jackie Robinson and Babe Ruth. No one was ever as good as Robinson in as many sports. Ruth might have become baseball's greatest pitcher if he had not changed course and become baseball's greatest slugger. Could Ruth rebound? Could Robinson play soccer? If they had to, I believe they could. What about Ruth at high jumping and water polo? Discussion here can go on for some time.

My own prejudice holds that to qualify as the greatest athlete you have to be able to hit Charlie Dressen's public enemy number one, the curve. Others disagree. About the only way to impose closure on the debate is to cite the infamous gambit devised by William Jefferson Clinton: "Depends on what you mean by 'athlete.'" This, to be sure, looses further debates, but that is another story for another book.

Who, then, might be the greatest pitchers since the dawn of baseball? Here is a list, opinionated, subjective, and personal.

1. **CHRISTY MATHEWSON.** Branch Rickey said he could learn any pitch in an instant and, with Matty's matchless gamesman's mind, work it into his assortment just as quickly. Forget 1910. Mathewson today would throw splitters, circle changes, "Atlanta-quality breaking balls," and all the rest, and outthink the Griffeys, the McGwires, and everyone else. Plus he looked like Apollo—not a bad thing.

2. **SANDY KOUFAX/BOB GIBSON/JUAN MARICHAL.** For all his flaws, Pete Rose knew how to read pitchers. I respect his ratings: Koufax, hardest thrower; Gibson, best competitor; Marichal, most complete pitcher. Gibson dissents from Rose's evaluation. "I threw harder than Sandy," he says. This is a high-level debate, which I leave right here.

5. **ALLIE REYNOLDS.** As Casey Stengel—whose view encompassed sixty major league seasons—put it, "the greatest two ways, which

is starting and relieving." That Reynolds is not in the Hall of Fame speaks to the vagaries of fortune and the myopia of many who make lists.

6. **GROVER CLEVELAND ALEXANDER.** Sixteen shutouts in one season, three times a thirty-game winner, his sinking fast ball seemed fashioned from cement. No one consistently hit it into the air. I should add that Alexander was an epileptic, though he never suffered a seizure on the mound. "Ol' Pete" gave Ronald Reagan a great film role in *The Winning Team,* where Doris Day, with blond hair and brunet eyebrows, plays Mrs. Alexander as the wife all pitchers ought to have. "He was also a drunk," Mr. Reagan told me at a White House screening, "but Jack Warner wouldn't let me touch that in the movies. And no, I didn't fall in love with Doris, beautiful as she was, because I'd just fallen in love with Nancy."

7. **BRUCE SUTTER.** The best relief pitcher I ever saw. Not in the Hall of Fame, either. If I start Reynolds and finish with Sutter, I might defeat any team the Hall of Fame could field.

8. **BOB FELLER.** Some prefer Walter Johnson as the ultimate fireballer, since Johnson pitched longer. Feller won 107 games before his twenty-third birthday, then went into service after Pearl Harbor and spent four of his prime years in the navy. When asked why he didn't try to delay his induction, Feller said simply, "We were at war and we were losing." The tough Feller/Johnson call is about to be made easier.

9. **WALTER JOHNSON.** In twenty-one seasons with mostly bumbling teams, he won 416 games and—in 1925, at the age of thirty-seven—"the Big Train" won twenty and batted .433.

10. **SAL MAGLIE.** No one on any mound was any meaner. Like Iago, he didn't know the meaning of the word "remorse."

11. **WARREN SPAHN.** He has to be here, even though he could not beat the Dodgers at Ebbets Field, even though in my heart I'd rather here place Early Wynn. But do you exclude a 363-game winner? I can't.

12. **JERRY SOLOVEY OF LAKE MOHEGAN, N.Y.** Played in the Giants chain, never escaping low minors. Why is he here? As I remarked, lists are subjective. Solovey could almost always get *me* out.

B I B L I O G R A P H Y

Adair, Robert K. *The Physics of Baseball*. New York: Harper & Row, 1990.

Coberly, Rich. *The No-Hit Hall of Fame: No-Hitters of the 20th Century*. Newport Beach, CA: Triple Play Publications, 1985.

Durocher, Leo, with Ed Linn. *Nice Guys Finish Last*. New York: Simon & Schuster, 1975.

Honig, Donald. *The Greatest Pitchers of All Time*. New York: Crown, 1988.

House, Tom. *Fit to Pitch*. Champaign, IL: Human Kinetics, 1996.

Jacobson, Steve. *The Pitching Staff*. New York: Crowell, 1975.

Johnson, Rick L. *Jim Abbott: Beating the Odds*. Minneapolis: Dillon Press, 1991.

Jordan, Pat. *Pitching*. New York: Harper & Row, 1985.

Marx, Doug. *Relief Pitchers*. Vero Beach, FL: Rourke, 1991.

Mather, Paul, and Alfred Slote. *Hang Tough*. New York: Harper & Row, 1973.

Mathewson, Christy. *Pitching in a Pinch, Or, Baseball From the Inside*. New York: Grosset & Dunlap, 1912.

Mazzone, Leo, and Jim Rosenthal. *Pitch Like a Pro: A Guide for Young Pitchers and Their Coaches, Little League Through High School*. New York: St. Martin's Griffin, 1999.

McGarigle, Bob. *Baseball's Great Tragedy: The Story of Carl Mays—Submarine Pitcher.* Jericho, NY: Exposition Press, 1972.

Palmer, Jim, edited by Joel H. Cohen. *Pitching/Jim Palmer.* Hillside, NJ: Atheneum, 1975.

Quigley, Martin. *The Crooked Pitch: The Curve Ball in American Baseball History.* Chapel Hill, NC: Algonquin Books, 1984.

Richter, Ed. *The Making of a Big-League Pitcher.* Philadelphia: Chilton Books, 1963.

Ritter, Lawrence S. *The Glory of Their Times.* New York: Macmillan, 1966.

Seaver, Tom, with Steve Jacobson. *Pitching with Tom Seaver.* Englewood Cliffs, NJ: Prentice-Hall, 1973.

Shapiro, Milton J. *The Don Drysdale Story.* New York: Messner, 1964.

Sowell, Mike. *The Pitch That Killed.* New York: Macmillan, 1989.

Sullivan, George. *Pitchers: Twenty-Seven of Baseball's Greatest.* New York: Atheneum, 1994.

Sullivan, Michael J. *Top 10 Baseball Pitchers.* Hillside, NJ: Enslow Publishers, 1994.

Thorn, John, and John Holway. *The Pitcher.* New York: Prentice-Hall Press, 1987.

Tunis, John R. *The American Way in Sport.* New York: Duell, Sloan and Pearce, 1958.

Young, Ken. *Cy Young Award Winners.* New York: Walker & Company, 1994.

ACKNOWLEDGMENTS

For boundless help and encouragement in bringing my labors into final form, I offer millennial thanks to Walter Bode of Harcourt. Like Ol Hoss Radbourn, Walt Bode possesses a firm work ethic and expects no less from his authors. He believes, I suspect, that a word processor will rust out before it wears out. Provided you spill no Chablis on the keyboard, that seems to be so.

Susan Kilgour assisted with many interviews and provided important research assistance. The Baseball Hall of Fame in Cooperstown is justly famous. The National Baseball Library, perhaps less well known, is a realm of gold for those looking backward at baseball and America. I am grateful to Dr. James Gates, director of the library, and two historians there, Tom Shieber and Tim Wiles, for their help. At the Hall itself, Dale Petrosky, the president, and Jeff Idelson, the director of communications, proved staunch allies in my journey across three centuries of baseball; and a millennium, when one factors in all those games of cricket, rounders, and creag. Absent friends, notably Don Drysdale, were generous with time and knowledge. So were Bob Feller, Warren Spahn, Johnny Sain, Bruce Sutter, Bob Gibson, Buck Showalter, Gene Michael, Tom Glavine, Greg Maddux, and Leo Mazzone.

Stanley Woodward, the late sports editor, called copy editors "the Comma Police." Ms. Anne Lunt of New Hampshire was comma cop here, doing the same fine work she did with *A Flame of Pure Fire*. Bill Deane of Fly Creek, New York, a most meticulous baseball historian, handled fact checking with his usual expertise. Finally, Robert N. Solomon, the author's literary agent, provided support, advice, and encouragement, always with high good humor. John Mattis prepared the bibliography.

My thanks to all.